Everything about

Rudyard Kipling

Everything about Rudyard Kipling

Mallikarjun Patil

GNOSIS

Nurturing the Aspirations

Worldwide Circulation through Authorspress Global Network
First Published in 2012
by
GNOSIS
(An Imprint of Authorspress)

Editorial
Q-2A Hauz Khas Enclave
New Delhi-110 016

Marketing
E-35/103, Jawahar Park
Laxmi Nagar, Delhi-110 092

e-mails: authorspress@rediffmail.com; authorspress@hotmail.com
Website: www.authorspressbooks.com

Everything about Rudyard Kipling
ISBN 978-93-81030-33-2

Printed in India at Tarun Offset, Delhi.

Preface

This book on Rudyard Kipling is an adventure. It is an intellectual adventure on one of the most controversial writers in the history of English literature. One must know that Kipling is both loved and hated for his finest writings and political ideas about Britain. As an Anglo-Indian writer, he stayed in India for many years and he had his boyhood here. After his education at Southsea and Westward Ho! he joined the *Civil and Military Gazatte* at Lahore and then he worked for the *Pioneer* in Allahabad. He travelled in other parts of the country like Kolkata and Rajasthan and studied India as no other Anglo-Indian writer could do. His writings are better than Forster's and Paul Scott's.

Kipling began to write of India and the East in the best possible way at that time. Later he settled down for some years in the USA and then in Sussex, England. He visited many countries like Japan, Sri Lanka, South Africa and Brazil. He was a globe-trotter. As critics like T. S. Eliot and Edmund Wilson think, he has depicted India in the best possible manner. His poetry and short stories depict India like nobody else could do. His poetry is really wonderful. It is melodious, folksy and, even at times, vulgar. One must read his poetry in the *Barrack Room Ballads*. Chapter 5 deals with his poetry.

If chapter 1 deals with Anglo-Indian literature, chapter 2 deals with Kipling's life and works. Chapter 3 is a critical analysis of Kipling's novels. His *Kim* is a picturesque work. Chapter 4 is the seminal chapter in the book. It is an analysis of Kipling's entire body of short fiction. Chapter 5 has details about his non-fictional prose. The last chapter has glimpses about his vision of the British Empire.

Mallikarjun Patil

Introduction

Rudyard Kipling was a great writer of the British Empire. He was a fine journalist, short story writer, poet and political thinker.

However people, even great writers, think that Kipling was a crude British imperialist, a jingo, cruel and arrogant, a thumper of banjo melodies, but he was a great genius, with concern for mankind. Fellow writer Bonamy Dobree thinks he had "a layer of human consciousness". Kipling was oppressed with the fact that man is a lonely creature. This is a thought about man as the existentialist thinkers like Jean-Paul Sartre worried. Sartre said that man's life is an accident on earth, and still man can survive and live happily, because he is a social and rational human being. His painful schooling at Lorne Lodge, South Sea (as it is evident in the story "Baa, Baa Blacksheep" and also his autobiography *Something of Myself*) made it clear. Then the next question was about how this lonely man was to live by. This depended on what and how he had to work. Action is the remedy for happiness, and in the first part of *The Light that Failed*, where the picture of his exiled childhood is again drawn, Maisie says to Dick in their misery, "Let's find things to do, and forget things."

Kipling's feeling of despair, like that of Thomas Hardy's (or Schoupenhouer's) streak of pessimism, upset the contemporary society.

Kipling's ancestry may help us as to understand why he had this melancholic strain in his life and work. His father, Lockwood Kipling, was a learned and cultivated man, curator of the Museum at Lahore, and himself an artist. His mother was the eldest of a group of very beautiful and intelligent women, two of whom married other artists—Burne-Jones and Poynter—and the third of whom became the mother of Stanley Baldwin, future Prime Minister of England. Further—and this is important—like his own Aurelian McCoggin, in the story of that name (*Plain Tales*) his grandfathers on both sides had been Wesleyan preachers, and the preaching strain came out in his mind. Kipling, like C. A. Swineburne, lost interest in religion quite early. Kipling lived by stoicism.

Kipling was not a philosopher, but an artist with impulses and intuitions, growing deeply over the years. He had a great zest in life. Yet he asks "what is it that makes living possible? And what is that man has to adhere in life?" He answers these questions in his poem "Recessional," and the story of Purun Bhagat. It's most notorious use is in "Recessional," the hymn where he rebukes the British Empire, and refers to "The lesser breeds without the law." There is, of course, the simple law we meet in the *Jungle Books*; but even in those volumes another dimension shows itself in the story of Purun Bhagat, who had a great statesman, and was going into retirement to meditate, as an ageing Hindu will. At Simla, where he appears as a beggar, a Mahomedan policeman tells him to move on: "and Purun Bhagat salaamed reverently to the Law, because he knew the value of it, and was seeking for a Law of his own." Bonamy Dobree observes, "For Kipling, moreover, the Law by which man lives, whether the law of his religion, of his tribe, of his craft, is always a law which demands of a man the total surrender of himself. He admired the British Empire which made rules for man's survivalism and quest for the self.

Two extracts from *Limits and Renewals* will perhaps illustrate the way in which the intuition grew to be merged in the sense of life as it comes to men to live it. The first is from the story "The Tender Achilles," in which a brilliant surgeon, strained beyond endurance by having to do hurried and second-rate work at the battle front, is saved from collapse. He is brought back to an illuminating piece or research which he alone can perform. The two friends who undertake his cure are talking, and one of them says:

> . . . I told him we were all alike, and the conditions of our job hadn't been human. I said there were limits to the machine. We were forced to go beyond'em, and we ought to be thankful to be able to do as much as we had. Then he wrung his hands and said, "To whom much has been given, from the same much shall be required." That annoyed me. I hate bookkeeping with God! It's dam' insolence, anyhow.

No, there shall be no book-keeping with God; a man must give everything freely, even self, though he may hope that God will give him back himself. Or so St. Paul said in that remarkable poem in the same book, "At his Execution," of which the last two stanzas read:

> Since I was overcome
> By that great Light and Word,
> I have forgot or foregone
> The self men call their own
> (Being made all things to all men)
> So that I might save some
> At such small price, to the Lord,
> As being all things to all men.
>
> I was made all things to all men,
> But now my course is done –
> And now is my reward –
> Ah, Christ, when I stand at Thy Throne
> With those I have drawn to the Lord,
> Restore me my self again!

In some ways what we might call his religion is best exhibited in the story "The Children of the Zodiac" (*Many Inventions*) where he tells us of the need of work or love or laughter to cure the fear of death, and of the need to despise pain. Beyond this morality lies the metaphysic of existence, and in this respect Kipling is almost wholly a late Victorian. In this sense, Kipling reminds us Mathew Arnold, George Meredith, and Thomas Hardy.

As an artist, Kipling cares for "life force"—a Tennysonian sense of "some far-off divine event / To which the whole creation moves." Man has to follow this force. Kipling insisted on change as the law of nature; and lo! he welcomed science and technology for man's welfare. This change and this progress is slow and painful, as we see it in the story "The Eye of Allah" in *Debits and Credits*. Kipling even prophesized new governments, and new law. Of course, man has an illusion that his creation is stable and permanent. But it is not so. All our pomps of to-day will no doubt in due course be one with Nineveh and Tyre, but the smaller things will remain, the smoke of sacrifice, a chosen myrtle-wreath, "the smell of the wattle by Lichtenberg," or finally, "the unconquerable grass."

Man can reach a final destiny, but he cannot stay there for long. His prosperity and peace are short-lived. His happiness is as short as his sorrow. Kipling curiously believes in man's fated life or predestination. He writes in *Something of Myself*, "Looking back in my seventieth year, it seems to me that every card in my working life has been dealt me in such a manner that I had but to play it as it came. Therefore ascribing all good fortune to Allah the Dispenser of Events, I begin.'

Kipling hated and even criticized anarchy. He loved law and order. Huxley spoke of three things—order, sanity and proportion—for an ideal civilization. He hated all kinds of bad people, particularly the politician, and the lazy people -, and even snobbery. The titles of his latest books—*Actions and Reactions*, *Debits and Credits*, and *Limits and Renewals*—were brilliantly chosen to define the subject matter of the bulk of the tales, and reveal his preoccupations in his later days.

Kipling, just like Hardy, thinks that man's lot is a burden. He says, ". . . we find / The Gods have no such feeling / of justice toward mankind." Still as Sartre reiterated, man has to stand and stare.

Kipling was a born writer. His headmaster Carmel Price at Westward Ho! knew it; and his parents who published his poems early discovered his natural genius. Like Emerson, he had love for life, and love for recording that life. His many years of Indian experience as a boy, a journalist, taught him what can interest man as a man. Verse and tales alike came abundantly from his pen, but, with considerable reading behind him, he knew that craftsmanship was of the first importance;

with his father's precepts and example to help him, he realized that a man's integrity depends upon his loyalty to his task.

Confessedly he could not make plots, construct in the grand way; but, given his intuitions, and his mastery over the word, his short stories carry a depth of implication which make them, in his mature phase, far more than anecdotes or clever sidelights. A notable instance is "The Strange Ride of Morrowbie Jukes" (*Wee Willie Winkie*), a tale in which an extraordinary atmosphere is created, as though all humanity were trapped in life.

Kipling loved life in its varied manifestations. Like Emerson, he loved ordinary life as the three-fourth staff of man's existence. A famous Kannada writer from Mysore De. Ja. Gow spoke to me of this recently. Much of our life is ordinary. Kipling loved this "ordinary life" in Lahore and Simla, in England and America, in South Africa and the rest of the world like Japan in one end and Brazil, the other end. In the fort at Lahore he met his three soldiers, the immortals, Mulvaney, Learoyd, and Ortheris; and everywhere in India, in the bazaars, on the teeming roads, on the slopes of the Himalayas, and in the Native States, he met the incredible diversity of creatures which go to make up the same old and rotten India.

Kipling's first stories appeared in the *Civil and Military Gazette* in India. Here, we see his stories, sometimes excellent, sometimes, bizarre. These stories depict man's life as sense and sensibility, as brash and animalistic. Most of the stories are uneven. His early ones suffer perhaps from too mechanical a structure, too evident a twist—the defects rather than the virtues of the Maupassant method. His characterization however is always beautifully clear, in his immature years brilliantly etched in by description, later on fully modelled by the phrases and gestures of the people themselves. Again, the stories are in a sense all "adventure" stories.

Kipling's deepest sympathies were already exhibited in his *Soldiers Three*, which appeared on the railway bookstalls in India in the late 1880s. Stories about these characters recur from time to time.

Kipling lived in India for seven years and then visited it sometimes. Indian life provided him much material. The first six books like *Plain Tales*, *Life's Handicap* and *Wee Willie Winkie* were shaped out of that. America shaped his next book *Many Inventions*. Later books—*The Jungle Books* and *The Day's Work*—also contain his Indian yarn. This is also true of his only good novel *Kim*. In the 1890s, he began to speak of rather criticize the British Empire. The death of his dear daughter Josephine made him a semi-mystic. "They" is an example.

But in the meantime, after his return to England, Kipling had discovered his own country, and entered upon what for him was a perpetual voyage of exciting exploration, not only as to the England of his day, but of the enthralling past. He produced not only the enchantingly vivid stories of *Puck of Pook's Hill* and *Rewards and Fairies*, but also the Roman and other tales in later books, such as "The Church at Antioch" and "The Manner of Men," both of them in *Limits and Renewals*. The romantic element which runs strongly through all his work, in the earlier phases as physical adventure such as we are superbly given in "The Man who would be King" (*Wee Willie Winkie*), is later diverted to the spiritual adventure of "A Madonna of the Trenches" (*Debits and Credits*): it develops from the schoolboy fun of "Judson and the Empire" (*Many Inventions*) to the grammar of life of "Sea Constables" (*Debits and Credits*), a story about "neutrals" who trade meanly in death and betrayal. So far; little has been said about Kipling's comic writing. Laughter for Kipling was an essential element of living, and equal in value with work; but we may well sometimes feel that with him the laughter is excessive. Nevertheless, "Brugglesmith" (*Many Inventions*), "The Village that Voted the Earth was Flat" (*A Diversity of Creatures*) and "Aunt Ellen" (*Limits and Renewals*) can be enjoyed as sheer high farce. But many of the tales have a moral purpose.

Moreover his sea-stories—those which centre round the inimitable Pyecroft—contain more than an element of criticism. They are Kipling's revolt against the stuffily moral, the ordinary, against the subservience to the code of "things that are not done."

Kipling is a great poet, indeed. We can say that he is a great poet-story teller. Because his stories and poems go together. His prose is poetic too as we find it in the *Bible*. Like the saying "Can we separate the dancer from the dance?" can we separate Kipling, the poet from Kipling, the story-teller? It is indeed, difficult. Bonamy Dobree says, "We can be certain only that he has done in verse what could not be done in prose, and in a way that nobody else has done. He was a master of versification, and it is clear that he had deeply studied the sixteenth and seventeenth century poets. Much admittedly is jingle; but he can handle all sorts of forms, all sorts of metres; while his rhythms are complex and inventive, sometimes indeed subtle. At all events he is at home in the heroic couplet, common measure, the ballad form, the sestina, the English Sapphic, the iambic measure or a rollicking anapest, the octosyllable, or the sixteener; free verse or a version of the *terza rima*, the seventeenth century stanza or an imitation of Swinburne."

It is sometimes said that Kipling's poetry is the poetry of statement, as though it had no overtones, no quality of evocation. The beauty of his verse can be seen in "My Boy Jack' in *Sea Warfare* (1914-18):

> "Have you any news of my boy Jack?"
> *Not this tide*
> "When d'you think that he'll come back?"
> *Not with this wind blowing, and this tide*
>
> "Has anyone lass had word of him?"
> *Not this tide.*
> For what is sunk will hardly swim
> *Not with this wind blowing, and this tide. . . .*

Certainly Kipling can put metrically what we may if we like call a statement, but much of his poetry is sheer charm-writing.

Most of the common English readers have hailed Kipling as a great genius. But the critics, the highbrow, and the conservatives have not yet given their marks. Not one would claim that he ranks among the great artists of the first towering order either in prose or in poetry; but he was an intuitive as well as a markedly able man, a man of wide and extremely vivid sympathies for individuals, himself a distinctive individual, and a very great craftsman, indeed.

The present book deals with Rudyard Kipling's life and works. There are separate chapters on Kipling's novels, short stories, poetry, non-fictional prose and the life.

Mallikarjun Patil

Contents

1

Anglo-Indian Literature

The English ruled, almost half of the world, for a century and more. They ruled many other lands for more than two centuries. Still, countries like Canada, Australia and New Zealand are England's dominions. Then the English ideas and ways of life, and the English language are reigning the world forever. After all, the big boss America is just an offshoot of England.

The English ruled India and other parts in the East for two centuries. Well, the Indian English rule has left two permanent legacies–one the impact of Western way of life, and–two, the use of English as an international language. English literature is a part of this interface.

English rulers bequeathed English language upon the Indians with the purpose of training Indians for clerical work. Great men like Lord Macaulay and Raja Ram Mohan Roy made English the medium of education in India. So the Indians began to use English as if it were the gift of Saraswati herself, as C. Rajagopalachari recalls later.

Now this English is playing the role of emancipating and empowering the weak and helpless everywhere. The Englishmen not only ruled India, but they also trained Indians in cultural and civilizational practices. They made us one nation. We learnt many things from them, and from the West. Mahatma Gandhi himself has admitted this profusely. These Englishmen also cultivated arts and literature in the subcontinent. Many of them wrote fine literature. Mr. Rudyard Kipling is just one of them, and, of course, the best of them.

The so called Anglo-Indian literature was, for a century, cultivated by the Englishmen in India. Bhupal Singh who is an authority on Anglo-Indian literature observes, "Anglo-Indian fiction covers a period of about a century and a half. It may be divided into three periods. The first period begins with the Governor-Generalship of Warren Hastings and ends with the Indian Mutiny; the second period ends with the death of Queen Victoria and the publication of *Kim* in 1901; the third period begins with the Partition of Bengal in 1905 and goes upto 1947. Meadows Taylor and W. D. Arnold are the chief novelists of the first period; Sir Henry Cunningham and Kipling of the second; Edmund Candler, E. M. Forster, and Edward Thompson of the third. The novels of the first period are mainly romances of Indian history, or descriptive sketches of English society in India; those of the second period are portraits of the official life of Anglo-India, mainly satirical; those of the third period show a vast range in the choice of subjects and a true reflex of the varied life and problems of India in transition."

Some of the characteristic features of the Anglo-Indian literature are as follows. This literature begins with the description of the Englishman visiting India. The hero of the story will be an honest and hard-working Englishman, and an Indian raja, or a nawab will be the villain of the piece. The hero is responsible for the British honour. The heroine enlivens the dull and dreary pages of Anglo-Indian literature.

The literature also describes Indian topography, the Himalayas, the overcrowding, the scorching heat, dust and evils. The mood in which this literature is written is one of the disgust, boredom and sorrow. The sense of the Englishpeoples' being exiles haunts the pages. The narration is mainly of the ephemeral. Most of these writings are done by people who are not professional writers. The style, language, characterization are all mediacare. Not to speak of, some writings are just propagandist.

The earliest Anglo-Indians were known as nabobs in English literature. India was an el Dorado (a lower kind of New World) for them. It was a second America for them. But still, as in the seventeenth century's colonialism in America, Indian life was low and mean. The *Oriental Memoirs* of Forbes furnishes the best picture of the cheerless life of young English adventurer on his arrival in Bombay.

Sydney C. Grier (Miss Hilda Gregg) has described the lives of her countrymen in India in the seventeenth and eighteenth centuries in *In Furthest Ind* (1894). They were semi-Orientals in their habits and manners of life, loving splendid sloth and languid debauchery. They married Indian women or entered into liaisons with them. Even Englishwomen succumbed to the eastern environment. They smoked hookahs, drank claret, and left their children to the care of Indian servants. Expensive dinners and horse-racing involved young writers in debts.

According to Warren Hastings English officers passed their time in sports, parties, and occasionally in arts. Historians think that the early Englishman was a naturalized Hindustani. The next phase Englishman whom he calls *Qui Hai*, retained his English habits and mode of life. Thackeray's sketch of James Binnie is an example for Qui Hai. Old Indians were dissolute soldiers, corrupt civilians, or usurious merchants. Qui Hais (of the period 1850 to 1900) were not isolated savages dwelling in a remote country. *The Baboo and Other Tales* (1834), a novel descriptive of society in Calcutta, portrays a number of characters who may be taken to represent the *Qui Hais*.

This is also seen in Mrs. Sherwood's *The Lady of the Manor* (1844). After the Mutiny and the institution of the Bengal Civil Service, the Qui Hais began to die out. In several books we find echoes of rivalry between Qui Hais or Anglo-Indians of the 'old school' and what the latter contemptuously styled 'Competition Wallahs.' The Qui Hais were trained for service in India at Haileybury. Constance Howell's *Married in India* (1910) speaks of Englishmen's difficult and isolated life in India.

Mr. Wetherall, the subaltern, is a typical soldier of the time. To him all Indians are niggers and lying rascals, who can be brought to their senses only by means of the whip. Mr. Alexander Allardyce gives a portrait of a Qui Hai in the person of Eversley in *The City of Sunshine* (1877), while Sir Henry Cunningham gives a pen-portrait of an Anglo-Indian of the new type in the character of Desvceux. Cunningham acknowledges that the vile corruption which characterized the East India Company in its earlier days, which fired the righteous wrath of Burke, had disappeared, but Indian Governments had long remained the home of jobbery. Kipling's Anglo-India is the India of Englishmen of the new regime. With the beginning of the twentieth century the Competition Wallahs begin to be referred to as 'heaven-borns' by members of other services. Next Anglo-India is the India of the I.C.S.. Likewise, military Anglo-India has lost much of its importance in the days of peace.

The Anglo-Indian of later day has not that profound contempt for natives which distinguished his countrymen of the post-Mutiny period, nor is he so deliberately ignorant of the language customs, and history of India and her people. Mrs. Barbara Wingfield-Stratford similarly writes in *Beryl in India*: "The whole white community in India was, as a whole, hopelessly narrow-minded, unimaginative, and lacking in dignity.' The Anglo-Indian of the last stage is discriminately hospitable. In times of trouble and need he is prepared to receive under his roof comparative strangers who may have little or nothing in common with him beyond the fact of their being Englishmen. Mrs. B. M. Croker in her first novel *Proper Pride* (1882), speaks of the proverbial hospitality of the Anglo-Indian. Kipling in the *Phantom Rickshaw* thinks that globe-trotters who expect entertainment as a right, have, even within living memory, "blunted this openheartedness, but none the less to-day, if you belong to the Inner Circle and are neither a Bear nor a Black Sheep, all houses are open to you."

Several writers speak of the snobbery of Anglo-Indians. Ross Church writes of this in *Gup*. Alexander Wilson divides the people of India into three divisions, sahibs, snobs, and sinners. Bhupal Sing observes, "In spite of the intoxication of power Anglo-India is not altogether happy. The English soldier pines for the sights and sounds of London, the mother for her children, the husband for his wife, the toiling official for the opportunities lost, the statesman for contact with minds more cultivated than his own, and the epicure for the joys of the English table." In "The Madness of Private Ortheris,' Kipling has given expression to it in unforgettable words. Coulson Kernahan speaks this in *The Woman who Understood.* John Travers' (G. H. Bell) is full of this note in *Sahib-log*. According to Duff-Fyfe India is no place for a white man with slender means and no certain and heaven-born position. Sir Francis Younghusband says that their life without home attractions is dreary and depressing. Mr Thompson's disappointment is great; as his love for India was great. Among other characteristics of Anglo-Indian literature we may notice its conservatism. While Anglo-India is very unconventional in some respects, it is strangely conservative in others. Savi draws attention to this peculiarity of Anglo-Indian life in *The Unattainable*. Norah K. Strange, in *Mistress of Ceremonies,* speaks of what is ordinary and quite harmless in England takes a very different complexion in Eastern eyes. Edward Thompson says in *Night Falls on Siva's Hill,* that it is not often that Englishmen quarrel in India in the presence of native servants. Considerations of prestige are chiefly responsible for the almost complete exclusion of Indians from English clubs. Talbot Mundy writes in *Om* that the members of the Delhi Club were proud of the fact that no Indian, not even a Maharajah, has ever set foot over its threshold. Anglo-India has definite views on the marriage of its countrymen in India. It does not approve of the marriage of an official at the commencement of his career, and condemns it as an unpardonable piece of stupidity. Military Anglo-India is still more strict in this respect. Anglo-India condemns mixed marriages in no uncertain terms. An Englishman who marries an Indian girl is pitied, and Anglo-India does all it can to prevent such a mésalliance.

Meadows Taylor in *The Story of My Life* refers to the indifference of his contemporaries to religion. Apart from missionaries, the average Englishman in India calls himself a Christian more for political than other reasons. Church attendance on Sundays is necessary more to show the solidarity of Englishmen in India than to satisfy their spiritual needs. Here is a characteristic passage from, Y. Endrikar's *Gamblers in Happiness*, typical of Anglo-India's attitude towards religion. Sir Francis Younghusband in *But in Our Lives* says that living in India with Hindus and Mohammedans had made him realize that Christianity had never sunk into the very marrow of the bone of an Englishman like Islam and Hinduism into the Indian.

In order to understand Anglo-Indian life, it is necessary to understand its peculiar constitution. In Anglo-India young children have to be sent to England to be educated there and old ladies accompany their husbands after their retirement. This leaves Anglo-India with girls and wives. Secondly, these ladies have nothing serious to do. A third feature is that its menfolk are either very busy or very idle. The assistant Magistrate, the civil surgeon, the engineer, and the Superintendent of Police are examples of busy people. The young unmarried subaltern, on the other hand, has very little to do. Fourthly, the climate of India separates the toiling husband from the wife, who spends the greater part of the year at one of the hill stations and comes down to the plains only in the cold weather.

Wingfield-Stratford, writing in 1921, thus describes Anglo-Indian life: "Once or twice it struck her that the lives of most of the women she met were singularly aimless ones. She was also surprised sometimes at the matter-of-fact way in which somebody's husband and somebody else's wife almost invariably paired off together. Every lady in the station, except herself, seemed to have what Mrs. Tukeson knew as a 'Boy,' and were surprisingly frank about it."

However, Anglo-Indians worked very hard, lest they would lose their Indian dominion long ago. They were dedicated and serious people. Sylvester of *The Price of Empire* and Delahey of the *Shadow of Abdul* resemble Henry Lawrence and remind one of the ancient Spartans and Romans. Even Sir Henry Cunningham, who has so mercilessly exposed the faults of Anglo-Indian society, acknowledges that Hannibal's soldiers did not have to work so hard as the English officials at Elysium. Another book which embodies this ideal of silent service and worship of work is *But in Our Lives* by Younghusband. One finds a subdued echo of the same in Edward Thompson's two books, *An Indian Day* and *A Farewell to India*. Hamar, Findlay and Alden are his heroes; they suffer but do their jobs.

India attracted the West from time immemorial. Greece and Rome had trade relations with India before the Christian era. The Middle East was the mediator between the East and the West. Then Vasco de Gama found out his way to India. This was followed by the European incursions into India, as the fabulous country, known for its *Vedas*, as well as its spices attracted every nation. Cosroe in Marlowe's play *Tamburlaine* says this:

> Men from the farthest equinoctial line
> Have swarmed in troops into the Eastern India,
> Lading their ships with gold and precious stones,
> And made their sports from all our provinces.

Shakespeare describes the Field of the Cloth of Gold in the following terms:

> and tomorrow they
> Made Britain India; every man that stood
> Show'd like a mine
>
> (*Henry* VIII, I. i.)

Lord Clive gave a voice to the Western nations. He began real relations with India. The magnificence and wealth of the Anglo-Indians, their eccentricities and vulgarities, first attracted the attention of the public and writers in England in 1772, the first year of Hastings's Governor-Generalship, when Foote produced *The Nabob,* a play picturing the discomfiture of Sir Matthew Mite, a returned Anglo-Indian. Already John Dryden had written his play *Ourangazebe*. In 1780 was published *Intrigues of a Nabob* by N. F. Thompson. *The Disinterested Nabob, a Novel,* is mentioned by R. Sencourt, and may be regarded as the first Anglo-Indian novel. 1789 saw the publication of *Hartly House* as the first journal written by a woman for her friends in England. Sydney Owenson, later Lady Morgan, published *The Missionary*, an Indian tale in three volumes.

More important than Owens is the name of W. B. Hockley of the Bombay Civil Service who had, by 1828, published three interesting books of fiction, all dealing with Hindu life: *Pandurang Hari* (1826), *Tales of the Zenana* (1827) and *The English in India* (1828). Sir Walter Scott, one of the greatest masters of romantic fiction, published his romance *The*

Surgeon's Daughter. In comparison with Scott's other well-known novels, it is no better than a cheap melodrama, rambling and ill-constructed. But The *Surgeon's Daughter* still deserves close study. It shows how Scott's imagination was fired by India, the true place for a Scot to thrive in. In the preface to the book he tells us why he was attracted by India. In India he could find as much shooting and stabbing as ever took place in the wilds of the Highlands.

In making Jonas Chuzzlewit the secretary of the Anglo-Bengali Disinterested Loan Company, Dickens, like Thackeray, satirizes the formation of bogus companies by means of which many Chuzzlewits exploited the ignorant. In *Dombey and Son* there is a reference to the long distance between England and India. In *David Copperfield* we learn that the young husband of Betsey Trot-wood went to India and there rode an elephant along with a baboon, which in the opinion of David Copperfield was a mistake for a baboo, or a begum. Thackeray was born in Calcutta and had Anglo-Indian blood in his veins. He remembered the land of his birth.

In his famous English novels *Vanity Fair*, *The New-Comes,* and *Pendennis*, Thackeray has created a few Anglo-Indian characters who even to this day remain as models for Anglo-Indian writers to copy. Joseph Sedley, the fat and vain Collector of Boggley Wollah—a fine, lonely, marshy, jungly district, famous for snipe-shooting and where not unfrequently you may flush a tiger-is a skit on Indian civil servants of the days of Barwell and Holwell.

Meadows Taylor visited England in 1838, just after his recovery from a severe illness in India. The whole journey through Persia, Arabia, and other countries took about nine months. This visit is important because it was in England that he published his first famous book *Confessions of a Thug* (1839), which laid the foundation of his literary career and brought him into public notice. The suggestion to write the *Confessions* came from Sir Edward Bulwer.

Other books followed soon. *The Scribbleton Papers* is an amusing record of Scribbleton's experiences in India, in the form of letters to a friend in England. *The Indigo Planters* is an illuminating record of the days when indigo plantations were a coveted possession. Another interesting and human book is *The Lady of the Manor* (1844) by Sherwood. Among other books we may mention a novel by Sir J.W.Kaye, *Long Engagements* (1846), which is meant to show that there is very little real difference between society in India and society in England. In 1853 there appeared two novels, *The Wetherbys* by John Lang, and *Oakfield* by W. D. Arnold. Both of them show the vices of Anglo-Indian society

Edward Money wrote the novel *Woman's Fortitude—A Tale of Cawnpore.* Major Charles Kirby's *Arcote Rupee* (1867) speaks of India when Wellesly was subduing Tippu Sultan. Florence Marryat's *Veronique* (1869) describes South Indian Life. Phil Robinson's *Nugae Indicae* (1873) is a new kind of writing. His *The Gnome of the Hillock* is a story describing the simple and superstitious Indian village folk. His style is like Kipling's. It is not improbable that Kipling in his youth read *Nugae Indicae,* and imbibed much of its spirit. *The Chronicles of Budgepore* in two volumes (1871) by Iltudus Prichard, is another remarkable book of the pre-Kipling period. The author informs the reader in the first chronicle that Budgepore is a typical place and that the Budgeporeans are both natives and English. Sir Henry Stuart Cunnningham's *Chronicles of Dustypore* is written in a light, airy, satiric vein. It is a clever and refreshing book with a hot and dusty country as its subject, where, as the author tells us, there is sand everywhere and a good deal of it in the heads of the officials. Cunningham's second novel, *The Caruleans* (1887), is a work of high merit.

Alexander Allardyce's works deal with Bengal. Bhupal Singh observes, "The humour, satire, exquisite workmanship, and intimate knowledge of official life and of Anglo-Indian society, whether in the plains or on the hill-top, which characterize the novels of Phil Robinson, Iltudus Prichard, and Sir Henry Cunningham mark them out as worthy predecessors of Kipling." Kipling's work relating to India was mainly done between 1888 and 1891 and is embodied in *Plain Tales from the Hills, Soldiers Three, Wee Willie Willkie,* and *Life's Handicap*. These four volumes cover 96 stories, taking the eight scenes of the story of the Gadsbys as a single story. No treatment of Kipling as a writer of Indian stories would be complete without an examination of *Kim* and *The Naulahka*. These novels may be so called because each covers more than four hundred pages. Edward Farley Oaten would even go so far as to say that to call it (*Kim*) a work of fiction is a little misleading. He regards it as the greatest masterpiece of journalism.

Kipling has been a force in the history of Anglo-Indian fiction. Much of what has been written since the publication of his Indian stories, and especially *Kim*, has directly and indirectly been influenced by Kipling. Before Kipling Anglo-Indian fiction was amorphous. It had no distinctive place in the history of English literature. Its recognition is due to Kipling. *Indian Dust* (1909) by Otto Rothfeld and *The Wayside* (1911) by 'Andrul' are two other volumes of short stories reminding us of Kipling. Another writer of merit but in marked contrast to 'Andrul' both in temper and style is Edmund Candler. *The General Plan* (1911) is his book of nine well-written short stories. His description of the journey from Kalka to Simla, from Simla to Kotgarh, Nachar, Warytu, Chini, Dankar and thence to Galdang Tso is one of the best pieces of Anglo-Indian prose, recalling Kipling's description of the Grand Trunk Road.

Sir Edmund Cox, Herbert Sherring and Richard Dehan have written excellent short fiction. Ethel Dell, A. T. Marris, T. P. Pilcher, Leonard Woolf, John Eyton and others have written much about India as the East. Eyton's object may be judged from the last stanza of a poem of his own, in his book, *The Dancing Fakir* (1922):

> If you would gather pictures of a land that never changes—
>
> Where Brahmans, though three thousand years have
>
> passed, are Brahmans still
>
> From sunny Coromandel coast unto the Northern ranges—
>
> Then come as I would guide you, and see history from a hill.

Some of Eyton's stories, such as 'The Ugly Calf,' 'A Philosopher

Stag' and 'The Pale One,' are reminiscent of Kipling's *Jungle Books*. C. A. Kincaid has won some reputation as a writer of stories of Hindu life and religion. *Shri Krishna of Dwarka* and *Tales of Tulsi Plant* (1922), illustrate his intimate and sympathetic delineation of Hindus of southern India. *Five Indian Tales* by F. F. Shearwood consists of artless stories written by a zealous missionary in India. Hilton Brown, in *Potter's Clay* (1927), has collected some stories of South India. The Potter bears testimony to the richness and abundance of the clay, and leaves his readers to judge the Potter for themselves.

Humfrey Jordan in his *White Masters* (1929) takes the reader to the jungles, swamps, and creeks of Burma, and shows, like the Ranee of Sarawak, "the sinister influence of the East' on the lives of white men and women. Talbot Mundy shows the influence of Kipling both in the substance of his stories and style. His book *King of the Kyber Rifles* (1927) is a mingling of the plots of *Kim* and *The Naulahka*. It is a complicated romance of secret service and German-organized jehad on the Frontier. 'Ganpat,' in his *Mirror of Dreams* (1928), shows himself to be a worthy chela of Kipling. Alice Eustace, in *A Girl from the Jungle* (1928), is also a close imitator of Kipling. Capt Bedford, Mark Somers and A. E. R. Craig have written just as Kipling did. H. K. Gordon, in the *Shadow of Abdul*, gives a picture of the Grand Trunk Road and of Simla in 1928 and notes the changes that have come over Kipling's India during the past fifty years.

Croker, whose literary career extends from 1892 to 1919, has written over thirty novels. Most of them describe Anglo-Indian life; most of them have their plot partly laid in the East and partly in the West; most of them have for their theme the trials and difficulties of loving couples who are destined to be happy in the end. Mrs. Maud Diver occupies an honoured place among the novelists of military and frontier life.

Of writers who mark the reaction against Kipling and yet are fascinated by him, G. H. Bell is the most important. She has published nine novels. In her first novel, *Sahib-log* (1909), she protests against the common view of Englishmen towards

Anglo-Indian women, made popular by Kipling's stories and novels. Alice Perrin, whose literary career covers about a quarter of a century, is a prolific writer of Anglo-Indian fiction. E. W. Savi is a prolific writer of fiction, mainly Anglo-Indian.

Out of the large number of other Anglo-Indian writers who are distinguished neither by the quality nor the quantity of their work, a few may be noticed here. O. Douglas gives us an amusing and readable book in *Olivia in India* (1913). *Just Because* (1915) by Peterson is a tale of misunderstanding between a husband and wife. Mary Julian in *Where Jasmines Bloom* (1917) attributes the unhappiness of married life to environment. Victor Rickard's *The Frantic Boast* (1917) is a poor imitation of Galsworthy's *The Man of Property*. *The Leopard's Leap* (1919) by 'Boxwallah' is a crude book, having for its plot the seduction of a married woman by an Indian Army officer. Barbara Wingfield-Stratford writes with sincerity though she shows very little skill in handling her plot. *The Red Flame* (1920) by Lady Miles is a fascinating study of a fascinating flirt with red hair. The scene of *The Jungle Girl* (1921) by Gordon Casserly is laid in Rajputana. H. Vaughan-Sawyer's book, *Sport of Gods,* is remarkable for the portrait of an Indian havildar and Waziri politics.

Shelland Bradley deserves separate notice on account of the brilliance of his style, his gift of humour, power of character drawing, and variety of his themes. His first book, *An American Girl in India* (1907), illustrates all his qualities to great advantage. S. S. Thorburn has written two novels of Frontier life, *David Leslie* (1879) and *Transgression* (1899). Younghusband, the great soldier and explorer, has a deeply religious and mystical soul. All the books he has written are artistic attempts to interpret Nature and his varied experiences in a spiritual sense. His *Wonders of The Himalayas*, though not a novel, possesses the interest of a book of fiction.

Most of the novels describing missionary life in India, when not written by missionaries, are satirical in tone. Kipling's short story 'Lispeth' is a satire. Perrin is evidently no great admirer of missionaries. Henry Bruce in two novels, *The Song of Surrender* and *The Temple Girl*, satirizes the Ritualist Mission in India. Margaret Wilson's *Daughters of India* (1928) is certain to rank among the rare classics of Anglo-Indian fiction. *Yet A More Excellent Way* (1929) by Dr. Mary Scharlieb is a missionary novel. *The Splendour of God* (1930), by Honoré Willsie Morrow, is the latest of the missionary novels Savi and Henry Bruce show how missionaries do not scruple to kidnap pagan children in the service of the Lord.

Miss Isobel Mountain undertakes to describe another aspect of Anglo-Indian life, the life of the mem-sahib in the *mofussil*. A book similar in substance, but better written, is *Dictators Limited* (1923) by Hilton Brown, describing the experiences of a new Assistant Collector and his wife in the south of India. A considerable number of Anglo-Indian novels deal with mixed marriages and the problems arising out of them.

Many Anglo-Indian novelists describe the life and character of Eurasians. Almost all of them emphasize their lack of moral backbone or draw a contrast between the English and the Indian side of their character. All authors pay a tribute to the beauty of Eurasians. They represent Eurasian girls as always manoeuvering to capture some Englishman for a husband. In the eighteenth century, the French were the chief rivals of the English in India; in the nineteenth century it was Russia who disturbed their political equanimity. When Kipling wrote, "The Great Game,' played throughout the borders of India, he was directed by a constant fear of Russian intrigues in Afghanistan and on the North-Western Frontier of India. Down to the end of the nineteenth century Indian politics possessed no interest for the writer of fiction. It is with the partition of Bengal in 1905, and the all-India agitation that resulted there from, that Anglo-India first began to be conscious of a disturbing element in the country.

The evolution of Indian nationalism in the twentieth century may be divided into three periods: (i) the pre-War period ending with Morley-Minto Reforms, (ii) the Non-Co-operation Movement of 1919-20 and the demand for Dominion status, and (iii) the period of what Mr. Edward Thompson has styled aggressive nationalism, in which India's right to independence was formally put forward by the Indian National Congress.

In the first period the attitude of Englishmen in India, as depicted in the novels of the time, was one of arrogance, perhaps mingled with a little fear. F. E. Penny's novels depict this. Penny refers to the Congress as "a mere bladder inflated by cheap gas, without even the power of causing an explosion.' E. W. Savi, though she wrote later on, refers to the change in the political atmosphere after the partition of Bengal. In *A Prince of Lovers*, she notices the changed attitude of village folk who, only a few years ago, were "full of kindly smiles and readiness to help the sahibs, but who were becoming hostile to Europeans and were taking every opportunity to humiliate the white race.'

The works of Everard Cotes, L. J. Vance, and Kenneth Combe depict Indian unrest. In 1912 appeared another book *Sri Ram, the Revolutionist* by Edmund Candler, which may be regarded as the best of the novels dealing with this stage of India's political agitation. Savi, Col W. P. Drury, R. J. Minney, G. H. Bell, E. M. Forster, Edward Thompson, H. K. Gordon, A. C. Brown, Y. Endrikar, Beatrice Sheepshanks, Nora Strange and Theodore Pennell have depicted the 1920s India full political agitation.

Bhupal Singh thinks, "Mr. Forster's *A Passage to India,* is an oasis in the desert of Anglo-Indian fiction. It is a refreshing book, refreshing in its candour, sincerity, fairness, and art, and is worth more than the whole of the trash that passes by the name of Anglo-Indian fiction, a few writers excepted."

A very large amount of Anglo-Indian fiction consists of books illustrating some phase of the history of India, past or present. Most of these books have one characteristic in common; if they are good history, they are bad novels, and if they are good novels they are bad history. Most of them imitate Scott or Bulwer Lytton, and have no higher aim than that of reproducing picturesque scenes or sensational incidents. The story of Buddha and Buddhism has attracted several writers. Paul Carus in his story of Buddhist theology, called *Amitabha* (1906), contrasts Buddhism with Brahmanism. *The Pilgrim*

Kamanita: A Legendary Romance (1911), by Karl Adolf Gjellerup, translated by J. E. Logie, is a story of the last days of the Buddha and gives a moving description of his death.

Some of the historical novelists are L. Adams Beck, Flora Annie Steel, L. H. Myers, Ena Fitzgerald, Meadows Taylor, Louis Tracy, Michael Macmillan and others. Miss Hilda Gregg ('Sydney C. Grier,'), has romanticized the history of British India in a series of historical novels. Richard Gamon, G. F. Macmann, G. H. Bell, V. E. Banmsdale, G. A. Henty, and Percy Groves have also written historical novels. W. B. Goddey, F. P. Gibbon, G. A. Henty, Maud Diver, Herbert Hayen and H. M. Wallis have written about India's regional history. George Chesney, D. H. Thomas, Robert Sterndale, Col Harcourt, Louis Tracy, Charles Pearce, H. C. Irwin, J. N. H. Maclean, and R. E. Forrest have written about the 1857 Sepoy Mutiny.

Mystery novels in which the element of mystery is connected with priceless diamonds or rare pearls have been very popular. Perhaps it was the success of Wilkie Collins's *The Moonstone.* Marion Crawford, A. M. Jacob and, of course, Kipling have written mysteries. Quite a number of mystery novels derive their inspiration from the occult, the esoteric, or the spiritual element in Indian life. John Henry Willmer in his book *The Transit of the Souls* (1910), says: "Although modern civilization has worked and is working many changes in India, yet the echo of the past remains, the spirit of departed grandeur, of magnificent follies, hovers over ruined mosque and temple.'

Mme Z. L. Cavalier's *The Soul of the Orient* (1913) is an original story of astrology and eastern mysticism. Mrs. L. Adams Beck is the most important among those writers who have been attracted by oriental occultism. Many novels are devoted to Indian sedition and Bolshevist conspiracies to engineer a revolution in India. In *Sentenced to Death* by R. Mackray, Holiday Browne, the hero, grapples with sedition and saves India. Mr. Percy James Brebner's *The Gate of Temptation* (1920) is a meaningless tale in which Bocara, an Oriental Professor of Languages, looks forward to the day when Indians and other peoples will rise in revolt and drive out all foreigners.

Red Vulture (1923) by Mr. Frederick Sleath deals with a great Oriental conspiracy to destroy the British Empire. Another story of Bolshevist attempts to create trouble in India is *The Devil's Tower* by 'Oliver Ainsworth' (Sir Henry Sharp). As a thriller the book may well be compared to Scott's *The Surgeon's Daughter*. S. B. Bannerjee, Hazel Campbell, Andrew Brown, Fredrick Turner and Henry Sharp have written detective fiction.

About the end of the nineteenth century several writers of minor importance, under the influence of Kipling, selected Indian life as the theme of their novels. These writers are R. W. Frazer, R. E. Forrest, W. H. G. Kingston and others. Penny who has written many zenana novels observes: “”A zenana, according to Mrs. Penny, is a place where the daylight even at the best of times does not penetrate to any extent, where enquiry from the outside world is baffled by the all powerful influence of *Gosha rules*, the gosha covering “in addition to women's faces and figures, injustice, tyranny, favouritism, cruelty, and crime; where tears are common and self-restraint never known, where old and young cry like babies, and where no one takes any notice of an extravagant display of grief; where the mother-in-law uses stick, fire, and sack to subdue the recalcitrant daughter-in-law, and where the enraged daughter-in-law, seizing her by the hair, tries to bite her; where the women are busy only with their tongues, or quarrel over the preparation of the daily meals.”

Even Edmund White and R. S. Minney have done much fine writings about the 1950s India. R. J. Minney has been acclaimed by some reviewers as a second Kipling.

2

Rudyard Kipling's Life and Works

Kipling in old age remembered his being brought up in Bombay. He played with native children, visited Hindu temples, and watched the Arab dhows and Parsees' worship of the sunset at the Towers of Silence. This was the atelier of his father's (J.J.) School of Art.

John Lockwood Kipling was one of the pioneers of art education under government auspices of India. He became a modeler and designer of terracotta. He worked at a time in an artist's studio. His father died in 1862, while his mother (the Skipton grandmother) survived until 1886. In 1865, he married Alice Macdonald, daughter of a well-known Wesleyan preacher, George Browne Macdonald. As he says, "Alice was keen, quick and versatile!' Kipling was the name of his village and Kipling got his name from it. George's son Henry befriended Edward Burne-Jones who was a friend of William Morris in London. In fact, George's daughter Georgiana married Burne-Jones in 1860. Then George's sons moved to 'The Grange' where Sr Kipling spent his last years. Georgiana arranged her sister Alice's marriage with Kipling at St. Mary's Abbot's Church in 1865. The writers Swinburne and Mr. Rossetti attended the wedding.

Lockwood was already appointed as professor of Architectural Sculpture in the School of Art at Bombay which he developed as he developed the Mayo School of Art in Lahore later. The Kiplings came to India in 1865 and their son Rudyard was born within a year. His mother spent six days of agony in a dangerous and protracted confinement, "as long as it took for the creation of the world.'

Kipling's father's old surname had no 'g' in the final, and his relations founded Baltimore in the USA in 1633. His maternal ancestors had joined Wesley's Methodism. James Macdonald, his son George (Sr Kipling's wife's father) and his son Frederick all served as Methodists for 144 years. George had five beautiful sisters Georgriana (married to Burne-Jones, the Pre-Raphaelite), Louisa (married to Prime Minister Stanley-Baldwin's father Alfred Baldwin), Agnes (married to the artist Edward Poynter) and Edith (with whom Kipling corresponded throughout his life). Of course, Kipling's mother Alice makes the number five.

Lockwood and Alice started their life in Bombay. Kipling passed in the teeming Indian city. There are photographs of Kipling as a baby. Alice returned to her parents' house in Bewdlely in 1868. Rudyard was very noisy then. Alice gave birth to her daughter, also called Alice. Lockwood said the baby was 'tricksy' and called her 'Trix' later. The Madras Ayah served the family in Bombay. Alice gave birth to one more girl child which died soon. In April 1871, the children—Rudyard now five and Trix, three—left Bombay for South Sea, in England, where they were left with the Holloways' boarding for education. Because Bombay's summer was harsh, and the Kiplings were not in a position to keep their children in Simla for that season.

This is how the Kipling children were bewildered for five years at the Holloways in South Sea. Critics call this "The House of Desolation.' This 'Lorne Lodge' was congested, and had little comforts. Its owners Aunt Rosie and Uncle Harry were mean and low, mistreating the little ones. 'Discipline' was aunt's favourite word. She had no daughter and she had a soft corner for Trix, but she treated the boy harshly.

The Holloway's son Harry—'the Devil—Boy,' as Rudyard thought of him—was the children's most painful cause of sufferings. Harry would mistreat Trix, and beat Ruddy. The maid Jain tried to protect the two. Mr. Holloway, the retired and wounded sea captain died in 1874. The aunt weakened the relationship between the two children as Trix recalled later. Moreover, Mrs. Holloway censored their letters sent to Bombay.

This harsh treatment affected their maturity. Mrs. Holloway taught the children the art of reading together. There were not many books in the 'House of Desolation,' but Rudyard found books like Mrs Ewing's *Six to Sixteen, the Old Shikari*. There were books that described nine white wolves coming over the world. Once Ruddy was taken to Oxford, and Trix to Brighton. It is strange that not one of the 'beloved aunts' visited the children, nor sent them any Christmas gift. But the grandma paid some visits and Ruddy visited 'The Grange.' This was the house in which Samuel Richardson wrote his novels like *Pamela*. The Grange had an orchard. Burne-Jones's daughter Margaret noted that the children were happy, and Ruddy's imagination was active. William Jones (Uncle Topsy) would visit the Grange and would tell the children a story. His friend Burne-Jones spent his time in the studio. Ruddy had a close relationship with his uncle. Ruddy somehow developed his hatredness for these Pre-Raphaelites and their political credo. The Baldwins (other relatives) bought a house in Albert Street in 1875 where Charles Reade had once lived. The Kiplilng children visited this house.

Ruddy began a little schooling at South sea, and he lived a desolate life with the Holloways. There was an ugly scene, but Trix met Aunty's threats by saying that she would tell everybody how cruel she was to the children and how they hated her. 'Aunty blustered: You don't know anyone to tell.' 'Yes, there's the doctor—and you can't stop me telling the vicar. I'll stand up in Sunday School—and I'll tell the postman, and the policemen on the corner of Palmerston Road.'

Alice visited Southsea and her sad children in March 1877. Then the children's Southsea episode ended. Kipling wrote of this episode sadly and bitterly. When he visited the place 40 years later, his wife noted that 'Kiplilng talks of it all with horror.' In India, as a young man, he was to deliver that bitter castigation 'Baa Baa Black Sheep' against the Holloway family.

But Rudyard was undisciplined, clumpsy, argumentative and slow.

'Baa Baa Black Sheep' was written eleven years after Kipling left 'Lorne Lodge.' He was living at the time with

Professor and Mrs Hill, and it is probable that he deepened the shadows to enlist Mrs Hill's sympathy. Biographer Edmurid Wilson has described this painful episode in his book *The Wound and the Bow.*

Mrs. Kipling took the children to the house of Pinder, the chief of Mr. Lockwood for a visit. The children enjoyed the wild stay. The farmer Mr Dally said the children and they could do anything on the farm and learn the farmlore. This was the Epping Forest. Their celebration of All Hallows E'en was extended as far as Guy Fawkes' day. With the winter this exciting holiday came to an end. But there was another happy period in front of him at a small lodging house at No 227, Brampton Road.

The children played, enjoyed and Ruddy was rather mischious. For example, Ruddy sat in the window upstairs and threw down on road small pockets containing wooden pieces. The walkers picked them up in curiousity and threw them away in disgust. This should have amused the boy. He teased animals. But Trix said he, like his father before him, loved all kinds of animals, and never owned a gun. Mrs. Kiplilng showed them the London Museum.

Then Rud and Trix joined schools from 1878 to 1882. They were in the care of three ladies Mrs Winard, Misses Mary and Georgina Craik.

In January 1878 Rudyard arrived at the United Services College, Westward Ho!, for which he was soon to find that the draconian regime of Mrs Holloway had been no bad preparation. The various accounts of Kipling's schooldays are clouded by irritating differences on points of detail. One of these was written by L. C. Dunsterville, the original of 'Stalky' in Kipling's later book *Stalky and Co.* ; another was the work of George Beresford, called 'M'Turk' in that book, and a third version was that of Kipling's autobiography *Something of Myself.* To these may be added such moments of historical truth as occur in *Stalky and Co.*

The old retired Navy and Army officers had started this school for educating their children. The school was, established to eliminate 'Crammers,' the costly school. There was a strong

Anglo-Indian ambiance about the place. The atmosphere was general and seculiar. Kipling's friend and biographer L.C. Dunsterville was also there.

Kipling was happy in the college. At 16, he was quite mature as Mrs. Pindar observed. He had the wisdom of '26' then. He was called 'The Beetle' and 'Gigger.' Kipling described his first term as 'horrible! The school had a position at the little seaside resort called Westward. Ho!, after Kingsley's novel.

The head Master Cormel Price was a strict disciplinarian. Clearly, the Headmaster of *Stalky and* Co., was a fiction of Kipling's mind, that 'nursing mother of jingos, a trainer, a guide, and an inspirer of Imperial fuglemen, and stimulator of prancing frontier officers, who was cheered wildly by the school for flogging them *enmasse.'* There are many differences in the various accounts of Kipling at Westward Ho! Kipling in *Stalky and Co.* writes about fags, and Beresford objects that the institution of fagging did not exist at the United Services College. The school could not have best teachers, and the first few batches were called 'a job lot!' J.C.Campbell, the chaplain was a sadist. His successor Willes passes as 'Gillete' in *Stalky and Co.* But the most dominating influence of Kipling, after Cormell Price, was William Crofts, who appears as 'King,' in *Stalky and Co.* and who instructed Kipling in Latin and English. In Dunsterville's words 'Crofts was a fine man in every way both mentally and physically. Kipling pays a right tribute to him in *Something of Myself.*

At the end of Kipling's painful first term he was told that his parents could not come to England for the Easter holidays. He spent them, not unhappily, at Westward Ho! Lord Birkenhead writers, "For compensation Rudyard was given a holiday when his father returned from India, and they went together to the Paris Exposition of 1878 where Lockwood was in charge of Indian exhibits. Rudyard was allowed to wander alone through the city and the exhibition grounds, and his adoration for France began from that moment."

The originals of 'Beetle,' 'M'Turk' and 'Stalky' soon came together at Westward Ho!, and the alliance was formed before the end of the first year. Here we should emphasize again that much of *Stalky and Co* is fiction. There were no such boys, and no such Napoleonic maneuvers. 'The three characters, however,' said Dunsterville, 'correspond more or less to the characters of Kipling, Beresford and myself.'

The first year was hard for Kipling. Then he did not participate in games. Because he had weak eyesight. Yet he enjoyed the sea-baths and sights.

Cornell Price was satisfied by 1880 that Kipling would be a writer, and prepared to help him. His freedom from compulsory games was a priceless asset. His first published juvenilia had appeared in the *Scribbler,* a home magazine organized by the younger members of the Burne-Jones and William Morris families in 1878. Kipling, then thirteen, made several contributions, including poems, signed 'Nick-son.' The good headmaster also appointed Kipling as the editor of *The United Service College, Chronicle.* Price taught him Russian, précis writing and craftsmanship. Kipling paid this debt to Price by looking after his son with kindness.

Kipling had widely read already. He had read Tennyson, Browning, Swinburne, Smollet, Fielding, Thackeray, Dickens, Bunyan and Defoe. The influence of Poe, Whitman, Emerson, Longfellow, Mark Twain and in particular Bret Harte, was also there. Kipling edited the *Chronicle* for two years and acted in Sheridan's play *The Rivals.*

Kipling had enough youthhood experience. He spoke of the fish girls of Appledore. He met Miss Florence Garrard at Lorne Lodge later (when Trix stayed there two more years later) and loved her. Maisie of *The Light that Failed* is based on her. He had an interest in her from 1879 to 1891. He helped her. She did not marry and she died in 1902.

Lockwood Kipling published Kipling's early verse as *Schoolboy Lyric* in 1881. These poems are derivative and not so famous. 'An Echo' reflects that of Browning's craft of versification. The first stanza is as follows:

> Let the fruit ripen one by one
> On the sunny wall;
> who is it suffers. What harm is done?
> None at all.

Other poems are 'Ave Imperatrix' and the sonnet 'Discovery.' The former speaks of Kipling's early imperialist moods so brilliantly.

Kipling finished his education at Westward Ho! by July 1882.

Cormel Price then told Kipling that he had to go to India as a journalist and work monthly for Rs150. This was Lockwood's decision too. At one time, Kipling had thought of doing medical study, while his father could not send him to Oxford. The young man, however, could not understand what to do.

'Stalky' and 'M'Turk' were also going to India, but Dunsterville was going as a soldier, and Beresford as a civil engineer. India would offer them both wide opportunities; but Rudyard already saw himself as a writer, and believed that his proper place was London, and not as a cub reporter in Lahore. Kipling's interests were entirely literary. His mind had already taken this turn when he wrote *Stalky and Co.,* and it was the mind of young 'Kuppelleen Sahib,' with his civilian's passion for the Army already strong within him.

Kipling arrived in Bombay in October 1882, and soon left for Lahore. The museum (which the Indians called 'the wonder house'), the walled city and the Shalimar Gardens mystified the young man. He soon became a member of the Punjab club. He was just to begin his work as Assistant Editor of the *Civil and Military Gazette.* James Walker and William Rattigan had founded this paper. They had also bought George Allan's paper *Pioneer* in Allahabad. These papers were already India famous for their news and views.

Kipling lived in an old building called 'Bikanir House.' Now he had his own office, and his own work. He did much of the editorial work. His chief Stephen Wheeler ('Amber Toad') guided him rather disagreeably. It was Kipling's duty to prepare for press the telegrams of the day; to provide all extracts and paragraphs; to make headed articles of official reports; write editorial notes; and be responsible for sports, outstation and local intelligence

Kipling found the work quite tiresome. Kipling could not impress the Lahore English people warmly as at his Westward Ho! Education was below the line. He was a little less cultured one. He had a 'caddishly dirty tongue.' He was bumptious. Aggressive and casual. Lord Birkenhead quotes the following incident:

> Sir Henry MacMahon recalled a military exercise in the middle of which he found himself in Lahore, and retired to the Club. Here he soon reached the bar, which was the centre of social life in all Indian clubs. There, among a group of men, was a small figure with a heavy moustache in civilian clothes. Someone said: 'Kipling, I want you to meet MacMahon.' Kipling replied: 'Why should I want to meet Mac-Mahon?' and turned away. This was said with such gratuitous insolence that MacMahon said angrily: 'Well, whether you like it or not you have met me, so come outside, and I will give you the biggest thrashing you ever had in your life.' This he said, he fully intended to do, but a stand-up fight was averted by the other members.

Let it be as it might have been. Kipling liked the country-life as he wrote:

> I'm in love with the country (he wrote to a friend) and would sooner write about her than anything else. Wherefore let us depart our several ways in amity. You to Fleet Street (where I shall come when I die if I'm good), and I to my own place, where I find heat and smells and oils and spices, and puffs of temple incense, and sweat and darkness, and dirt and lust and cruelty, and above all, things wonderful and fascinating innumerable.

Kipling travelled everywhere genuinely. As an Anglo-Indian remembered, he acquired in the bazaar an immense knowledge of Indian ways, language and trade customs. He was extraordinarily accurate in his Indian details, what he could not get from personal exploration, he was able to get from his father. Kipling loved to see night life, watch dances and gambling and write about them. He took his midnight prowls, and he loved it all, the stink, the oven-heat, the lust, the cruelty. His sister joined him in 1883. He wrote Aunt Edith that he made his first public speech in January 1884.

Kipling began to love the Army. This interest stayed with him for life. He wrote sometimes as though a soldier. It is clear that Kipling derived a vicarious delight from the atmosphere of a military ante-room, from the orderlies, the regimental trophies, and the army 'shop.' He regretted that he could not join Army because of poor eyesight. The story "The Man who was" speaks of his enormous interest in it. He sympathized with the soldier. 'I came to realize,' he said, 'the bare horrors of the private's life, and the unnecessary torments he endured on account of the Christian doctrine which lays down that "the wages of sin is death.

The soldiers also remembered him. One wrote:

> My old Battalion, the 2/5 Fusiliers, were stationed in 1885 in Mian Mir, near Lahore. I was colour sergeant, acting Sgt. Major, when one evening in May I was asked by the orderly officer 2 Lt. Hill to introduce a friend of his, who was with him, to typical scenes of barrack room life and to afford him the opportunity of coming into contact with the men. Mr Kipling, then a man of 19, just out from school in England, explained that he had been commissioned to turn out a series of articles descriptive of army life gathered in from personal contacts and experience.

Kipling befriended QMS Ban Croft in Solon near Simla and got materials about 'Mulvaney' and the story of 'Snarleyow.' He might have got the clues about the three soldiers—Mulvaney, Ortheris and Learoyd. It is rumoured that he joined the 'B' company of the Punjab volunteers for a time. He met Viceroy Lord Ripon in April 1884.

In September, 1884 Kipling was a little uneasy because of the spread of cholera in Lahore. In such bleak times, he would visit the famous Shalimar Gardens, and he would remember Tennyson's description of the garden of the Princess Ida by moonlight. His book of parodies *Echoes* appeared in August 1884. Trix was also its collaborator.

Kipling would visit Simla for a month at a time. Here he would devote every spare moment into the study of his fellowmen as the raw material for his books. It seems he had a veiled affair with one 'Maisie.' He called her 'this-Tillie Venner,' who happens to be an empty-headed girl in *Plain Tales from the Hills*. Trix recalls an event:

> He rode and danced with married women, observing them narrowly, and often using them for a copy, a circumstance which they understandably resented. He sent them verses, sometimes indifferently using the same lines twice.
>
> 'Once I remember he was attracted by the face of a girl seen in church. A chaplain's daughter-small, dark and slender with fine eyes. He used to go to church to look at her—I was eighteen then. I found her pretty and commonplace——though of course I did not tell him so—I introduced him to her at one of the afternoon dances. The next dance began; I looked for Rud and the dark-eyed maiden; they seemed to sitting out. Came the third dance—and she was sitting out alone. No sign of Rud—and he did not drive home with us.

Kipling lived in Lahore a rough life. He had often troubles with white people. Once two lawyers almost kicked him in the Punjab Club. In another occasion, Michael O'Dwyer (later Lieut Governer of the Punjab) wanted to beat Kipling. Kipling thus had many unpleasant episodes. The debates about Ilbert Bill disturbed him. Then the poor Lockwood family could not have an attachment with the Viceroy circle in Shimla.

Kipling spent the hot weather of 1885 in Simla, his second season in the summer capital, and July found him special correspondent for his paper, his salary now raised to £420 a year. For that sum he was supplying editorial notes, reviews, articles, and social Simla letters. To his Aunt Edith he sent, in facetious vein, the first of a lifelong series of complaints about the pirating of his work. Kipling refers for the first time to his novel *Mother Maturin,* which was never published:

> Further I have really embarked the June of 237 foolscap pages on my novel *Mother Maturin*—Like Topsy 'it growed' while I wrote, and I find myself now committed to a two volume business at least. It's not one bit nice or proper, but it carries a grim sort of moral with it, and it tries to deal with the unutterable horrors of low-class Eurasian

> and native life as they exist outside reports. Mother says it's nasty, but powerful, and I know it to be in large measure true.
>
> 'In vain,' said General McMunn, 'have several of us looked and hoped for it, for it promised to be the story of stories. I have however ascertained that *Mother Maturin* kept a questionable house of entertainment for sailors of the South China at Saigon.

The last reference to this unpublished work is on 3 July 1900, when Kipling's wife Caroline was to enter in her diary that the manuscript of *Mother Maturin* had been sent to Kipling by his literary agents, A.P.Watt. Later, parts of this book were used in *Kim*.

Lord Birkenhead describes Kipling's Simla as a wonderful place. He writes:

> Kipling found Simla an almost inaccessible town, clinging to the mountains like a swallow's nest amid peaks thick with firs and deodars. Here was a wonderful refuge for men driven to the limit of their endurance by their labours in the baking inferno of the plaint beneath. There was a delicious coolness in the air, and log fires in the evening. It was a place of incessant entertainment, of striving for social supremacy, of place-hunting, of petty intrigue and eager gossip. The fact that it was the summer seat of Government, and the distinction of the Viceroy's presence, which lent it something of the atmosphere of a court, raised Simla in the eyes of the English to supreme social position among all the Indian hill-stations.

The ever-bustling Mall, the sports-ground Annandale, and the amateur theatre in which Rud and Trix took part were always overcrowded. Pelitis was a gathering place and Benmore was for public assembly. The whole ambiance of the place pleased the whites. The Indian Empire was administered from Simla in summer. Lord Dufferin stayed at Peterhoff. The Kiplings befriended the Viceroy, and the latter's son Clandeboye fell in love with Trix. Stepher Wheeler was replaced by E-Kay Robinson, who was not happy of Kipling.

In 1886, in the cool weather, Kipling began to write the satirical verse and the short stories which were published daily in the *Civil and Military Gazette* and brought him instant fame all over India. He was modest about his first volume of verse, saying: 'It's a tiny little book, but we hope to get it decently reviewed, and as it's anonymous no harm will be done.' He had been contributing verse to the paper for some time, verse born out of the life about him, of the backslidings of Government officials and their jockeying for position, of the scandals of Simla life, of the bazaar and the places he visited.

Men in the Army, the Civil Service and the Railway wrote to Kipling saying that the rhymes should be made into a book. They had been sung to the banjo round campfires and bivouacs, and had penetrated as far as Rangoon and Mandalay. By December 1886 the name of Kipling was known all over India, and he wrote to Aunt Edith with exultation:

> Then a strange thing happened. The little booklet just hit the taste of the Anglo-Indian public for it told them about what they knew. . . . I got some lively reviews comparing me to. . . all sorts of people whose shoe-latchets I am not worthy to unloose. Then I had the book published by Calcutta firm. *Vanity Fair* reviewed it; Andrew Lang in Longman's said some of the work was worthy of Bret Harte, and again the public bought. And Thacker Spink & Co. write to say that the second edition is nearly exhausted. The Viceroy and divers other people have written and said all sorts of sweet things to me about the book.

In 1886 itself Kipling began to write stories, maybe to fill up space in the *Gazzette*. Trix also wrote stories. Oscar Wilde laughed at, while reading these of Kipling stories. Although Kipling's name was now known in India, he failed, for the moment, to impress those critics in London to whom specimens of his work had been shown. Sir Ian Hamilton, who was a friend of Kipling and had quickly realized his genius, had sent a manuscript of *The Mark of the Beast* to England in 1886, to be shown to Andrew Lang and William Sharp, and to the editors of two magazines, in an attempt to launch Kipling in London. Both Lang and Sharp disliked the stuff of Kipling's stories. Even the book *Plain Tales from The Hills* made a slow move in 1886.

In 1887, unwelcome orders reached Kipling to move to Allahabad to serve on the *Pioneer*, hundreds of miles to the south-east. His new position made it necessary for Kipling to make a number of visits to northern India. And in Rajaputana, in November 1887, he found the material for *Letters of Marque,* a series of articles which afterwards appeared in the volume *From Sea to Sea,* and for the background of *The Light that failed* and other stories. Here Kipling befriended Prof Aleck Hill and his wife Edmonia, both American photographers. Kipling wrote 'Baa Baa Black Sheep' now. Hill noted: 'Mr Kipling looks about forty, as he is beginning to be bald, but he is, in reality, just twenty-two.' Elsewhere she described him as 'a short, dark-haired man of uncertain age, with a heavy moustache, and wearing very thick glasses.'

Kipling became famous. The Viceroyo admired his genius. Now Kipling asked Hill whether he could leave for professional writing career in England. He had authored one book of poetry; six books of prose and readied six books of short stories. The Indian railway bookstalls controller Emile Moreau was ready to help him for publishing his books of stories. Moreau, however, proposed to take all the risk and to pay Kipling $1,000 and a royalty of $20 per 1000 copies, after the sale of the first 1,500, for the rights of publication of *Soldiers Three, Wee Willie Winkie, Under the Deodars, The Story of the Gadsbys, In Black and White* and *The Phantaom Rick-Shaw.* The books were published in India in green paper covers with designs by Lockwood Kipling at one rupee per volume, and in England in 1890 by Sampsom Low, Marston & Co., where they were also an immediate success.

Many unhappy things happened to the Kiplings now. Trix decided to marry John Fleming, a soldier in the Survey Department and Kipling's cousin Margaret was to marry an Oxford don. Rudyard was unhappy of his life. A captain called Hearsay thrashed Kipling. Hill, rather ill desired to go back to America.

Kipling decided to leave India at once, not even waiting for Trix's wedding, and in February 1889 paid his last visit to Lahore to make his farewells to the family. He was to sail in company with the Hills on *SS Madura* bound from Calcutta to Rangoon. He traveled via Rangoon, Singapore, Hong Kong and Japan, and was happy. He reached with the Hills the city of San Francisco. He was unhappy with media people there. He stayed with the Hills in Pennsylvania for a month.

Kipling described this journey in *From Sea to Sea*, and, according to Trix, surprisingly he became engaged at this time to Mr Hill's younger sister Caroline. The engagement was broken off, and she returned to India with her father, a congregational minister, who objected to Kipling's creed.

Kipling then journeyed to London in October 1889.

Critics think that Kipling's early work contains his enchantment of India. 'He went up in the sky like a rocket'—it was said—a 'rocket out of the magic East, scattering its many-coloured jewels in the bowl of the night.'A huge readers and admirers of all classes welcomed him. They found something strange and un-understandable in him. Edmond Gosse said Kipling's poetry 'disturbs and attracts me'; William Archer said, 'this man ought to be another Shakespeare' and 'whoever except Whitman,' asked George Moore, 'has written with the hole language since the Elizabethans?' (Some like Mix Beerbohm hated him). The times were also ripe for Kipling.

It was into this gap that Kipling stepped with his exotic realism, aggressive and triumphant. Politically, too, he arrived in the nick of time. He came at the moment when the national imagination had suddenly grasped the vastness of the British Empire. Gosse found Kipling 'the master of a new kind of terrible and enchanting peep- show' which all crowd around wanted 'once more!' Like Byron, description was Kipling's forte, and many consider that he ventured far too often into the vernacular.George Orwell said, 'Kipling idealizes the army officer, especially the junior officer, but the private soldier, though lovable and romantic, has to be a comic. He is always made to speak in a sort of stylized cockney, not very broad, but with all the aitches and final g's carefully omitted. Very often the result is as embarrassing as the humorous recitation at a church social.'

Andrew Lang spoke of Kipling's blemish thus: "His faults are so conspicuous, so much on the surface, that they hardly need to be named. They are curiously visible to some readers who are blind to his merits. There is a false air of heartiness; there is a knowing air; there are mannerisms, such as 'But that is another story'; there is a display of slang; there is too obtrusive knocking of the nail on the head. Everybody can mark these errors; a few cannot overcome their antipathy, and so lose a great deal of pleasure." Kipling's forte lay in description of Indian lore. His remarkable range was to increase with the years, until he soon appeared to know everything, the organization of armies in the battle, the habits of wild animals in the jungle, and the function of tappet valves, in a detail as numbing as that in which he described the government of India, the building of bridges.

Kipling's first book of verse *Departmental Ditties,* appeared in 1886, and his prose stories were collected in 1888 when *Plain Tales from the Hills* appeared in Calcutta. In the same year appeared the Railway Library books, *Soldiers Three, The Gadsbys, In Black and White, Under the Deodars, The Phantom Rickshaw,* and *Wee Willie Winkie,* the collections that Kipling brought to London.

Lang said: "The literature of the sub-continent of India had been curiously sparse before Kipling's advent, its English conquerors seeing little in their exotic surroundings to kindle the imagination, and being intent upon governing, making war and love, and compiling official reports. For an author India was an unworked seam; the novels of the author of *Tara,* Cunningham's sketches, and Sir Alfred Lyall's poems—there was little else: 'that old haunt of history, the wealth of character brought out in the confusion of races, of religion, and the old and new, has been wealth untouched, a treasure-house sealed: those pagoda trees have never been shaken." Kipling described this strange India to the Englishmen's taste. Kipling like Pierre Loti, had made his countrymen see a new world. The people wanted to know the Englishmen's life in India. Kipling descried this old world.

Nevertheless Mulvaney, Learoyd and Ortheris are memorable figures, and they quickly gathered an enormous circle of admirers in such stories as 'The Big Drunk Draf,' 'The Madness of Private Ortheris' and 'The Taking of Lungtunpen.' When we turn over the pages of *Plain Tales from the Hills* we are struck by the technical efficiency of these stories. Constantly disfigured as they are by the faults we have noticed, many of them are yet models of their kind, and it is one of the curiosities of literature that these little masterpieces were tossed casually each week into the columns of an Anglo-Indian journal.

Kipling's early stories were weak particularly in ideology. Yet they reflect Simla society in the 1880s. Lord Birkenhead writes, "A grim but authentic picture is unrolled before our eyes, of balls and routs, and dated slant, of callow subalterns trotting beside the rickshaw wheels of faded provincial vampires, of picnics on ponies, of line officers showing off in the gymkhanas before the coy daughters of officials—all the snobberies and petty allegiances of a small second-rate society are petrified as in a stop-camera shot." For e.g., 'Thrown Away' depicts a memorable suicide. In the group of stories *The Phantom Rickshaw* and *Wee Willie Winkie,* we see a new and maturer Kipling emerging. These two books contain three of Kipling's finest stories, 'The Strange Ride of Morrowby Jukes,' 'The Man Who Would be King' and 'The Drums of the Fore and Aft.' Had Kipling died at this point and written nothing else, these three stories might well have snatched his name from oblivion.

Kipling wrote many other admirable tales at this period, some of which deserve reference. 'The Gate of the Hundred Sorrows' is a realistic version of 'The English Opium Eater' and 'The Return of Imray' is another essay in the macabre. There are also the stories that deal, always from Kipling's political angle, with the fusion between Asiatic and European blood. 'Namgay Doola,' a story of the red-headed son of an Irish soldier and a Tibetan mother, and 'His Chance in Life,' where Michel D' Cruz, the black telegraph signaler with what Kipling regarded as the saving dash of white in him, quells a riot—a story in which the author indulges his favourite theme of the relapse of the converted native. The sketch of Indian life in 'On the City Wall,' came as a revelation to English readers, bringing to them again the fruits of Kipling's minute observation, his acute vision, and his easy confidence in his extraordinary powers.

Kipling found many diverse and unpleasant things in London. The so called Aesthetic Movement was a hasty thing for him. This movement was the bohemian. Verlaine and Rimbaud supported this movement of a *beauty maudite.* The symbolist poets of Paris influenced London. Arthur Symons, Lionel Johnson, and Dawson followed this. Kipling found many other literary activities and he viewed it with distaste. Such great men with diverse ideologies like Hardy, Meredith, George Moore, Conrad, James, Arnold, Browning, Morris, Shaw, Yeats, Eliot, were rather active. Such crazy writers like Peter, Swinburne, Ruskin and Beerbohm were writing. Kipling followed realism as Aubrey Beardsley followed aestheticism. Beardsley was too familiar with the evil. Wilde was reckless and triumphant. But he fell and his Aesthetic movement fell, leading to Kipling's rise. His work *Soldiers Three* had got fine reviews in journals like *Spectator World* and *St James's Gazette.* Then Andrew Lang was the first critic to advise Sampson Low to publish Kipling's six railway books. So *Soldiers Three* appeared in 1890. The Anglo-Indian journalists Mowbray Morris (now the staff of *Macmillan's* magazine) and Stephen Wheeler (now the staff of *St James's Gazette)* encouraged him. Kipling's famous poem "Ballad of East and West" appeared in *Macmillan's* in1889.

Kipling was in the company of 'the three old ladies and loved Mrs. Hill's sister Caroline Taylor again. He stayed in Vallier's Street, Strand. He could see Charing Cross, Cleopatra Needle and Waterloo Bridge. He toiled for writing. But then, he said, 'I can watch the fire, and weave tales, and dream dreams.' He worked ten hours of the day. We find indications of the life Kipling led in Villiers Street in *The Light that Failed*, when Dick Heldar:

> leaned into the darkness, watching the greater darkness of London below him. The chambers stood much higher than the other houses, commanding a hundred chimneys—

> crooked cowls that looked like sitting cats as they swung round . . . Northwards the lights of Piccadilly Circus and Leicester Square threw a copper-coloured glare above the black roofs, and southward lay all the orderly lights of the Thames. A train rolled out across one of the railway bridges, and its thunder drowned for a minute the dull roar of the streets.

Kipling was lonely, and he managed life economically. He felt like a hermit's crab. He became a member of the Savile Club in 1890. But he treated other writers with suspicion. He spoke to John Symonds harshly. After the 'House of Desolation,' the drab schooldays, and his seven years drudgery in India, Kipling passionately wished 'to own himself' to be independent of the patronage and control of others.

Kipling believed in God at this time. He also entertained people. In 1890 Kipling earned at least 400 pounds a year and he informed it to Caroline. The papers encouraged him and *The Times* wrote an article on him. Here it said:

> India has given us an abundance of soldiers and administrators, but she has seldom given us a writer. There is no question, however, that she has done this in the person of the author of the numerous short stories and verses of which we give the titles below. Mr Kipling has the merit of having tapped a new vein, and of having worked it out with real originality. He is even now a very young man, in spite of his seven or eight small volumes.

Kipling befriended Wolcott Balestier, a rich American this time, and he married Caroline, his sister later. Like Kipling, Balestier took London by storm, for his background and name. He represented the American publishing firm of John Lovell. He wanted an English author for publication and copyright activities. He befriended Hardy and Gosse. Balestier's sisters Josephine, Caroline and brother Beatty were also there. Well then Kipling and Balestier became friends, and Lovell published Kipling's works for his importance, and Kipling married Caroline. Besides, the widow writer W. K. Clifford who was struck by Kipling's writings encouraged him.

Mrs Clifford was able to introduce Kipling to important figures in London's literary world. Editors and publishers helped him to negotiate the dramatization of *The Light That Failed*. That she helped to set the door of London ajar for Kipling, enlarged his narrow outlook, and did something to diminish his social uncouthness. But this man hurt Clifford as he hurt many others in life and literature. Ernest Hemingway also did the same.

By the year 1890, Kipling was the lion in the field of literature at least in London. He worked with W. E. Henley for *National Observer* (formerly *Scots Observer*). Henley's circle had Stevenson, Yeats, Barrie, Kipling, Wells and Conrad. Henley loved to read Kipling's poems of the book *Barrack Room Ballads*. The poems like 'Fuzzy Wuzzy' and 'Cleared' impressed any. The 'Cleared' attacked Liberalism,

> My soul! I'd sooner lie in jail for murder plain and straight,
> Pure crime I'd done with my own hand for money, lust or hate
> Than take a seat in parliament by fellow-felons cheered.
> While one of those 'not provens' proved me cleared as you are cleared

The poem concluded bitterly:

> We are not ruled by murderers, but only—by their friends.

Henley found Kipling as a new poet, and Kipling found a supporter in the other. Kipling was not happy around 1890. Trix had left the family on marrying Fleming. His liaison with old Caroline Taylor was over. Flow Garrard showed more interest in her painting than in Kipling. Now his parents got back to England and settled down in Kensington. Their presence helped him, rather. 1890 was said to be *annus mirabilis* for him. He published not only *Barrack Room Ballads* and Indian books of short stories, but also stories and poems in *Harpers's, Lippincott's* and *Macmillan's*. He published such stories as 'The Head of the District,' 'The Courting of Dinah Shall,' 'The Man who was,' 'Without Benefit of Clergy,' 'At the

End of the Passage,' 'The Mark of the Beast' and 'On Greenhow Hill.' However, his novel *The Light that Failed* failed. Lockwood as well as Alice and Trix guided Kipling in all these literary matters.

It is unnecessary to dwell on the light that failed, in which the hero, Dick Heldar, is overtaken by blindness. It need only be said that this work was largely autobiographical, that the 'house of desolation' is closely described, and the character of Flo Garrard thinly disguised as 'Maisie.' This unsatisfactory and ill-knit book suggested to a discerning eye a fact that was afterwards confirmed by "Captains Courageous," that the short story, not the novel, was Kipling forte, and the less he ventured into this genre the better for his own reputation.

Kipling became very famous just at his age of 24. His fame spread abroad. His fame spread to Australia, where the south Australian gazette described him as 'the literary sensation of the day.' And to America where the *New York Mail* and *Express* inquired in a banner headline; 'Will success turn his head?'

Once in 1890 his health broke and he visited Italy. He met Lord Dufferin and spoke to him about Indian rule. He also worried about piracy of his books in America. Soon Lovell published all of Kipling's books with a foreword by Henry James. Walter Besant advised Kipling to have A. P. Watt as his literary agent. Later Watt's son did it. Besant asked Kipling to avoid literary squabbles, factions and cliques. Kipling yet had a good admiration in literary circles as his poetry was quite popular. As George Orwell quotes, Kipling's poem 'The English Flag' is one in the context:

> Winds of the world, give answer! They are whimpering to and fro- And what should they know of England who only England know?

For the first time, in this poem, the wild scenes and strange distant places over which the English flag waved, thrilling with wonderful virtuosity in the language of the extent of their empire.

In June 1891 Kipling visited America. He had a bad encounter with the press as Charles Dickens had it earlier.

Kipling got fame so easily and so early, but he could not face its consequence. He got back. He journeyed by the *Union Line* to the Capetown in 1891. Kipling traveled to Tasmania in the SS *Doric* and to New Zealand. He enjoyed the official protection as a sacred cow. He soon journeyed to Colombo and traveled to Lahore. This was his sentimental journey. Henry James wrote a month later; "Kipling strikes me personally as the most complete man of genius..... that I have ever known."

Kipling was staying with his parents in Lahore when, to his unspeakable grief, he received a telegram from Caroline Balestier telling him that Wolcott was dead. He had died in Germany from a virulent typhoid germ brought with him from London. Balestier was writing his part of the novel called *Naulahka* (in collaboration with Kipling) at this time. Balestier was writing the American scenes, Kipling the Indian, and Balestier had reported progress from time to time by cable. The work was nearly finished when Balestier went to Leipzig on the business of the English Library. He fell desperately ill in Dresden, and died on 6 December. *Naulakha* was one of Kipling's least successful books. An alien hand lay heavy on him, and reading the dry, stilted chapters contributed by Balestier about life in the Middle West, one is again astonished by the spell that this man exercised.

Kipling rushed back to England and mourned the friend's death. Kipling and Caroline got together and marred in 1891 at All Souls, Langham place. The wedding was quiet. Henry James stood for Caroline and Ambrose Poynter for Kipling. Edmund Gosse was also present. James did not like Caroline, nor liked the match.

Kipling decided to continue his travel around the world. He left London in February 1892. The couple sailed for New York in *Teutonic*. He reached Battleboro, the Balestiers' home, and Beatty Balestiers, the formidable tough guy who was to play painful part in his life later was there.He found New England in snow, and liked the country. The beauty of Mt Monadnock pleased him, remembering Emerson's remark 'the wise old giant busy with his sky affairs.'

After a few day reconnaissance the Kiplings resumed their wedding tour. From New York they set out again for St Paul,

Chicago, Winnipeg, and Vancouver, where they embarked on 4 April in the *Empress of India* for Japan. In Vancouver he bought 20 acres of land, which he discovered later, had belonged to another party.

The Kiplings travelled in Yokohama and experienced the beauty of the island country, and also an earthquake. He lost his money in a bank there. Kipling's gloom increased. Still they boarded the *Express of China* on 27 June, and Kipling read his story 'The Taking of Lungtungpen.' He sent his accounts of the travels to *The Times*. Back again, the stormy American period began. At the family estate 'Maplewood,' Beatty lived a harsh life with his wife Marjorie. Then the couple lived in 'Bliss Cottage,' here he wrote 'Love o' Women.' Kipling actually belonged to no country, and here he liked to stay for long. Daughter Josephine was born here on 29 December 1892. Later he had one more daughter and she died soon. Kipling was disturbed by the event of death. Kipling loved farming and animals, and the wild northern climate.

Here, at last, was home—Kipling's first and his own, and how different it was from the bungalow in India with its tamarisks and eucalyptus trees. He referred to the house as a ship, with the propeller the material provision of the furnace and kitchen at the stern, and his own study as the captain's bridge at the bow, opening on the south and east. Before the house was finished Lockwood Kipling, now retired, but with many active years before him, arrived in Vermont, to the delight of Rudyard and Carrie. He took an immediate interest in 'Naulakha.' The father advised the son-writer about the books *The Jungle Books, The Seven Seas* and *The Day's Work*.

As in all his writing for children, Kipling gave these stories a particular loving care, his daemon soaring to new heights of inspiration. And his reward has been that generations of children have since been enthralled by them, so that they have become the greater part of many an adult's memories of childhood. Well Kipling might have told his wife that he had received an access of power, "the return of a feeling of great strength," for into the Jungle Books are poured the full glory of his imaginative genius, untainted by bitterness, and unalloyed by special pleading. Had he written nothing else, these inspired stories would have made a powerful claim to immortality.

In the 'Bliss Cottage' Kipling wrote many vulgar verses. But 'The Sergeant's Wedding,' 'For to Admire' and 'Follow me One' are very superior. Kipling developed an interest in athletics. His friends were also few. He met such men like Charles Eliot Norton, a Harvard professor, Browning's son Pen Browning, and Arthur Conan Doyle. Kipling's best friend was Dr James Conland. He also had parties in the house. Likewise, Kipling's only work was writing, and Caroline took care of the house. She took care of his publications. 'I'm no more than a cork on the water when Carrie is with me,' said he once.

There is much gossip about Kipling's shyness, and desire for seclusion. Though once he was a journalist, he never liked publicity. Therefore, many Americans disliked him. He also disliked Americans. Lord Birkenhead quotes this: He discussed these matters with John Hay from the State Department, who replied in a phrase which remained indelibly in Kipling's mind: 'America's hatred of England is the hoop round the forty four staves of the Union. So, when a man comes out of the sea we say to him: 'See that big bully over there in the east? He's England. Hate him, and you're good American.' Kipling's attitude towards America and Americans was always curious, not to say touchy and explosive (wrote an American friend). One minute he would load us down with compliments; in the next, attack with vicious precision. If I said something about the ruthless measures which produced the British Empire, he would turn on me like a bull, and bellow that Americans had no cause to boast. Who fell upon decadent Mexico, after she had been beaten by a 10,000 handful of Texans on their own, and marched victoriously over her prostrate armies, snatching New Mexico, Arizona and the Southern half of California with scarcely the decent pretence of a fair purchase? Who tore the Philippines and Porto Rico from a Spain too poor to fight a single battle? Who ran into a hornet's nest of revolution in the Philippines, and made un unholy mess of governing even miserable little Porto Rico?"

The year 1893 ended fruitfully for Kipling. The Kiplings visited England meanwhile, and the elder Kiplings had settled down in a Wiltshire village. In July Kipling revisited Westward Ho! While he was in London, he transacted an important piece of business, closing a contract with Wheelers by which he bought back the English copyright of his first six Railway Bookstall books for £1200, while Wheeler retained the Indian sales for himself.

Meanwhile Kipling published the novel *The Brushwood Boy* in the *Century Magazine* in 1894. He was paid 354 pounds for it. At this time, he befriended Theodore Roosevelt, the future president of America. Kay Robinson the old boss in India and the Doubleday publishers met him. On 31 December he added his usual end-of-year note to Caroline's diary: "And so ends our fourth and best year. The Lord had been good to us beyond telling, and we have taken delight in all the days of our life."

Beatty, Kipling's brother-in-law lived at 'Maplewood.' This man picked up a quarrel with Kipling very brutally so that Kipling left for England. Beatty's main passion was for offering hospitality to others, and his only serous enemy drink, under the influence of which the darker side of his character would emerge with sudden and alarming violence. He was a brilliant talker and raconteur, and a dangerous man to argue with, quick as lightning on to a weak point, swift and brutal in repartee. Wolcott had worried about this scapegrace brother. Kipling had a difference of opinion with him once. Two persons of exceptional strength and determination, and precisely antipathetic character, were now opposed to one another. The fatal quarrel, then between Kipling and his brother-in-law had its origins in a Balestier family feud, beginning in childhood with an early collision between Beatty's wayward character and his sister's love of domination.

Kipling continued his writing in 1896. He was asked by the New York Paper *Sunday World* to write an article "Armenia could never Conquer England." He attended Yale Students Kipling Club and wrote the poem "Attend ye Lasses" for the occasion. This year he wrote the book *Captains_Courageous* about cod-fishing. He now had the feeling that the novel was a failure. He thought it was not his forte.

In one such occasion Beatty encountered Kipling and said "' See here-I want to speak to you.' He looked terrible. Kipling said, 'If you have anything to say, say it to my lawyers." The other came with anger: 'By Jesus; this is no case for lawyer's. This bad episode affected Kipling. Later he kept a pistol. He took the case to sheriff and ordered Beatty's arrest. The trial was still worse.

Kipling's testimony was so contradictory that had first been given to laughter, and the sympathy that had first been given to him by the townspeople ebbed towards Beatty. The case left Kipling prostrate for days. Caroline wrote in her diary on 12 May: 'Beatty's trial comes on in the a.m. and lasts until 5 p.m. leaving Rud a wreck. The lawyers play to the reporters. May 13: Rud a total wreck. Sleeps all the time dull and listless and dreary. These are dark days for us.'

The American period was nearly over. Pan was soon to be driven from Vermont. Kipling knew that he could never again recapture the tranquil happiness of those first years, and Vermont must for ever remain for him a place of evil associations. When the time came to go, Caroline was in tears, and Kipling seemed broken-hearted. He said: 'I love 'Naulakha,' and as he spoke of the touch of autumn already on the distant hills, tears filled his eyes.

The Kiplings arrived in London by Lloyd streamer *Bremen*, and they felt happy to be in their native land. Soon they leased a house 'Rock House' in Torquay. Kipling's energies revived and he published *The Seven Seas*, a collation of verse. The Kiplings passed time, riding the new thing called bicycle or attending a naval office programme. The Navy people liked his poem 'Mc Andrew's Hymn.'

Soon Norton published an article on Kipling's poetry in the *Atlantic Monthly*, and the poet replied: "True it is, most sadly true that I have not been true to my duties, but I did not know that I had been so untrue. As you know I love the fun and the riot of writing (I am daily and nightly perplexed with my private responsibilities before God.) and there are times when it is just a comfort and delight to let out with the pen and ink—so long as it does not do anyone any moral harm I don't believe very much in my genius. Then there is the danger it seems of a man running off into William Waston's kind of wordy rot if he at a comparatively tender age consider himself a poet."

In December 1896 Kipling completed the book of stories *Stalky & Co* which annoyed 'Stalky' himself. He read these stories as he wrote them, and his cousins roared with laughter. The stories seem to describe school life. 'In *Stalky & Co.,'* wrote Edward Shanks, 'Kipling took his life as an author in his hands. It could not have been other than a violent shock to readers brought up on *Tom Brown's Schooldays*. The venture succeeded because the stories were superb of their sort.' In this book Price is 'Head Sahib', the parson is 'Padre Sahib' and the school is a forcing House for the militia whom he had admired in India; the book has the so called motif of 'wish-fulfillment.' Kipling loved Indian experience as he thanked Lord Roberts for his copy of *Forty-one Years in India.*

Kipling liked March as the climate remembered him the climate of Brattleboro. Kipling remained hard at work, refusing to write a Jubilee poem, saying : 'It's rather outside my beat and if I tried, I am afraid I should make a mess of it, but surely London is full of loyal poets who are all getting odes ready against May.' All was not well for the Kiplings at Torquay. It was, he thought, the *Feng-Shui* the spirit of the house itself. His own health was not so good. In 1897, the Jubilee year, the Kiplings left the place for London. They stayed in a hotel overlooking Hyde Park. As Carolina became pregnant they moved to a house near Brighton. Kipling felt like a houseless gypsy.

They came in June to 'North End House,' Lady Burne-Jones's home in the little fishing village of Rottingdean, where Kipling had spent his last days before sailing for India fourteen years before. Kipling's cousin, Baldwin, had married the eldest daughter of the Ridsdale family who lived in 'The Dane,' the house on one side of the green. On the other was Burne-Jones's 'North End House' and in the centre, opposite the church, 'The Elms,' the house into which Kipling was soon to move.

Meanwhile, as we have seen, the Lockwood Kiplings had some time before left India for ever and settled in a small stone house near Tisbury in Wiltshire. Here Lockwood erected a building for his portfolios and architectural books, modelling tools and varnishes, and lived happily, immersed in his work and visiting his neighbours.

Kipling visited Balliol College in Oxford and interacted with the students. He engaged in angry discussion with Bleyber. The latter would criticize the British Empire which hurt Kipling. So acrimonious did these discussions become that Bleyber would be left gasping with a dangerously quickened pulse, while Kipling strode angrily out of the house, warned in the end by the local doctor to cease these conversations "unless you want to murder him." Kipling from this year 1897 developed his views about the aggressive intentions of Germany. He thought England could save herself only by her own exertions. 1897 was the year of Queen Victoria's Jubilee. Kipling felt strangely uneasy about the news that came to him from abroad. There had been trouble in South Africa after the Jameson Raid, and he was warned of further disturbance.

Kipling now decided to write the world famous poem 'Recessional,' as a *nuzzur-wattu* (*nuzzur-wattu* means an averter of the Evil Eye). He wrote it again and again as Prof Norton's daughter Sarah attests it. Sarah requested the poet not to throw away the rough draft and asked him to retain the repetition of the last couplet (as a retrain) of the first stanza. The first stanza of the poem which first appeared in *The Times* is quoted here:

> God of our fathers, known of old,
> Lord of our far-flung battle-line,
> Beneath whose awful hand we hold
> Dominion over palm and pine-
> Lord god of hosts, be with us yet,
> Lest we forget—lest we forget!

Many people congratulated Kipling for this best Kiplingiana. Arthur Sullivan decided to set it to music. Some also said that the poet copied the metrics of Cordial Newman's 'England.' It was further suggested that another famous line:

Beneath whose awful hand we hold
Dominion over palm and pine-

derived from Eemerson who had written:

And grant to dwellers with the pine
Dominion o'er the palm and vine.

'Recessional,' which has so often been criticized as typically arrogant and brutal, was in fact, at a moment of national apotheosis, an unusually humble admonition to the English people to keep the law as a special obligation. Of the line "or lesser breeds without the law," George Orwell wrote years later:

> This line is always good for a snigger in pansy-left circles. It is assumed as a matter of course that the 'lesser breeds' are natives,' and a mental picture is called up of some pukka sahib in a pith-helmet kicking a coolie. In its context the sense of the line is almost the exact opposite of this. The phrase 'lesser breeds' refers almost certainly to the Germans, and especially the pan-German writers who are 'without the law' in the sense of being lawless, not in the sense of being powerless.
>
> The whole poem, conventionally thought of as an orgy of boasting, is a denunciation of power-politics, British as well as German.. . . (Kipling) still believes that pride comes before a fall, and that the gods punish *hubris*.

Kipling got a son John on 17 August. The whole Kipling family was over- joyed. Now the Kiplings were living at 'The Elms.'

The Kiplings had a visit to South Africa. They were happy and the Cape brought back vividly his childhood in India. They met Cecil Rhodes, the empire-builder. Kipling spoke to him about the expansion and preservation of the empire. The Kiplings visited Kimberley, Bulawoyo and Johannesburg. They returned to England after four months. Then America was in war against Spain, and Kipling wrote about this sister nation:

Take up the white man's burden
Send forth the best ye breed-

Go bind your sons to exile
To serve your captives' need

It was a call to that great sister-nation, the United States, to join in the vast civilizing movement which in Kipling's eyes England had spread across the world. Their time had also now come to

. . . . . wait in heavy harness
On fluttered folk and wild -
Your new-caught sullen people,
Half devil and half child.

It was exhortations of this kind, always less offensive when carefully analysed than at first sight, that so enraged men and women of liberal habits of thought, and they were the main cause of the steep decline in Kipling's reputation.

Kipling added some more pieces to *Stalk & Co*, wrote an article on his African tour and begin his work on *Kim.* In June his novel *The Light That Failed* became a drama, 'a vivid and agonizing play.' The book of stories *The Day's Work* was published in October.

The first of September 1898 found Kipling on HMS *Perlorus* for naval manoeuvres off the Irish coast as the guest of Captain Norbury. He remained, through the firm control of Caroline and the vigilance of A.P. Watt, an author well defended from the commercial angle. Contracts were strongly fought out, and infringements of copyright decreased.

The students of Horsemander School in Kent requested Kipling for two verses each for three pences. He wrote for them and their school magazine was well-sold. Later Cambridge undergraduates asked Kipling a poem for their *Cantab,* and he replied:

There was once an author who wrote:
'Dear Sir: In reply to your note
Of yesterday's date,

I am sorry to state
It's no good at the prices you quote.'

They asked him for a photo, and he refused it in a veiled but aggressive manner.

Kipling had a series of disasters now onwards. His sister Trix become insane. The death of 'Uncle Ned' (Edward Burne-Jones) saddened him. Caroline wished to see her mother, and the family sailed to America on 25 January 1899. Kipling, who was tired of England, embarked on his holiday in mood of juvenile zest. I've had enough of grey skies and boiled potatoes. I'm going to where the sun shines and oysters is cheap. I shall have 'em on toast, likewise stewed *and* roasted and fried; and I shall have grapefruit for breakfast and nineteen different sorts of bread.'

They docked in New York on February and Kipling was again surrounded by reporters, his old enemies. They asked him for an interview: He said, briefly: 'Every effort of art is an effort to be sincere. There is no surer guide, I am sure, than the determination to tell the truth that one feels.' The reporters unhappy of Kipling left, singing:

We've met with many men from overseas,
An' some of 'em was shy and some was not.
The Frenchmen and the Germans and Chinese,
But Kipling was the hardest of the lot.
Some of 'em talked in English and the rest
Would talk from early winter to the fall,
But the Mowgli-man we found the greatest pest,
For the bloomin' sod 'e wouldn't talk at all.

The Kiplings American tragedy began simply thus. First Caroline fell ill, and then the daughter and the father. Dr. Dunham who had recently married Caroline's sister Josephine treated them with care. Kipling had delirium, and was assonated of " dog- tread in the underground." It was sleep, and recovery had begun, in the meantime the world outside held its breath. Telegrams poured in and were filed by his publisher

F. N. Doubleday. The Kaiser sent an anxious inquiry, and far away in London Arnold Bennett, who was giving a musical party and reading the programme aloud to his guests, ended by saying 'God save Kipling' instead of 'God Save the Queen.'

This time the Kiplings stayed at friend de Forest's house in Long Island. Fortunately Kipling recovered, and his dear daughter Josephine passed away. Both Caroline and publisher F. N. Doubleday had been a tower of strength in the trouble.

By 26 March Kipling was allowed to see a few friends. He lay changed and thin, and his voice was hoarse. Sallie Norton sat by the bed with his hand in hers and saw a look of profound sadness about his face. Critics think this cruel blow was the beginning of his intellectual maturity.

The Kiplings were to find the house and garden at 'The Elms' full of the lost child. Rudyard told his mother that he saw her every time a door was opened, and every time a place was empty at table. Kipling spoke of Josephine to the end of his life as of a catharsis for his sorrow. In such stories as 'They' and 'Merrow Down' that we shall find the intensity of Kipling's passion. Staying near Guildford with Lockwood's friend, St Loe Strachey, two years later, and wandering about the countryside, he could not look at Merrow Down or any part of the Surrey landscape without thinking of his daughter:

> But long and long before that time
> (When bison used to roam on it)
> Did Taffy and her Daddy climb
> That down, and had their home on it.

Kipling's cousin, Angela Thirkell, wrote of Josephine's death: "Much of the beloved cousin Ruddy of our childhood died with Josephine and I feel that I have never seen him as a real person since that year."

Kipling visited a hotel of Lakewood. He stayed with Mrs. Catlin of Morristown. Caroline visited America again for collecting odds and ends. She reported that their 'Naulakha' was still at peace and green everywhere. Kipling spent much time with Philip Burne-Jones. In July Philip Burne-Jones began his famous portrait of Kipling : "It's just me at my writing table, and as like as one pea to another down to the flap of my pocket and the pipe at my side." The painting was a welcome break in Kipling's enforced idleness.

Kipling visited Sutherlandshire in August. The broad valleys and harsh solitude of the hills soothed him. The estate belonged to Andrew Carnegie.

Stalk and Co appeared on 6 October. Yet Kipling's suffering did not help him work more. He had an interest in volunteers and ordered for a car. The postscript ended "One year ended and I owe my life to Carrie. R. K."

In 1899 the English Govt in South Africa was doing badly. The Boer war was in the offing. Kipling did not believe that the Boers were fighting for liberty. He thought that they were a republic only in name, in reality a one-man despotism, feebly tempered by a corrupt and ignorant oligarchy. He would have agreed with his father's words: 'Since we have an Empire, needs must we hold it; it is our existence that is at stake.' He was here referring to the verses entitled 'The Absent-Minded Beggar.' A rhymed invitation, of singular vulgarity, to subscribe to a fund for soldiers' wives and children which appeared in the *Daily Mail* and became the most talked of publication of the hour. Lord Newton in his autobiography gives us an interesting glimpse of Kipling's touchiness in connection with this poem.

On 14 December Kipling was offered and refused a KCB. On this occasion Lord Salisbury's secretary came down to offer the distinction, but Kipling "felt he could do his work better without it."

On 20 January 1900 he and Carrie left for South Africa, and landed at Cape Town on 5 February. Next day he had an hour's talk with Lord Roberts, who had him a pass to go anywhere in South Africa. He wasted no time in using it to visit military hospitals and see conditions for himself. Here he met a group of journalists—L.S. Amery, who had represented *The Times* at Kruger's capital, Bennet Burleigh of the *Daily Telegraph*, Julian Ralph, an American who was in Africa on behalf of the London *Daily Mail*, and two men who were to become friends for life—H.A. Gwynne of Reuter's and Perceval London of *The Times*.

In mid-February Kipling heard that the siege of Kimberley had been raised. He was particularly please by this good news. Rhodes told Kipling that while shut up in Kimberley he had made plans to build a house on the 'Groote Schuur' estate for the use of artists and writers. As a beginning he offered it to the Kiplings for as long as they wished to stay. The thought of working in this heavenly climate in such lovely surroundings appealed to Rudyard. Carrie, too, welcomed the idea and went with Rhodes's architect, Herert Baker, to choose the site for a house to be built in the Dutch Colonial style.

The Friend was established as a paper for the troops, taking over the name and office of a small local paper, and Kipling joined the staff in March. Kipling was appalled by the sanitary arrangements revealed in the war, which had led to 8,000 cases of typhoid in Bloemfontein, to which was added the sickening stench of dysentery, he devoted himself to cheering the wounded in tours of the hospitals and trains from the front. At one of the daily meetings of the editors he suggested that they should have a club with a ritual something like that of Masons. On 29 March 1900 he had an experience in the army. The battle was raged between the English and the Boers. It stirred his pulses to watch the troops marching into Bloemfontein. The following verse shows a glimpse of this:

> From the corn and wine of the Lowlands to the stubborn hill of the North
>
> The word that heralds your coming shall call your army forth,
>
> With the voices of many cannon where the ordered legions pace,
>
> They shall give you welcome befitting the House of the Kings of our race.

Kipling returned to England on 3 April, and found that many people disliked the Boer war. He dismissed Englishmen's criticism of the empire with pity and contempt.

Kipling's Boer war experience, were bitter. Yet he talked of the common soldier as in 'Boots.' Look at the poem:

Don't—don't—don't—don't—look at what's in front of you
(Boots—boots—boots—boots—moven' up an' down again);
Men—men—men—men—men go mad with watchin' 'em,
An' there's no discharge in the war!

Try-try-try-to think o' something different
Oh-my-God-keep-me from going lunatic!
(Boots-boots-boots-boots-movin' up an' down again!)
There's no discharge in the war!

Kipling remembered the bitterness of Boer war even in his old age. It is said: "We charged ourselves step with the care and maintenance of all boredom. Whence horrible tales of our atrocities in the concentration camps. Eventually the 'war' petered out on political lines. Our men did not see why they should perish chasing stray commandoes, and then followed a sort of demoralizing 'handy-pandy' of alternate surrenders complicated by exchange of army tobacco for Boer brandy which was bad for both sides."

In India Kipling had seen the administrators of the Indian Civil Service grappling with their tasks in the baking oven of the Indian summer, spanning river, quelling epidemics, surveying jungles, and restraining native princes. From this had sprung his admiration "the strong man ruling alone."

Kipling never liked the new creed of democracy and in his poem 'Pagett MP,' he wrote derisively:

And I laughed as I drove from the station; but the mirth died out on my lips
As I thought of the fools like Pagett who write of their 'Eastern Trips.'
And the sneers of the traveled idiot, who duly misgoverns the land;
And I prayed to the Lord to deliver another one into my hand.

In Tokyo Kipling had argued with his Japanese hosts about the new constitution:

> 'You've a Parliament, have you not?'
>
> 'Oh yes, with parties—Liberal and Radical.'
>
> 'Then they will both tell lies to you and to each other.

Kipling as a successful writer, began to think of the empire. He was as great as Dickens and Tennyson before. He was assured of immortality. He became an authoritarian in his conception of civil government. He believed that the 'job belongs to the man who can do it.' He disliked radicalism 'which would always support a German artisan against an English nobleman, a negro against a white overseer, a mutinous soldier against his officer. He disliked Japan as it became strong against British empire. He had regarded the shrill chatter of the Congress Party in India with contempt, and the vulgarity of Congress in the USA with horror.

Democracy to him was a system conducted by unpractical people who tended to obstruct those who were properly equipped in the art of government. Kipling believed that the British ruled India for its uplift. He felt that the end of British rule would lead to a civil war and corruption in India. This is partially true today.

That is why in *The Jungle Books*, those inspired stories of animal life, there penetrates into the enchanted glades of the forest the antiseptic discipline of the public school. Mowgli is the district officer, or the prefect; although a child of the Jungle, he is a white man, and must therefore have predominance over even the most capable native colleagues—Bageera the Panther, or Kaa the Python; in a later story Mowgli is pressed into the service of the British Raj in the Forestry Commission.

Kipling finished *Kim* in South Africa. He worked on it for seven years and had his father's advice for its finishing. This more successful novel was his farewell to India. He published it in 1901. Years before in Vermont, he had an idea that an Irish boy was born in India and he immersed in native life. The novel is a full-length story, enchanting, intensely moving and authentically great. There is all of India in this inspired *tour de force*. The novel is an artistic triumph.

Kipling criticized the lethargy and lapses of the civil government in India, and this naturally upset the editors and the Anglo- Indian community. Yet Kipling admired and encouraged the works in the field--the bridge-builder, the doctor struggling with a cholera epidemic and the district officer. Alfred Milner was his ideal in South Africa. Kipling believed in the supremacy of the British Empire as Cecil Rhodes did. According to Lord Birkenhead, his hatred of liberalism was returned in full measure, as can be seen in these sentences:

> The rocket that rose in the East completed its arc in the Transvaal. Mr Kipling in a word was the poet of the great reaction. Through all the amazing crescendo of the nineties, with its fever of speculation, its Barney Barnatos, its Whitaker Wrights, its swagger and its violence, its raids and its Music Hall frenzies, the bard of the banjo marched ahead of the throng, shouting his songs of the barrack-room, telling his tales of the camp-fire and jungle, proclaiming the worship of the great god Jingo.

Kipling hated the Indian Congress as well as its " university trained mules." Orwell disliked Kipling's violent strain in writing and his intellectual interest in cruelty. Orwell said, "Kipling is a jingo-imperialist, he is morally insensitive, and aesthetically disgusting." Kipling had a wrong idea about war as a necessary instrument of policy. He best thought that English men must give more importance to war-practice than to cricket. This view is explicit in his story 'The Army of a Dream' and the poem 'The Islanders. He thought war helps for law and order. This is why the first World War took a revenge on him when his only son John was killed in it. Kipling's stories 'Many Inventions' and 'The Head of the District' show his intellectual brutality. Lord Birkenhead observes "Kipling believed that the word 'wall' was a symbol of protection. He thought that the wall should not be breached."

Kipling hated the politicians and lazy rulers for this reason; he said they wanted only money. He lashed out at his indifferent countrymen thus:

> Now we can only wait till the day, wait and apportion our shame.
>
> These are the dykes our fathers left, but we could not look to the same.
>
> Time and again we were warned of the dykes, time and again we delayed:
>
> Now it may fall, we have slain our sons as our fathers we have betrayed.

The Kiplings visited South Africa again in 1900. They stayed in the Rhodes' house 'The Woolsack' on the 'Groove Scours' estate. They revisited this place every winter for some years. They liked the land as it looked like a paradise. "No one seems to explain the fascination of Africa," he said. 'We unite to curse it root and branch and yet we love it. I wish you could ever have seen the sunlight and the space of it and the great breadth of wine-dark sea where I am going to lunch with Carrie.' Here Kipling wrote the book *Just So Stories*.

Kipling's veneration for Rhodes was profound, as was his gratitude for Rhodes's generosity, but Jameson's wit matched his own and could draw a spark from him, and he adopted the character of Jameson for the poem 'If.' Kipling liked and once admired Rhodes as if God. The Kiplings dined with Rhodes and the discussion about the British Empire grew. Here also grew the plan of the Rhodes scholarship.

One bad event took place at this time. A lunatic followed Kipling in order to shoot him. He shot him lightly, of course, the same not hitting Kipling. The man was arrested. We do not know why this so happened. Here Kipling and friends started a rifle- range club, another war in mind.

Kipling back in London for summer resumed his work. He was pestered by visitors. He clearly disliked them. Caroline was not well over the years, in spite of their visits to South Africa. He also bought a car drawn by horses, and enjoyed rides. Kipling's poem 'The Islanders' of the year 1902 was too bitter for the Englishmen. It begins thus:

> And ye vaunted your fathomless powers, and ye flaunted your iron pride
>
> Ere-ye fawned on the Younger Nations for the men who could shoot and ride!
>
> Then ye returned to your trinkets: then ye contented your souls
>
> With the flannelled fools at the wicket or the muddied oafs at the goals.

On 26 March they heard that Cecil Rhodes was dead. Kipling was deeply stricken by the lonely agony of Rhodes's death-struggle, when with suffused face and bursting heart he staggered from room to room in his little cottage built on the rocks at St James's gasping for air.

The Kiplings purchased a house called 'Bateman's' (built in AD 1634) at Burwash in Sussex, with 33 acres for 9,300 pounds. This was his last house-moving. The house stood near a stream, and his had a mill there for electricity. Here Kipling did a lot of writing. *The Five Nations,* his book of South African verse appeared in 1903. He wrote the stories 'Bathurst,' and 'They.' He was a sort of science-fiction writer. His story 'With the Night Mail' he described an Atlantic crossing by air in the year 2000. He envisaged radio- telephony also before Bleriot flew the channel seven years later. 'As Easy as A. B.C.' describes a new technology. 'Wireless' is his inventive story. This is Kipling's finest short story.

Kipling studied British history and wrote of it. He wanted to write about the Roman Britain. *Puck of Pook's Hill* and *Rewords and Fairies* evidence this amply. But the real inspiration came from Kipling's own children, John and Elsie, who were to become Dan and Una in *Puck of Pook's Hill.* 'Bateman's' provided Kipling a strong inspiration as if a place of magic. This book *Puck of Pook's Hill* speaks about the ageless Puck appearing from the thickets to Dan and Una, friendly yet immortal, and, by bringing before their enraptured eyes figures from bygone centuries, presenting to the children in a series of episodes the unfolding history of England. Marcus Crouch observes, "Kipling is an intuitive historian, but generations of children have come to see through his eyes the moving pageant of England's story." In the *Puck* stories one sees Hal Dawes "dear, dear land," the long process of change—the God of the Knife, and the unchanging country ways, 'seely Sussex for everlasting.' J. I. M. Stewart in his article "The Unfading Genius of Rudyard Kipling" wrote, 'Kipling's vision of the procession of the generations, centuries, epochs and their millennial gravure upon the face of England is surely the deepest, the strongest ever to have been achieved in terms of literary art. . . . It is a vision that to this day enriches England for us.'

Kipling's son John grew into a young man. This time supporters asked Kipling to stand for MP election, which he refused. His criticism of Liberalism and Politicians continued. Kipling is of the view that politicians side with the winning causes. In 1906, Jameson lost his position in South Africa. Kipling now decided to forget South Africa, as he forgot America before. Kipling at this time pressed for compulsory national service.

Kipling, however accepted a doctorate from Durham, a D.Lit from Oxford, and an honor from McGill University, Montreal, Canada. In September 1907 he embarked on an arduous tour of Canada, covering the country in exhausting train journeys—Prairie Country, Regina, Calgary, Vancouver, Ottawa, Toronto—speeches, reporters and receptions. Kipling thought Canada was a better country—safe, clean and orderly. He remained interested in that Canada, and two Canadians Andrew Bonar Law and Max Aitkin became his friends. Soon he got Nobel Prize which Kipling received with pleasure from King Gustav V. John Gardner added: "At least one Liberal regarded Kipling's Nobel Prize with amazement and anger. He is the first Englishman to be crowned in the Court of Literary Europe.' He is chosen as our representative man of Letters, while George Meredith, Thomas Hardy, and Algernon Charles Swinburne are still amongst us. The goldsmiths are passed by and the literary blacksmith is exalted.'"

Kipling also visited Switzerland yearly from 1908. Kipling's old teacher Carmel Price died in 1910. His own mother died in 1910 followed by his father the next year. He remembered his mother's wit and father's mellow philosophy. Kipling soon destroyed their letters and we do not know why. Many of his other old friends had gone—Ned Burne-Jones, Aggie Poynter, Alfred Baldwin, Henley, Conland and Charles Eliot Norton. Trix had several nervous breakdowns and was of little comfort to him, and from now on he would rely mainly on Perceval London, with whom he had worked on the Bloemfontein *Friend*, and H.A.Gwynne, who was to become editor of the *Morning Post* in 1911, and whose extreme right-wing opinions perfectly matched his own.

Kipling felt miserable, and made a trip to Vernetles Baines for change. He bought a Rails-Royce. He wrote of the war minister Hal Dane badly. He criticized coal strike. He visited Venice in March 1912. Meanwhile he was exploring with fascination a new world, the Royal Flying Corps. Here again his foresight was remarkable. He realized that he was standing on the threshold of a revolution, like primitive man when he first launched his canoe. Kipling threw himself with almost despairing ardour into any cause likely to promote national virility. Kipling visited Egypt in February 1913.

Kipling had anticipated the World War I, and it came at last. He offered his only son John just 16. He joined the Irish Guards. At this time, there was a rumour that the Kiplings may visit America, and the English government stopped such a thing, as the same government evicted D. H. Laurence from south-west of England in 1914. Kipling was now up to making recruiting speeches, raising funds, visiting wounded soldiers and autographing books. He had been revolted by the terrorism, deliberately chosen, as he thought, by the Germans and had retaliated with two savage stories that winter—'Swept and Garnished' and 'Mary Postgate.'

Now Kipling felt that the wall of the empire was ill-kept, because of people's trance and now its bricks collapsing. This sounded like the beginning of one more Dark Age. Kipling visited France for an account of the war. His son was there already. He met Princess Victoria of Schleswig-Holstein, and she spoke to him about the war's cruelty. He met Clemenceau, and both spoke of the war. Clemenceau, like Kipling, detested political compromise and cowardice and was to stamp them out in France with brutal severity. Both men were ardent patriots, and were further united by a common contempt for the doctrinaire obstinacy of President Wilson. Many people liked Kipling's *The Jungle Books*. He visited Rheims, now reduced to 2,000 people from 100,000. He saw how Germans destroyed the town.

When Kipling spoke to his friend Perceval London, he said the Germans were shelling the Alastian town Thom. The French loved Kipling and one man asked as to how the idea of the *Jungle Book* came. One shook Kipling's hand saying *Le grand Rutyar*. The bad news came on 2 October from war office to the effect that John was missing. No doubt, the boy was killed in the war. This was a second blow to Kipling. His countrymen had disregarded his warnings—even flinched in boredom from their hero's writings—and now Kipling had to pay this terrible price. Kipling was numbed by his son's death and his grief is apparent in the bitter couplet:

> My son died laughing at some jest, I would I knew
>
> What it were, and it might serve me at a time when jests are few.

It is apparent, too, in the poem, 'My Boy Jack,' put into the mouth of the mourning mother of a young seaman:

> 'Have you news of my boy Jack?'
>
> Not this tide.
>
> 'When d'you think that he'll come back?'
>
> Not with this wind blowing, and this tide.

Edgar Allan Poe's world famous poem 'Raven' has this kind of echoes. Kipling never forgave the Germans for the death of his son. He saw in the 1914 war a preparation for the next one, and was deeply wounded that he only bored people, particularly the young, by his habit of incessant reminder. In 1917, Kipling wrote a book about the Irish Gourds, as a memorial to his dead son. In April a collection of stories entitled *A Diversity of Creatures* was published, and the same month found Kipling writing to C.R.L. Fletcher, the historian, on the subject of the corpse-factory in which the Germans were supposed to process their war-dead for pig-food.

Kipling visited Italian front in May 1917. In Rome, he witnessed the Beautification of a Carmelite nun. Then he visited Udine. Later he visited the Italian Ypress. This time Kipling refused the appointment of him as a Companion of Honor. He refused OM thoughtlessly four years later. In 1917, Kipling was assigned the work of Commissionership for consoling the dead. He also became a member of Rhodes scholarship in Oxford.

Kipling had an inclination of hero-worship. He worshipped Cecil Rhodes then, and President Roosevelt later. In his letter to the American President, Kipling reveals America's stand in the World War I:

> Dear Roosevelt,
>
> Our letters from England will have given you an insight into things as they are here. But I wish you could spend half a day with the Belgian refugees as they come into Folkestone. The look on their faces is enough, without having to hear their stories which are like tales from Hell. When people congratulate each other that So and So's womenfolk were shot outright one realizes a bit about German culture. As far as one makes out the rapings etc. were (and are) put through as part of a set plan to strike terror into the world. Of course, we in England may have these things happen to us : but frankly we are aghast at there being no protest from the USA against the Belgian dealings. It seems almost incredible that America, which has always stood so emphatically against these horros, should be silent now. Neutrality is of course understood, but surely neutrality cannot bar her from putting herself on record as officially opposed to Louvainism etc.

On 21 October 1918, Kipling wrote an extremely frank letter about the activities of President Wilson, and proceeds to an onslaught on the Papacy. Roosevelt, however, replied Kipling about why America did not take much interest in the war :

> But now, friend do not overstate your case. It is strong, and it needs no overstatement. You say that 'the United States existed for 142 years under the protection of the British Navy.' As a matter of fact for the first ninety years the British Navy, when, as was ordinarily the case, the British Government was more or less hostile to us, was our greatest danger.

Kipling emerged from the war with four preoccupations in mind—the continuance of his work, Ireland, India and Germany. In the meantime he sought relief from private sorrow and public anxiety in his work for the Imperial War Graves Commission. On 19 November 1918 he met the Prince of Wales, found him "keen about it all, and successfully proposed the text for all altars in the cemeteries.

Kipling loved France now. He signed autographs there, without hurting any as he did in England and America. His poem 'France' has the following stanza:

> Furious in luxury, merciless in toil,
> Terrible with strength that draws from her tireless soil;
> Strictest judge of her own worth, gentlest of man's mind,
> First to follow Truth and last to leave old Truths behind–
> France, beloved of every soul that loves its fellow kind!

Kipling's work in 1918 was similar to that of 1917 in quantity, covering a fairly wide file. He spent much time on his Irish Guards history, produced a shilling volume of selected verse, and wrote a number of assorted verses including 'The Lathes,' which dealt with munition workers.

The Kiplings health remained bad, and they made a somewhat depressing visit to Bath in February 1919, where they were visited by a Mr Brooking from Warrington, with proposals to start a Kipling Society on a large scale, a project which filled Rudyard with apprehension and annoyance.

In February 1920, the Kiplings also visited 'The House of

Desolation' at South Sea. Still Kipling spoke of 'Lorne Lodge' with horror. It was in this year in May that he went to London to see John's memorial cast in bronze, dismissed it as a failure, and ordered it to be undertaken again: it was finished in June, and passed as 'most satisfactory.' They made a journey to France to visit the ground over which the Irish Guards had fought. They visited a tentative grave of their son. Kipling received doctorates from the universities of Paris and Strasbourg. The French called Kipling a hero. He holidayed in Cannes. He met Bonar Law.

Back in England Kipling turned again to work and politics. He was disappointed at a cinema version by Pâté of *Without Benefit of Clergy* which he felt missed all the essential points of his story.

The Kiplings visited Spain in March 1922, and France in May of that year. Kipling felt proud of his being a link between England, France and the empire. He wrote 'The Kipling Pilgrimage.' The King delivered the speech which Kipling had composed. At this time, Mrs. Clare Sheridan's interview with Kipling about America was published in *New York Evening World* causing a scandal. Kipling had said in it that America did not take part in the war in proper time. Kipling's cousin Stanley Baldwin became the Prime Minister of England in 1922.

The most important event for him in 1923 was the publication of his *History of the Irish Guards in the Great War.* He also delivered a speech at the Royal College of Surgeons, prepared the king's speech on Italy, and finished 'The Janeites,' begun in 1922. He wrote 'The Prophet and the Country,' 'A Friend of the Family,' 'London Stone,' and began that strange and macabre story 'A Madonna of the Trenches,' which he had had long in his mind. He began work on a brilliant, even stranger fantasy 'The Wish House,' at the beginning of 1924, with its recurrent theme of cancer, agony and death. In October 1923 he was elected Lord Rector of St Andrew's University, and seized the opportunity of expounding his philosophy of life to the students in the spirit of 'If,' a message which was ill received by the large section of the public which was now blind to his warnings and sick of his nagging.

Lord Birkenhead writes of the next blow to the Kiplings: “1925 was a flat and uneventful year for Kipling. He had lost his two children, and the third had gone. The poet was restless and unsatisfied. Now the poet heard the rumours that he might be successor to poet Lord Tennyson.”

Every spare moment from Kipling’s literary routine and frequent bouts of pain and illness was now devoted to politics. Kipling combined at this time an incongruous zeal of the emergent Fascist Italy, under ‘a strong man ruling alone,’ with a vigilant mistrust of a soon-to-emerge Fascist Germany. Kipling now regarded his cousin Baldwin as a despicable Prime Minister. He had been disgusted by the readiness with which Baldwin had speeded the emancipation of India and Ireland, which had caused him to move, if possible, further to the right in politics.

In 1927 Kipling fulfilled a lifelong ambition by making a journey to Brazil, arriving in Rio on 13 February. On 5 October he went to France, where the Secretary of State of India, Lord Birkenhead, unveiled the war memorial at Neuve Chappelle to the Indian dead, delivering a speech which Kipling described to Lord Lloyd as the finest funeral oration since Gettysburg. Afterwards, at a luncheon attended by many French and English officers, including Foch, Kipling made a short and moving speech about the Indian soldiers fighting for England, and crossing a sea to do so which many of them believed to be ignoble.

In the same year the Kipling Society was founded. Kipling at this time came into contact with a man whom, by every convention of his life, he should have admired—Lawrence of Arabia—yet strongly resented him. Lawrence was present at a dinner at Brown’s Hotel, and was by then protégé of ‘Effendi.’ According to Lawrence, the governing classes were all blood-suckers, living on the starving poor; no man should have more than £200 a year—otherwise he should be ashamed to look his fellows in the face.

As the years passed, the English winter crept more and more into Rudyard's bones, and he went each year in quest of sunshine. The pursuit took the Kiplings to Algiers and Egypt. His ship left Marseilles port for Algiers in hard pale sunshine on an oily sea which immediately suggested flying fish to him.

Rudyard found much consolation, at this somewhat depressing period of his life, in his London clubs, the 'Athenaeum' and the 'Beef-steak.' Although he had accepted a number of university distinctions, he was a difficult bird to snare for their public functions. He was particularly reluctant to give public addresses, and is believed to be unique in academic history in having refused to deliver the Romanes Lecturer at Oxford, the Leslie Stephen Lecture at Cambridge, the Gifford Lecture at Edinburgh, and the Reith Lectures of the BBC.

Kipling is a great writer, indeed. He got more fame in young age, and was soon forgotten as the young did not like his themes of duty, patriotism and military preparedness. Interestingly Kipling was more famous abroad. But he is sure of fame for ever. Maurice Baring observes, "He is 'safe in the Temple of Fame,' which once you have entered you cannot leave. For this Temple is like a wheel. It goes round and round, and sometimes some of its inmates are in the glare of the sun, and sometimes they are in the shade, but they are there; and they never fall out.

Kipling became famous for his stories and verse. But he also attempted his hand at fiction. He produced the novel *The Light that Failed* (1891) and *The Naulahka (*1892*)* with Wolcott Balestire. The first was a bad book, and critics said that it was 'The Book that Failed.' Kipling did not have enough patience to write characterization that would sustain readers' interest. *Kim,* by far the most successful of his longer works, is not by any normal standards a novel at all, but a series of linked episodes in the progress of the Lama and Kim. 'Kipling was rarely capable of creating a character,' wrote another critic. Lord Birkenhead writes, "We may test this undoubted truth by comparing Kipling's characterization with that of Somerset

Maugham. They were the two most widely-read writers of the short story of their day, but unlike Kipling, Maugham was also, at his best, a most capable novelist. And the reason for this difference lies in the fact that Maugham was profoundly interested in the quirks of human nature and fascinated by the good and evil at war in every human breast."

Kipling was at his best in writing short stories. Maugham himself says: "Kipling alone among the English writers of the short story, can bear comparison with the masters of France and Russia. Though he captured the favour of the great public when first he began to write, and has retained a hold on it ever since, cultivated opinion has always been somewhat scornful of him. He has identified with an Imperialism which as obnoxious to many sensitive persons, and certain characteristics of his style have always been irksome to readers of fastidious taste. But he was a wonderful, varied, and original teller of tales. He had a fertile invention, a merit in any writer, and to a supreme degree the gift of narrating incident in a surprising and dramatic fashion. His influence for a while was great on his fellow-writers, but perhaps greater on his fellow-men who led, in one way or another, the sort of life he dealt with. When one traveled in the East it was astonishing how often one came across men who had modeled themselves on the creatures of his invention."

Kipling's unpleasant public relations were based on his personal ill-health. He had unhappy childhood. He suffered from vomiting, haemorrhages and perforation. Even Caroline suffered in her last years. He suffered from gastritis in 1915. In 1922 Caroline found him "very ill, yellow and shrunken." Kipling was haunted by the dread of cancer. "He suffered," said his daughter, 'frightful and incessant pain over a very long period with the patience of an angel. He never complained. The most he ever said, when doubled up in agony, was: "Just leave me alone; I'll be all right soon."

Kipling's depression from now on was increased by a steadily deteriorating conjugal relationship. As his health declined, Caroline exercised upon him a more rigorous control. Kipling was timid, less social. Caroline's threats of self-violence terrified Kipling, and the terror made him even more submissive. All this, coupled with the constant physical pain, reduced him to a terrible condition. Kipling was devoted to Caroline, and he was intensely grateful for all she had done for him.

Kipling's troubled later life is said to have affected his writings. Lord Birkenhead observes: "Kipling's later stories had a change in characterization and narrative technique. They are not linear in details. They are rather obscure and abstract, his concentration being rested on the psyche of characters. First, when he wrote in Indian ink, he would write a story, edit it, and make it free from dead wood. The late stories are indeed pared to the bone to such an extent that we struggle to understand them. They are closely packed like the skin of an onion." In 'The Eye of Allah,' 'A Madonna of the Trenches' and 'The Gardener' four or five different interpretations can be placed upon the stories, which mean that four or five different tales are contained in each story, although the average reader will only notice the obvious one. But the public did not regard Kipling's 'late' manner as glorious fun. They wanted him to continue writing the sort of stories long familiar to them, like those in *Plain Tales from the Hills*. They were baffled by the ambiguity of the new ones. On one layer of 'The Gardener' we find a story of an upper-class Englishwoman, suffering agonies through her code of respectability; and on another a story of the mercy of God to sinners. The gardener in the war cemetery relives Helen of her terrible burden of deception by revealing his knowledge that the dead soldier whose grave she is seeking is her son. The revelation is equivalent to rolling away the stone of the sepulchre, as did the angel in the New Testament account, and that this was Kipling's meaning made clear in the accompanying poem :

> One day of all my years –
> One hour of that one day –
> His angel saw my tears
> And rolled the stone away.

The swing of some modern critics toward Kipling has been

largely based on these 'late' stories. "What narrative there is," said Lord Radcliffe in a lecture to the Kipling Society, '-often there is little—runs like a root below the surface of the story, and all that shows above ground are the shoots that tell by implication what lies underneath. Kipling had forged one more of his remarkable tools.

By 1930 Carrie's health was shaken as that of her husband's. She suffered from rheumatism and diabetic. The doctors advised them a foreign trip. They visited the West Indies, taking with them Lady Milner's daughter Helen Hardinge. Again Carry had to be put in hospital in Bermuda (in USA). Kipling decided not to have any further treatment for her in America. The Kiplings left Burwash on 20 February 1931 for Egypt, where they remained until April, dallying for a fortnight on the way home. Another visit to Paris in June, and one to Oxford in September, seem to have been the only excursions for other than the normal ones to London.

Kipling misunderstood many social reforms. He mistrusted extensive popular education. Lient Col Thwaites was surprised of Kipling's conservatism. Kipling disliked Baldwin's 'Safety Fist' slogan. He had a poor opinion of many classes of the community.

Kipling's last collection of stories *Limits and Renewals* was published on 8 April 1932, but although he continued to write, his mind was becoming increasingly engrossed in politics.

Kipling had a peculiar dislike for biography, which he often referred to as the 'Higher Cannibalism,' a fear which probably sprang from his deep reserves about his own private life, and which was increased by the stirring of dead memories. He had many slices of tragedies like Josephine's death, Beatty's violence, his son's fall, and his own ill-heath. He even refused to write a book about his dear aunt Lady Burne-Jones. His dog James died. Now Kipling prepared a selection of verse and prose *A Pageant of Kipling* for the American market, as well as the vast Sussex Edition of his works in 35 volumes. Now his annual income was 32, 831 pounds (and he paid a tax of 7989 pounds plus super tax of 9000 pounds).

As though realizing that his creative life was now over,

Kipling turned to the revision of old work. On 5 October 1933 he published his *Collected Verse 1885-1932*. His practical literary competence is shown by the fact that he undertook single-handedly the forbidding task of correcting the proofs of this vast mass of print, classifying the verses, indexing them, and arranging them in chronological order. He left a word saying that the biographers should not trouble him. He put it succinctly in the following verse:

> And for the little, little span
> The dead are borne in mind,
> Seek not to question other than
> The books I leave behind.

Kipling made his outbursts, telling that England is calling for peace, white, Hitler and Germany is training its youth for war. He visited France in March 1934. He continued his old nagging about politicians. This year he could not produce anything remarkable. His *Collected Dog Stories* appeared in September 1934. Alexander Korda offered him 5000 pounds for 'Toomai of the Elephants.' Kipling made a great speech at a meeting of the Royal Society of St George on 6 May 1935. The speech began thus:

> Great Britain's quota of dead in the War was over eight hundred thousand when the books were closed in '21 or '22. It would be within the mark to say that three-quarters of a million of these were English. Furthermore, a large but unknown number died in the next few years from wounds or disease directly due to the War. There is a third category of men incapacitated from effort by the effects of shock, gassing, tubercle and the like. These carry a high death-rate because many of them burned out half a life's vitality in three or four years. They too, have ceased to count.

Valentine Williams speaks of Kipling's generosity to young authors. In spite of the difference in their age and literary attainments, he always treated Williams on equal terms. During the summer of 1935 Kipling wrote a 'Just So Story,'

'Ham and the Porcupine,' for Princess Elizabeth's Gift Book, and a poem 'The King and the Sea,' which was widely circulated in the press.

Kipling began his work on his autobiography *Something of Myself* at the advice of Sir Alfred Webb-Johnson, President of the Royal College of Surgeons, who edited it. He entertained the friend Sydney Cockerel and spoke of his life. He wrote the poem about a strife between a Jew and an Arab (as he heard it in his visit to the Middle East) and the poem speaks of a history of the Jewish race. The following is the first stanza:

In ancient days and deserts wild
There rose a feud—still unsubdued –
Twixt Sarah's son and Hagar's child
That centered round Jerusalem.

Rudyard and Carrie voted at the General Election of 1935 which placed Baldwin again in office with a large majority. Kipling could not now conceal his contempt for his cousin. He was disgusted by Baldwin's attitude towards India, and regarded the policy of sanctions against Italy in the Abyssinian War as midsummer madness.

Kipling's mind and writings began to turn to the eternal verities. He assured his Aunt Edie that he had no fear of death: 'Bless you for your note which has just come in. He who puts us into this life does not abandon His work for *any* reason or default at the end of it. That is all I have come to learn about my life. So there is *no* fear!'" Suddenly on 9 January 1936 Kipling fell ill and was admitted to the Middlesex Hospital. The surgeon and friend Sir Alfred Webb-Johnson found that he was suffering from duodenum.

Three poignant entries close Caroline's diaries. These documents, amounting to nearly fourteen thousand pages, span the entire married lifetime of the couple. United in youth by the compelling bond of Wolcott Balestier, they had faced the world together. Quietly, finally and briefly her diary entries for 1936 read: *Jan.* 9 London. Rud signs his Will. *Jan.* 12 Rud taken ill and to hospital in the early morning for an operation.

Webb-Johnson sees him at 3 a.m. and later operates. *Jan.* 18 Rud died at 12.10 a.m. Our Wedding Day. Kipling was cremated at Golden Green crematorium and his ashes were buried in Westminster Abbey.

King George V also died that day. 'The King has gone," they said, 'and taken his trumpeter with him.' The *Daily Telegraph* wrote: 'In the midst of her greater sorrow, England was not unmindful yesterday of the poet who above all others has honoured her achievement in undying verse.' After the committal of the urn to a grave beside those of Charles Dickens and Thomas Hardy, the great congregation which filled the North and South transepts joined in singing 'Recessional.'

A backward glance can be as follows, about Kipling, the great artist and genius. Kipling was both loved and hated. He was, indeed, a controversial writer. George Orwell thinks five generations of readers have rejected him, nor forgiven him. His themes are brutality, sadism, abysses of folly and snobbery. He is aesthetically disgusting. But Orwell also adds that Kipling's poetry is a pleasure. Long ago, in his glorious emergent youth, his most vicious tormenter, Max Beerbohm, clearly recognized this genius, and his hatred was due to the fact that he believed that the gold had insensitively transmuted into baser metal, and a rare gift brutally squandered. Ruskin Bond, the Anglo-Indian writer speaks of this honestly. There were many others who continued to hold this opinion throughout Kipling's literary career. Kipling was, above all else, the poet of work, discipline and responsibility. He is hated for his Imperialism, subjection of man, pride in white race and Europe. He seems not to understand, or else not to care, that Mulvaney and Ortheris may derive a sadistic pleasure in inflicting punishment on men entirely at their mercy and denied the freedom to protect their rights.

Lord Birkenhead observes, "It has been said that no writer since Dickens has made an equal impact upon his age. Streets and frontier towns were named after him: branches of the Kipling Society thrived in five countries. All over the world were admirers of Kipling in their thousands, and the popularity of his ensured that he was a best-seller throughout his lifetime, and after his death. He is the most often quoted 20th century writer. His phrases are so abundant in the language. He is the only historian of the contemporary India." Kipling was a

3

Rudyard Kipling's Novels

The Light that Failed (1891), *The Bushwood Boy* (1895), *Captains Courageous* (1897), Kim (1901) and *Naulahka* ()

Kipling wanted to write novels, but he could not succeed in that genre. In India to begin with he conceived a story about the relationship of a young artist to his art. The result was his writing of his first novel *The Light That Failed*. In his autobiography *Something of Myself*, he calls it 'that *cante*,' and puts it in its place as "not a built book." The Kipling family discussed about his growth as a novelist. Kipling after *Kim*, however, decided that novel-writing was not his forte, and he felt that his short stories should be made as good as his novel (Critics think that Kipling did not have the knowledge as to how to elaborate characters and make the readers to read it with interest until the end. This experience of his reminds us Poe's experience too). This we see in his short stories 'The Story of the Gadsbys,' 'The Wish House' and 'Dayspring Mishandled.'

The Light that Failed (1891)

This is Kipling's novel in 15 chapters, ever chapter beginning with a verse. The novel begins with the dedicatory verse 'Mother o' Mine.'

> If I were hanged on the highest hill,
> Mother o' mine, O mother o' mine!
> I know whose love would follow me still,
> Mother o' mine, O mother o' mine!

The first chapter depicts the children Dick Heldar and his sister Maisie (their parents are in India). Both stay in a seaside town in England, reminding Kipling and his sister at 'Lorne Lodge' as depicted in the story 'Baa Baa, Black Sheep.' Mrs. Jennet, the landlady is just like Mrs. Holloway, very rigid and disturbing type. Chapter 2 opens on another beach—a sandbank in the Nile, where Dick is a war-correspondent, sending home his pictures for the illustrated papers. He meets Torpenhow, another correspondent, and is wounded on the forehead. This is exactly what Kipling did as journalist in India. Chapter 3 takes him to London where he has became famous (it is said Kipling assaulted London with fame). Here unlike Kipling this Dick Heldar is a painter and he takes a room at Charring Cross (Kipling took a room at Villiers Street, nearby) and exhibits his paintings.

In the next chapters Dick is shown as a successful man, and he encourages his lover Maisie for an initiation in painting. But she is slow. He is not happy to marry her as we see her in the next chapter. He meets Maisie, and her friend. The two spend a day at seaside revisiting the haunts of their childhood. Chapter 7 continues with Dick and Maisie discussing love, painting, and life, but she is selfishly inclined to continue with her painting and will not listen. Chapter 8 shows Dick, Torpenhow, and the Nilghai at ease at the Chambers. Dick tells that he did a fine painting with the help of a woman of very mixed ancestry (Kipling, like Laurence was helped by a rich lady).

Dick does no work for the rest of the week and sees Maisie on Sunday; she and her friend are off to their studies in France soon. Dick wants to paint Melancolia. He soon returns to his chambers to find Torplenhow with his girl Bessie. Dick thinks she is a model for his Melancolia (whom he calls 'Broke'). Then we see that Dick falls ill with weak eyesight (as Kipling suffered from weak eyesight) and the doctor only speaks of hopes. Bessie is uneasy. But his painting appears brilliant.

In the next chapters the war clouds gather (This is World War I). The picture is fine, though Bessie destroys it. Unfortunately Dick becomes blind. He curses himself for remaining alive, while the war-correspondents discuss the coming of war and send Torpenhow to France to tell Maisie. Maisie and her friend are in France; the former's Melancolia is not going well and she is angry at not hearing from Dick. The news of Dick's blindness frightens her. Maisie meets Dick but leaves him forever. Dick sits alone in dejection. His housekeeper Beeton takes him for a walk where Bessie meets him. She visits him and tells him that she destroyed his painting 'Melancholia.' He clears up his affairs with Beeton, makes his will and decides to sail to Port Said.

Bessie sees him aboard the ship. A doctor takes Dick to Binat's at Port Said. Next he moves to Tanai-el-Hassan. Then he goes to a war front. He is shot and dies in Torpenhow's arms. The American edition of the novel has a happy ending. The novel also became a play and film. But critics called it 'The Book That Failed.'

J. M. S. Tompkins thinks that the basis of the novel is personal. A great deal that befalls Dick in the earlier part of the book can be matched in Kipling's autobiography *Something of Myself.*

The Light That Failed is *a fin-de-siècle* decadent tale with death as its outcome but this would hardly matter but that the mode was not Kipling's. Much has been written about its debt to Scarron and to the Abbé Prévost's fine novel *Manon Lescaut*. One of its defects—a brutality, evidenced both in the scene with the cardiac publisher and in the treatment of the women characters. Angus Wilson observes, "The idea of the lasting destructive romantic attachment, which Kipling may owe either to Uncle Ned Burne-Jones, in his life and art, or to the family history of his failed uncle, Harry Macdonald, who had experienced such a passion in youth, must surely have been in his mind all through the pains and pleasures of his love affair with Flo. Yet in *Plain Tales from the Hills*, it is only once, the story of young Deckie Hatt's ruin through love for a shallow girl, that he lays blame on the woman. In 'The Other Man' and in 'The Phantom 'Rickshaw' he turns the idea to artistic success by treating it as a setting for Gothic horrors. Indeed, contrary to the critical opinion of the nineties which still lingers,

Kipling's early work is largely marked by his extraordinary understanding of the unfairness of women's lives, with his sympathy and liking for them. The blind, self-flattering misogyny of *The Light That Failed* comes, then, as a peculiar surprise and disappointment."

The Light That Failed was published first in America and England in *Lippincott's Monthly Magazine*, January 1891, a magazine that the previous year had published another inferior autobiographical fantasy by a major author—Wilde's *Dorian Gray*. Kipling's novel in these versions had a novelettish conventional ending in which Maisie repents of her rejection of Dick and they are married. In March 1891 what the author called the original conception appeared in book form published by Macmillan—in November 1890 it had been used by Lovell in America in the copy they deposited in Washington for copyright. Here, as we have seen, Maisie is peremptorily dismissed from Dick's life and he goes blind to die amid the glorious sands of the Sudan battlefields. A most interesting article by Margaret Newsom in the *Kipling Journal*, drawing upon an earlier article by Charles Carrington, suggests that the first more conventional and surely less objectionable version was urged upon Kipling by his mother. This was what an old friend of the Kipling family had told Professor Carrington. Mrs Newsom goes on to suggest that when Kipling then published the more objectionable version of the novel, he appended as an attempt to appease his mother, the famous poem, 'Mother O' Mine':

> If I were damned of body and soul,
> I know whose prayers would make me whole,
> Mother O mine, O mother o' mine!

This poem has usually been seen as a comment that when other women fail, a man's mother may be relied upon.

According to Angus Wilson, "The usual explanation of the two versions of *The Light That Failed*, namely that Wolcott with a knowledge of the magazine market persuaded Kipling into publishing first in a conventional happy form, is very likely.

Lionel Johnson thinks "the story has a double interest: the interest of character in Maisie, the heroine, and the interest of dramatic life and action in Dick, the hero and in his friends. Now the first thought that occurs to one well acquainted with Mr. Kipling's work, upon reading this, his longest book, is of this sort: why is the interest of character so slight and the interest of action and of life so strong? Scenes of superb vigour and animation, passages of wonderful force and movement, these have struck us and taken hold upon us; but the characters, emotions, the mind and soul of Maisie and Dick have not been felt, and do not remain with us. We remember how they looked, talked, bore themselves in various situations; we still hear their characteristic phrases, we still see their attitudes and motions; but themselves, their inner reality, for all the power and mind of the book, are strange to us. Perhaps this may be the reason. Mr. Kipling, before all things, is an observer, not a thinker."

It is a London in its hateful aspect largely of streets and of literary or smart salons—the claustrophobia of the outsides of buildings and their insides. One senses him like an animal unsure of its own strength and of its new territory, venturing forth with all guards up, retiring to its den to hide and lick its wounds, driving all intruders angrily out of that den. This jungle aspect, indeed, is the one overall impression of life as portrayed in *The Light That Failed* which reveals that that unhappy novel is the mistaken work of a young man of genius.

Lord Birkenhead observes, "It is unnecessary to dwell on *The Light that Failed,* in which the hero, Dick Heldar, is overtaken by blindness. It need only be said that this work was largely autobiographical, that the 'House of Desolation' is closely described, and the character of Flo Garrard thinly disguised as 'Maisie.' This unsatisfactory and ill-knit book suggested to a discerning eye a fact that was afterwards confirmed by *Captains Courageous,* that the short story, not the novel, was Kipling's forte, and the less he ventured into this *genre* the better for his own reputation."

***The Bushwood Boy* (1895)**

This is a small novel by Kipling. *The Bushwood Boy* is a fantasy about a locale in England and India. The major characters are Georgie Cottar and his lover Miriam Lacy. The story is about the career of Georgie, who is haunted by the same dream about a lovely girl from his infancy through his adult years. He thinks she grows with him, sharing his dream experience. These dreams always start the same way. Near a beach is a pile of brushwood. Around this heap of brushwood Geogie runs and plays with other boys and girls. Strange and beautiful things happen in his dream story. Iron railings turn soft and can be walked on; houses fill with grown-up people and are pushed over by the children. These wonderful things happen, however, only so long as Georgie knows he is dreaming. When he sees her he thinks he is waiting for her. The story reminds Hardy's novel *The Well-Beloved* in its essentials.

The princess of his dreams, and his fävorite, he calls by the two names he thinks the most beautiful in the world, Anna and Louise. These he runs together and pronounces Annieanlouise.

When Georgie is seven he moves with his family to "Oxford-on-a-visit." While there he is taken to a magic show, where he sits next to a little girl who in a lisping voice admires the cut in Georgies' first knife. He hopes it might give him lockjaw. His conversation with little girl is cut short by his nurse, who tells him he must not talk to strangers. Georgie knows his friend is not a stranger, but he cannot explain the fact. That night he has a new dream, and at the brushwood pile the girl of the theater waits for him; they play wonderful games around the brushwood.

Georgie spends the next ten years at an English public school. He becomes a boy's leader there. Then he goes to Sandhurst where he does well. Later he receives a commission as a subaltern in Her Majesty's regiment.

Georgie's training for leadership during his school years serves him well in his new position of minor authority in the Indian service. His natural way with men make him a good leader. In India Georgie's dreams start again. They begin like his dreams of old by a brushwood pile. A sea lies beyond the brushwood pile, and on it he will travel far. Somewhere there is a lamppost, at which any wonderful thing can happen. Sometimes he races for that lamppost in his dreams, for he knows it is a place of safety. Once a policeman waits there for him and fills him with terror, just as the policeman had terrified him in his babyhood dream. He sails in a clockwork steamer, stopping by lilies labelled Hong Kong or Java. He knows that he has reached the world's end.

Georgie is promoted, and under his leadership his men win an important battle. As a reward he is given a year's leave in England. Throughout his furlough his dreams continue. Now a girl with black hair combed in a widow's peak, is his companion in most of his dreams. As a companion she helps him back to the lamppost and the brushwood pile.

At home Georgie is pampered by his parents and people. Mother brings her daughters to parade before the eligible Georgie, but he is immune to them. Then Miriam Lacy is brought for a visit. Before he sees Miriam he hears her singing a song about the policeman, from the land of his dreams. His heart stands still; he knows here is the girl of the brushwood pile. When he meets her he sees the black hair, the widow's peak, and she speaks with a concealed lisp.

On a ride, that evening, Georgie speaks to Miriam of the Thirty-Mile Ride and the lamppost. At first she pretends ignorance, but her song has given her away. Then two young people break all barriers and share in real life dreams they had shared so long. Miriam, too, has seen all the wonderful things Georgie has seen. The companion of his dreams, through all the years, she is his Annieanlouise. Now they will marry and be together in real life. In the darkness, each of them wonders what the other would look like in the light.

Hardy's novel referred to above *The Well-Beloved* is a semi-allegorical Platonic fantasy based loosely on Plato's idea that "all men are pursuing a shadow, the unattainable." The main character is Jocelyn Pierston, a sculptor obsessed by the concept of ideal beauty. The name of Avice, the heroine (who appears in three manifestations, as Avice I, her daughter Avice II, and her granddaughter Avice III) is taken from a daughter of the Talbots family the family that once owned Talbothays farm, one of the settings of *Tess of the d 'Urbervilles*. Hardy remarks in the *Life* that the kernel of the novel is his wish to trace 'the story of a face which goes through three generations or more.'

Captains Courageous (1897)

In *Captain Courageous* Kipling says he tried to record a "rather beautiful localized American atmosphere that was already beginning to fade." The narrative substance of the novel is so small that it is little more than a way of organizing the descriptive substance; we become acquainted with the conditions, physical and moral, of life on the fishing schooner.

This is a story of the Grand Banks. The novel has ten chapters. How King Solomon intervened in a quarrel between a butterfly and his wife and thus reduced his own importunate wives to peace. He prepared a meal for all the animals in the world which is eaten by Small Porgies. This imagery is felt in the novel.

Chapter 1 introduces the unpleasant Harvey Cheyne *enroute* to Europe with his mother (his father, a millionaire, is much occupied with business), and shows him attempting to smoke a cigar; this, coupled with sea-sickness, causes him to fall overboard, to be rescued by a fishing-dory manned by Manuel from the schooner *We're Here*, of Gloucester, Mass.

Harvey does fishing and other things. The story prolongs up to chapter seven. Chapter 8 is the climax of the trip: the fishing-fleet is on the Virgin where the *We're Here* is, as usual, the first to be filled to capacity and makes a triumphant return to Gloucester and ties up at Wouverman's wharf. Harvey sends his parents a telegraph. Chapter 9 shows Cheyne senior attempting to attend to his affairs at his house at San Diego despite his own heartache and his wife's near-madness. The telegram arrives and the secretary, Milsom arranges the epic dash across to Bostom in the private railway-carriage *Constance*. The boy meets them at Albany, where his father is delighted at the change in him, but his mother has some misgivings. The *Constance* takes them to Gloucester where

Harvey is in time for his last work for Troop—checking the fish as it is weighed on the wharf. Cheyne Sr meets Troop without disclosing his identity until the latter gives the boy a good character.

Cheyne Sr is happy of Troop's help and offers his son a job in his shipping company. Chapter 10 gives an account of Cheyne Sr and his son. The ship goes ashore for fishing, while the boy remains bound for college. The story ends with Cheyne Sr's meeting his son. An account of the origin of the novel is given in Kipling's autobiography *Something of Myself* (129-30).

J. M. S. Tompkins observes, "*Captain Courageous* was constructed by agglutination, but here every fact is structural, every word purposive. The expansion, where the brief statements and their implications gradually ripen and shed their contents."

Admiration for the self-made American industrialist, indeed, is one of the two central themes of Kipling's purely American work of distinction, *Captains Courageous*. This novel, in which the spoiled American boy who had so disgusted Kipling on his journey from Calcutta to San Francisco in 1889 is redeemed in the person of the hero, Harvey Cheyne, is marred by a little too much undigested technicality about cod-fishing, Kipling's one book that can truly be called 'a book for boys.' It is filled with a real love of the vigour and mixedness of America as represented by the cod-fishermen with their various national origins and by the spoiled boy's self-made millionaire father, as it is by hostility to American lawlessness and self-indulgence as exemplified by Harvey's spoiled upbringing by his mother. In February 1896 Kipling made some fact-finding trips for this book with his Brattleboro doctor friend Conland, to Gloucester, Massachusetts and to Boston where the cod fleets lay at anchor. These were his happiest American days, but also some of his last American days, for by the end of August he had left America in distress.

The tracts or parables on the education of the young Kipling were published in *Captains Courageous*, the chief character of which was also a youth in his teens. The book, as he said later, was not, all reporterage, but Kipling is very frank in relating how it was pieced together.

***Kim* (1901)**

Kim is the only novel Kipling attempted at fiction most successfully. Angus Wilson in his book *The Strange Ride of Rudyard Kipling, His Life and Works* observes this: "The story of Kim and the Lama is...the culmination and essence of all the transcendence that Kipling gained from his Indian experience. In it alone of all his works he does ask 'Who is Kim?' although he cannot answer the question. In a sense, his answer is the book itself, for it is the best thing he ever wrote."

Rudyard Kipling's *Kim* is an adventure romance set in the late nineteenth century British India. The principal characters are Kimball O'Hara (Kim), a street boy, a Tibetan lama as Kim's teacher, Mahbub Ali, a horse trader, Col. Creighton, director of the British Secret Service, and Hurree Chunder Mookerjee, a babu.

Kim grew up on the streets of Lahore. His Irish mother had died when he was born. His father, a former color-sergeant of an Irish regiment called the Mavericks, died eventually of drugs and drink, and left his son in the care of a half-caste woman. So young Kimball O'Hara became Kim, and under the hot Indian sun his skin grew so dark that one could not tell he was a white boy.

One day a Tibetan lama came to Lahore in search of a holy river Arrow. Kim liked the lama's adventure and joined him as his esteemed pupil. The same day, a Lahore horse trader Mahbub Ali gave Kim a cryptic message to deliver to a British officer in Umbal (in Haryana). Kim did not know that Mahbub was a member of the British Secret Service. Later he found out that his message meant 8,000 men would go to war.

Out on the big road the lama and Kim encountered many people of all sorts. Conversation was easy. One group in particular interested Kim, an old lady travelling in a family bullock cart at tended by a retinue of eight men. Kim and the lama attached themselves to her party. Toward evening, they saw a group of soldiers making camp. It was the Maverick regiment. Kim, whose horoscope said that his life would be changed at the sign of a red bull in a field of green, was fascinated by the regimental flag, which was just that, a red bull against a background of bright green.

Caught by a chaplain, the Reverend Arthur Bennett, Kim accidentally jerked loose the amulet which he carried around his neck. Mr. Bennett opened the amulet and discovered three papers folded inside, including Kim's baptismal certificate and a note from his father asking that the boy be taken care of. Father Victor arrived in time to see the papers. When Kim had told his story, he was informed that he would be sent away to school. Kirn parted sadly from the lama, sure, however, that he would soon escape. The lama asked that Father Victor's name and address, and the costs of schooling Kim, be written down and given to him. Then he disappeared. Kim, pretending to prophesy, told the priests what he had heard at Umballa. They and the soldiers laughed at him. But the next day his prophecy came true, and 8,000 soldiers were sent to put down an uprising in the north. Kim remained in camp.

One day the lama sent enough money for Kim's education, having asked him to join St Xavier's school. Mahbub Ali met Kim. While they were thus engaged, Colonel Creighton came up and learned from Mahbub Ali, in an indirect way, that Kim would be, when educated, a valuable member of the secret service. Kim joined the school and met lama often there. Kim did not like being watched by. He joined Mahbub Ali again on trips. He saved the horse trader when a party conspired to finish him.

At Simla, Kim stayed with Mr. Lurgan, who taught him a great many subtle tricks and games and the art of make-up and disguise. For, as Mahbub Ali had said, he was now learning the great game, as the work of the secret service was called. At the end of the summer Kim returned to St Xavier's. He studied there for a total of three years. Now Kim joined the lama who was still in search of a sacred river.

A little later Kim was surprised to see the babu, who told him that two of the five kings of the north had been bribed and that the Russians had sent spies down into India through the passes that the kings had agreed to guard. Two men, a Russian and a Frenchman, were to be apprehended, and the babu asked Kim's aid. To the lama Kim suggested a journey into the foothills of the Himalayas, and so he was able to follow the babu on his mission.

During a storm the babu came upon the two foreigners. Discovering that one of their baskets contained valuable letters, including a message from one of the traitorous kings, he offered to be their guide, and in two days he had led them to the spot where Kim and the lama were camped. When the foreigners tore almost in two a holy drawing made by the lama, the babu created a disturbance in which the coolies, according to plan, carried off the men's luggage. The lama conducted Kim to the village of Sham-legh. There Kim examined all of the baggage which the coolies had carried off. Everything except letters and note-books he threw over an unscalable cliff. The documents he hid on his person.

Kim and the lama set out again. Then they came to the old woman who had befriended them in the past. When she saw Kim's emaciated condition, she put him to bed, where he slept many days. Before he went to sleep, he asked that a strongbox be brought to him. In it he deposited his papers; then he locked the box and hid it under his bed. When he woke up, he heard that the babu had arrived, and to him Kim delivered the papers. The babu told him that Mahbub Ali was also in the vicinity. They assured Kim that he had played his part well in the great game. The old lama knew nothing of these matters. He was happy because Kim had brought him to his river at last, a brook on the old lady's estate.

Masterplots adds, "*Kim* gives a vivid picture of the complexities of India under British rule. It shows the life of the bazaar mystics, of the natives, of the British military. The dialogue, as well as much of the indirect discourse, makes use of Indian phrases, translated by the author, to give the flavor of native speech. There is a great deal of action and movement, for Kipling's vast canvas is painted in full detail. There are touches of irony as well as a display of native shrewdness and cun-ning."

The novel explores a fictional India through the cultural

and geographical wanderings of its boy-hero. Kim somehow bridges the gap between the rulers and the ruled. Lama achieves his own nirvana and Kim does not yet. Andrew Sanders adds, "*Kim* poses questions about identity and the problems of race, religion, isolation, loneliness and courage."

The Naulahka (1892)

Kipling traveled India for many years. Once he visited Rajaputana and wrote his account "Letters of Marque." The novel *Naulahka* (actually Naulakha, the name of a fabulous necklace. Kipling called his house 'Naulahka' in America) depicts this story in all of its vivacity. The novel which has American lead characters might have enthused the American readers. J. M. S. Tompkins, however thinks that the novel resulted in artistic confusion and nullity.

The novel is subtitled 'A Story of West and East.' The authors are Kipling and Wolcott Balestier. The novel begins with the verse:

> There was a strife 'twixt man and manid—
> Oh that was at the birth o' time!
> But what befell 'twixt man and maid,
> Oh that's beyond the grip o' rhyme.
> 'Twas: 'Sweet, I must not bide wi' you,'
> And: 'Love, I canna bide alone;;
> For baith were young, and baith were true,
> And baith were hard as the nether stone.

Kipling has written many novels, sometimes alone and sometimes, with his brother-in-law Wolcott Belestier. Kipling and Belestier wrote together this novel called *The Naulahka* in 1892. Belestier wrote the first part, American scenes, and Kipling wrote the second part, the Indian scenes. The novel altogether has 24 chapters. 'Naulahka' is the name of a famous diamond of the times. Interestingly, Kipling built a house in Vermont, and called it 'Naulahka.' Actually, the word is misspelt. It is 'Naulakha,' meaning nine lakhs. The novel is subtitled as 'A Story of the West and East.' Again the story depicts the theme of the West's hegemony over the East. A brief critical analysis is as follows.

The novel begins with Nicholas Tarvin, a social worker and Kate Sheriff, daughter of a railway engineer, both from the town of Tapaz, Colorado, USA. Tarvin loves her. Tarvin, an up-and-coming young man with interests in politics, real estate, and anything that will promote the progress of his beloved town, tries to persuade Kate to marry him instead of going to India. She makes him promise not to follow her. Tarvin meets Mutrie, the President of the Three C's (a railroad co), the railroad that is considering running through Topaz—or the rival town of Rustler. The young wife of the president seems a good subject for Tarvin to work on, and he accordingly does so; in due course he learns that her weak point, for which she was searching, is jewels. He promises to bring her a magnificent necklace from India. The young wife of the president loves a Jewell, and Tarvin decides to please her by bringing a Jewel (Naulakha) from India. What he hopes from Mutrie is getting railways to his town Tapaz.

Tarvin arrives in India as much as his beloved Kate, who wants to improve the lot of women in India. He stays in the town of Rhatore (in Rajasthan), where there is a princely state, belonging to the widowed queen Sitabai (actually in-charge). Maharaja Kunwar, the late King's son is there. Tarvin hears about the Naulahka, and gathers conditions about it. He is now elected to the King's Legislature. Tarvin dreams in the uncomfortable rest-house and decides to call on Estes at the American Mission, where he is made welcome by the missionary and his wife who are expecting Kate to join them shortly. He enjoys an American breakfast and hears of the difficulties in Rhatore. He explains his presence in the town by saying that he is a prospector and learns that he must seek the permission of Colonel Nolan, the Resident.

Tarvin meets the nine-year old Maharaja Kunwar, and trains him in the martial arts. He meets Kate. Both do sight-seeing Tarvin goes with the Maharaj Kunwar to give her a present from the boy's mother—the real Queen—with a plea that Kate should try to save him from the gipsy Queen

Sitabhai. Kate writes to Tarvin, telling him not to see her for a while; he visits the Maharajah while Mrs. Estes takes Kate to inspect the hospital, which is badly run and filthy. A woman of the desert drags Kate off to see her sick husband. Tarvin tells the Maharaja that he came there to prospect gold in the nearby river. So they think of diverting the river. The king promises the foreigner the gift of the holy necklace—the Naulahka—for his efforts. He thinks it is kept at Gye-Mukh—the Cow's Mouth, a dreadful place. A European Ester provides information about it.

The work of damming the river for a diversion begins. Kate helps the prince in improving his health. Tarvin also hears that the Three Cs rail project may not cover his town. Unfortunately, there is an attempt on his life. The prince's wedding is in offing, but he appears ill and tired. Actually Sitabai has poisoned him.

A thug leader Juggut Singh is in nexus with Sitabai. He meets her for his share –the Naulahka. She is afraid of him now. The Naulakha necklace is with her now. She suggests him that he may remain the prime minister after her son Umr Singh ascends the throne. He threatens her for the jewel. Finally he gets the coveted Naulahka and runs off, thinking of Kate. Somehow there is firing on both Juggut Singh and Tarvin and Tarvin protects the conspirator. He then telegraphs Mrs. Mutrie and calls on Mrs. Estes to thank her for her hospitality and sees Kate. She will not marry him, but he cannot leave her as both their lives are now in danger. He returns to the rest-house, and she goes in to the Maharaj Kunwar, who is recovering from his illness. The Maharajah calls to see his son, who desires to go away to school. They decide to discuss this later and the father departs. A messenger arrives with a basket of fruit for the boy—a present from the Queen—but his pet monkey, Moti, eats a banana and dies. Kate begins to yearn for the protection of Tarvin. The wicked Sitabai is also in trouble. She wants Kate's help. Tarvin is in crisis. He has yet to get the necklace. Unfortunately, some people have him in their hit-list. He then meets the Maharaja, gets the Naulahka, destroys the dam, reverting the river, and departs with Kate.

The two have married at this time.

Kingsley Amis observes, "*The Naulahka*, was written and eventually published. It is by no means a bad book. The first four chapters, certainly Balestier's work, show an engaging light with that Kipling never attempted. If the former used the same style in talk as in writing, we would have a good unsensational reason for the latter's attachment to him." *Naulahka* has usually been dismissed as an inferior work unhappily written with an inferior writer. This conventional judgement is mistaken. *Naulahka* is not a masterpiece, but it is excellent reading. The American first section laid in Colorado, written by Balestier, who spent some time in the South West States after he left Cornell University, is very fresh and workmanlike. The hero, Nick Tarvin's determined wooing of Kate, the heroine, away from her supposed vocation as a mission teacher in India though a bit contrived in plot, is free of the misogyny and self-pity of Dick Heldar's story. It was easier for Kipling to engage in an informed attack on missionaries (old butts of his Indian stories) than on art students. And the Indian section, laid in a Princely State, gave free rein to Kipling's dark imagination of princely intrigues that had been roused by his visits to the ancient ruined cities of Amber and Chitor. It also gave him a chance to create one of his best child portraits in the Maharaj Kunwar, the ruler's son who is threatened with death by secret poisoning.

Mother Maturin

In most big cities natives will tell you of two or three Sahibs, generally low-caste, who have turned Hindu or Mussulman, and who live more or less as such. But it is not often that you get to know them. But Kipling did. He said, "I was admitted to the Jellaludin Mclntosh household—I and my good tobacco. But nothing else. Unluckily, one cannot visit a loafer in the Serai by day. Friends buying horses would not understand it. Consequently I was obliged to visit him by night. McIntosh the loafer makes a present to his observer of a huge manuscript—"my work ... being an account of the life and sins and death of Mother Maturin ... If the thing is ever published, someone may perhaps remember this story, now printed as a safeguard to prove that Jellaludin and not I myself wrote the Book of *Mother Maturin*."

Kipling's planned novel *Mother Maturin* never was published, of course, for Kipling wrote only a part of what was intended to be his great novel of the half-life and low-life of Lahore. From the names dropped in the course of the ravings of McIntosh in 'To Be Filed for Reference,' we can tell that, connected with it, is the poem 'The Ballad of Fisher's Boarding House':

> Since Life is strife, and strife means knife,
> From Howrah to the Bay,
> And he may die before the dawn
> Who liquored out the day,
> In Fultah Fisher's Boarding House
> We woo while yet we may.

All the characters are brought together in the script of the never-made film of the twenties, to be called 'The Gate of a Hundred Sorrows.' Mrs Carpenter, widow of the American collector of Kiplingiana, tells us that a friend informed her that in the final story of *Mother Maturin*, the old Irishwoman of the half-world would send her daughter to be educated in England, and that the daughter, married to a civil servant, would return to Lahore. Thus a connection would be established between The City of Dreadful Night and the Lahore of the Sahibs of the Civil Lines and the Cantonment. Out of this would come a tale of espionage and the selling of the secrets of the British Government. She adds, what Carrington also tells us, that Kipling's decision not to finish the book was much influenced by his father's disapproval. Lockwood's disapproval might have been because he thought it a bit garish and sensational, or he may have disapproved of its sexual freedom, or he may have doubted the wisdom of discussing the leaking of Government secret. Kipling made his own masterpiece, *Kim*, which is far more than any simple connecting of opium dens with Government House, the Club and the Mall.

4

Rudyard Kipling's Books of Short Stories

Kipling was a great short story writer. He began writing stories in India. His first book *Plain Tales from the Hills* appeared in 1888. Then he gathered as many as six volumes of stories– *Life's Handicap* (1891), *Wee Willie Winkie* (1892), *Many Inventions* (1893), *Soldiers Three* (1895), *The Day's Work* (1898) and took them first to England, and the publishers showed no interest in any of them. Likewise, the American publishers showed their indifference. Only after that the *Scotts Observer*'s Mr. Henley and Mr. Andrew Long noticed Kipling's genius. Kipling then came to limelight like Wordsworth, Dickens and Hemingway. He took hold of the audience gradually, but firmly. He became the voice of the people. His verses as well as stories brought him immense rewards. He became the balladeer of the British Empire.

Imperialism, as the label was a splendid thing while it was popular. But the Boer War came and the new century and the Old Queen died and there was talk of democracy and the rights of man, and as suddenly as he had been mistaken for a mouthpiece Kipling found himself a voice crying in the wilderness. But during the decade of the 'nineties, and particularly in these five books of short stories, his prejudices were the people's, his sentiments the Empire's.

Rupert Croft-Cooke observes the following about Kipling's short stories: "He was a best-seller, a public figure, a sort of institution, though in his own life he—as the people of Burwash say about him to this day—kept himself to himself. He seems to have been remarkably indifferent to the literary movements and cliques and tendencies of the time (the *Savoy* and the *Yellow Book*, Wilde and Beardsley might have belonged to another age), while he showed no influence from other writers, popular or esoteric. There he was with his stories, his countless good stories from India and America and London, and he seemed content to sit down and write them without a glance over his shoulder. Only he was no longer learning or experimenting, trying to give an impression or hoping to conceal inexperience. He knew now. He knew what to do and how to do it. He had learnt self-confidence though he was still as eager and enthusiastic as in his first newspaper sketch."

Kipling's Indian tales are dipped in Hindustani. Kipling learnt more than plot in India, and also a private philosophy.

Kipling may be compared with Edgar Allan Poe in his profession of writing stories. Both have many similarities. Critics also compare Kipling with Mark Twain, and particularly with Bret Harte. Kipling was an admirer of Harte and he imitated both Twain and Harte. The differences are also there. Harte was discursive, Kipling concise; Harte was sentimental, Kipling, detached and ironic; Harte wrote about mining camps and vagabonds for metropolitan audience, while Kipling wrote for the multitudes of the Anglo-Indian.

Early critics—and some later ones—likewise discerned an affinity between Kipling and Guy de Maupassant. Both are masters of brevity and precision; both are notable for their cold and detached treatment of their characters; both appeared misogynistic and, in that reticent age, too interested in illicit sexual liaisons. But claims for the influence of Maupassant are frustrated by obstacles.

Finally, Kipling's debt to earlier writers of Anglo-Indian fiction can be neither dismissed nor precisely ascertained. We have seen that he called attention to his general obligations to Anglo-Indian poetry, but in the case of fiction he left no such record. The first chapter of the book provides many details about Kipling and the Anglo-Indian literature.

Now the question about Kipling's approach to life and art remains. Critics are of the opinion that Kipling was both realist and idealist (who follows a streak of romanticism). In spite of a good deal of evidence of this kind, Kipling's claims to realism have been obscured by the history of fiction during his own lifetime. His English contemporaries realized in the 1880s and 90s that the development of the novel was proceeding in two different directions. By and large, the classic mid-nineteenth century English novelists, though predominantly realistic, were willing to include elements of the fortuitous and improbable for the sake of a good story. But with the demise of the three-decker and the growth of interest in French naturalism, readers began to demand a new realism in fiction and to manifest a new contempt for the improbable and romantic in novels that claimed to be 'serious.'

If we were required to assign Kipling to either the realist or the romantic school, one may think one could find plausible reasons on both sides. But in fact Kipling's achievement transcends such simple formulae. Like his great contemporaries Henry James, Conrad, and Stevenson, or like Zola himself, Kipling's traffic with the real world became a far more complex affair than the mere registry of sensory impressions. Because Kipling often sought out instances of the startling, the supernatural, the bizarre.

Plain Tales from the Hills (1888)

Plain Tales from the Hills deals mostly with Simla life. Kipling's picture is yet not a happy one, but it is realistic. His characters Mrs Reiver, Mrs Mallowe and, of course, Mrs Hauksbee represent Anglo-Indian society at large. Kipling developed his characteristic voice in this book of 1886. Here the narrator is a breezy, cynical reporter. Mark Twain, the American frontier journalist seems to be his model.

An anonymous reviewer in the *Saturday Review* in London in 1888 observes, "There are forty plain tales, of which twenty-eight have appeared separately in a newspaper, and the other twelve are, in the modest words of the author more or less new. Each tale is extremely short, the average length being just under seven pages. Nevertheless, for the profitable disposal of odds and ends of time or for a cross-country journey in stopping trains on Sunday it would be hard to find better reading. Mr. Kipling knows and appreciates the English in India, and he is a born story-teller and a man of humour into the bargain. He is also singularly versatile, and equally at home in humour and pathos. 'Thrown Away,' a story of a commonplace youth who killed himself in despair merely for want of proper training, is little short of genuine tragedy, and is full of a grim humour which is decidedly telling. 'The Three Musketeers' and 'A Friend's Friend' are farce of a high order. Four of the stories-and four of the best-concern the British private in regiments stationed in India. Another remarkable military story is 'The Madness of Private Ortheris.' Ortheris goes out shooting with his friend Mulvaney. The military stories happen to have been dwelt on here, but there are many tales of civilians, and indeed of natives, that are really quite as good."

Some of the most important stories are analyzed here.

1. Lispeth

'Lisbeth,' the heroine of the story that stands first in *Plain Tales from the Hills*, becomes half servant, half companion to the chaplain's wife in Kotgargh. She meets and saves a young English traveler who has fallen by the wayside with fever. He just flirts with her and leaves her though she wants to marry him. She returns to her own people as the woman of Shamlegh in *Kim*. The great Himalayas seems to protect her family.

Lispeth symbolizes her disenchantment with English civilization by putting on native rags.

2. Three and an Extra

This is the second story in the book. Mrs. Cusack Bremmil loses her baby and also loses her husband's respect. He flirts with Mrs Haucksbee. Cusack is unhappy and she participates in a ball. Here she makes a superb entrance and carries her husband off again.

3. Thrown Away

The Boy of 'Thrown Away' 'took all things seriously' and killed himself as a result; Dicky Hatt was "kidnapped in his early, early youth . . . by a girl so nearly of his own caste that only a woman could have seen she was just the least little bit in the world below it," and the mistake cost him his career.

The story is tragic in tone. The young man brought up on the sheltered life principle cannot stand alone in India. He takes his colonel's rebuke to heart and shoots himself. A friend informs his family, lying that the man died of cholera.

4. Miss Youghal's Sais

The character Youghal will not consider Strickland as a son-in-law, so the latter disguises himself as a groom and takes service with the family. He learns a lot of interesting things during his successful courtship.

5. Yoked with an Unbeliever

Phil Green who is sent out to plant tea, forgets the girl he left behind and lives with Dunmaya. Agnes Laiter, his beloved marries to please her parents; her husband dies, so she goes to India and finds Green and his mistress, who are quite nice to her.

6. False Dawn

The character Saumarez is enamored of one of the almost identical copleigh girls and, during a storm, proposes to the wrong one. The story speaks of the possibilities and passions of life. Cut down to the quick, it only tells how a civil servant, in love with one sister, proposed to another in the darkness of a dust storm. But the brief, vivid narrative; the ride to the old tomb in the sultry tropical midnight, 'the horizon to the north, carrying a faint, dun-coloured feather, the hot wind lashing the orange trees; the wandering, blind night of dust; the lightning spurting like water from a sluice; the human passions breaking forth as wildly as the fire from Heaven; the headlong race in the whirlwind and the gloom; the dust-white, ghostly men and women all these make pictures as real as they are strange. 'I never knew anything so un-English in my life,' says Mr. Kipling; and well he may. It is more like a story from another world than merely from another continent.

7. The Rescue of Pluffles

Pluffles, a young man with too much money, falls for the fascinations of Mrs. Reiver, about whom there is nothing good except her dress. Mrs. Hauksbee takes charge and saves the boy for a nice girl at Home.

8. Cupid's Arrows

Bar-Saggott loves Kitty Brighton. Bar is an actress and she arranges a tournament. She also has an eye on Cubbon and in the mood loses the game.

9. The Three Musketeers

This story is about the British disaster. It is not about the three musketeers, but about two drummer boys, Lew and Jakin. The two boys are drunk and they die. The British army is defeated by the Afghan army. The story is a criticism of the army practices. 'The Three Musketeers' plays an outrageous joke on Lord Benira Trig.

10. His Chance in Life

Two Eurasians are in love, and the man faces a riot and he is promoted. So he marries his lover. As with the love of Michele d'Cruze and Miss Vezzis in 'His Chance in Life' where some atavistic drop of Yorkshire blood in the girl imposes a demand, as a preliminary to marriage, of a basic salary far beyond the hopes of her telegraph signaller lover. Beyond the hopes, but not beyond the courage and the sudden sense of authority that Michele finds, when without any white man available to take charge, he quells a religious riot far south in Orissa. And so earns promotion and his love.

11. The Watches of the Night

The characters Platte and his colonel own similar watches which they accidentally exchange. This brings about a domestic estrangement.

In 'Watches of the Night' the whole community joins in a conspiracy against the colonel's wife.

12. The Other Man

Miss Gaurey marries Colonel Schreiderling—thirty-five years her senior—under parental pressure, although she loves the

'Other Man.' She loses her good looks through illness, and her husband tires of her. The 'Other Man' comes to Simla to recover from fever and heart-trouble. She goes out to meet his tonga, in which he is found dead.

13. Consequences

Tarrion on leave at Shimla calls on Mrs. Hauksbee who is studying a bundle of secret papers sent to her by mistake. He reports it to the officer, and gets a promotion.

14. The Conversation of Aurelian McGoggin

McGoggin is a brilliant but eccentric civilian who bores all the men at the club with his theories. He is suddenly stricken with aphasia; when he recovers he is a changed character.

15. The Taking of Lungtungpen

And what when battle or skirmish comes to make sense of the soul-killing tedium? With the *Soldiers Three* it is always in reminiscence-short, brutal, absurd, or effectively half-comic as in the Burmese's exploit in 'The Taking of Lungtungpen.'

16. A Germ Destroyer

The sixteenth story in the book which hinges upon the confusion of similar names—Mellishe and Mellish—whereby the wrong man meets the Viceroy and nearly chokes him with an anti-cholera fumigant.

'A Germ-Destroyer,' a minor 'Plain Tale,' provides an instance that may be taken as characteristic of one of the ways one's mind work. It is said to be a satiric comedy.

As Mr. Randall Jarrell puts it in one of the best recent discussions of the 'Plain Tales': 'The continual understatement, the continual contrast of form and content, the continual "writing short," all help to give the stories their particular force.'

17. Kidnapped

Peythroppe desires to marry a young Eurasian woman Miss Castries whom Hauksbee and his friends consider not suitable. He is therefore kidnapped until after the wedding. Kipling, indeed, seems disturbed at this humiliation of a half-caste girl deserted at the altar steps, for he gives as his reason, 'marriage in India does not concern the individual but the Government he serves,' and he makes the jilted Eurasian girl behave impeccably after her sorry treatment. 'Miss Castries,' he says, '*was a very* good girl.'

18. The Arrest of Lieutenant Golightly

The most successful story about an officer is, however 'The Arrest of Lieutenant Golightly,' in which a somewhat self-satisfied, extremely dandyish officer falls from his horse in a rainstorm coming down from leave in the hills. Filthy and unrecognisable he is arrested, despite all his protests, as a deserter from the ranks and treated accordingly. Perhaps it is natural that, as in 'The Strange Ride of Morrowbie Jukes,' Kipling seems most in his stride when the sahib's role is grimly and comically reversed.

'If there was one thing on which Golightly prided himself more than another, it was looking like 'an Officer and a Gentleman,' the reporter tells us.

19. In the House of Siddhoo

Siddhoo, an old man lets rooms in his house to Bhagwan Dass and a seal-cutter, also to people like Janoo and Azizun, the ladies. Siddhoo's son is ill in Peshawar. The seal-cutter receives information about the landlord's son and tells him that he will do magic for his well-being. The narrator attends such a scene.

The natives of India have been dwelling for countless centuries in the region which can make even Englishmen un-English.

20. His Wedded Wife

'His Wedded Wife' is about a masquerade. The ugly character called worm, Henry Faizanne is ragged by his regiment and finally has a bet with the senior subaltern that he will work a spell on him. One morning a beautiful girl claims him as her husband. The worm claims the bet.

21. The Broken-Link Handicap

Shackles was a certain winner so long as the jockey sat still. The owner of Regula Baddun had discovered a curious echo on the course, not unlike the whispering-gallery of St. Paul's, and used it to about a victory for his own horse.

22. Beyond the Pale

Christopher Trejago seeks reality in the native world rather than the white, in 'the City where each man's house is as guarded and unknowable as the grave.' 'He knew too much in the first instance,' says the reporter's warning voice, 'and he saw too much in the second. He took deep an interest in native life; but he will never do so again.' What Trejago finds in the City is love of a sort that British India cannot offer: the ultimate reward of this quest for India's hidden reality is not merely knowledge but Bisesa. To be sure, loving Bisesa is a dangerous adventure—Bisesa loses her hands in consequence of the affair, and Trejago nearly loses his life—but she is not hedged about with the dreary conventions of Simla flirtation.

Trejago becomes estranged with Bisesa, a young native widow. She is dreadfully mutilated as a result.

23. In Error

Moriarty, a secret drinker, meets Mrs. Reiver at Simla. He is not aware of her wickedness, and reforms himself. He later marries a better woman, but credits her with his reform.

24. A Bank Fraud

Reggie Burke, a two-sided man—very austere in banking hours, the reverse at other times—is saddled with Silas Riley, himself, with a very narrow outlook and no sense of humour. Riley is dying of a lingering illness; Burke does his best to keep him happy until the end.

25. Tod's Amendment

Tod, born in India, mixes happily with the locals and knows all about their problems. He strays into a dinner-party because he wants a drink (the old story!) and hears some talk on proposed changes in the local land acts. He asks a question that astonishes the Legal Member and then explains what the population have to say about the proposals. The latter makes inquiries, finds that the boy is correct, and so amends the legislation. The natives are delighted with the amendment, which they believe is due entirely to the child. Critics think that this story promises a new delineator of children. 'Tod's Amendment,' which as a curiously constructed piece of work, is in itself a political allegory. Edmund Gosse comments, "Mr. Kipling has sketched for us the attitude which he adopts towards babies. 'Only women,' he says, but we may doubt if he means it, 'understand children thoroughly; but if a mere man keeps very quiet, and humbles himself properly, and refrains from talking down to his superiors, the children will sometimes be good to him, and let him see what they think about the world.'

26. The Daughters of the Regiment

Mulvaney explains why Miss Jhansi McKenna, daughter of 'Old Pummeloe' and Colour-Sergeant McKenna, was so called, and how, as a little girl, she helped her mother take water to cholera-stricken soldiers. Mulvaney arranged for her to marry Corporal Slane when he was promoted to Sergeant.

J. H. Fenwick thinks, "In 'The Daughter of the Regiment,' the sadness of the central episode is modified by the gaiety of the frame, so that the total effect is one of slightly comic, yet poignant triumph in the face of conditions of life in India."

27. In the Pride of His Youth

Dick Hatt, secretly married a young girl, leaves her at home and goes to a job in India. He works hard but cannot earn much to get his wife to India. A baby is born and it dies. The girl gets an affair with another man. Then Hatt is offered a promotion that would solve his problem. However, he resigns and disappears.

28. Pig

Pinecoffin sells a bad horse to Nafferton who is injured by the brute. Nafferton takes revenge on the horse-seller.

29. The Rout of the White Hussars

A new colonel orders the old drum-house of this very exclusive regiment to be sold. Mutiny is avoided and Hogan-Yale buys the horse, which is supposed to be shot. When the regiment is watering houses one evening, however, the drum-horse appears with a skeleton rider. The regiment panics and flees. The colonel is persuaded to reinstate the animal and all is well. The narrator appears to have been party to the plot.

30. The Bronckhorst Divorce-Case

Edward Bronckhorst, married for fifteen years, treats his wife badly and makes his young son drunk. He starts proceedings for divorce, naming one Biel as co-respondent. Strickland comes to the rescue and finds that the evidence on which the case depends is to be provided by an ayah, a bearer, and a khitmatgar who have been coached by Bronckhorst. This is made plain in court. Biel gives Bronckhorst a thrashing outside the court and he returns to his wife.

31. Venus Annodomini

Young Grayson loves a lady who knows the secrecy of perpetual youth. The men's father visits the son and comes to know that his lover is the old flame of his youth. His son is finally left to console himself with Kitty's 19 year old daughter.

32. The Bisara of Poonee

The Bisara is a little eyeless fish, enclosed in a ruby-studded box; if stolen it brings its owner luck. If acquired by gift, purchase, or finding, its continued possession after three years will be marked by mishap or death. The tale recounts the experiences of Churton, who bought it off pack, who stole it, and another man who knew too much about it and rid himself of the latent danger when he was presented with it.

33. A Friend's Friend

The story tells of a globe-trotter named Jevon who makes himself objectionable at a Simla ball. He is punished in summary fashion, rolled up in a carpet, and placed in a bullock-cart. He is never seen again. The last verse of '*Hadra-mauti,*' slightly adapted, forms a heading to the story.

34. The Gate of the Hundred Sorrows

On the other hand in 'The Gate of a Hundred Sorrows,' the whole life of a half-caste opium smoker, all the spectacle of will and nerve hopelessly relaxed and ruined, is transparent and masterly. At first three pipes enabled him to see the red and yellow dragons fight on his neighbour's cap. Now it needs a dozen pipes, and soon he will see their last battle, and slip into another sleep, in 'The Gate of a Hundred Sorrows.' The tales of English existence, official and military, are often diverting and witty; occasionally flippant and too rich in slang. Mr. Kipling may have the vivacity of Guy De Maupassant, but he has neither his pessimism, nor, unluckily, the simplicity of his style.

35. The Madness of the Foreign Ortheris

Ortheris has an attack of homesickness, and, cursing the day he joined the Army, remembers a girl at home and the taxidermist's shop he might have had. Mulvaney is for once at a loss, but the narrator suggests desertion, promising assistance. As expected, Ortheris later comes to his senses and decides to remain a soldier.

The fit wears off, and Ortheris is as horrified as Mulvaney at the idea of deserting, but Kipling has shown us the terrible strain that is required to keep up one's public role in India.

Kipling's mastery of device of multiple narration, but the beginnings of his progress towards the technical and emotional subtleties of Soldiers Three. 'The Madness of Private Ortheris', for example, shows significant changes in the narrator's relationship with the three men, and in his attitude to military life in general.

36. The Story of Mohammad Din

Muhammad Din, young son of the narrator's Khitmagar, Imam Din, is given an old polo ball; a solemn and polite friendship develops. The child gets fever, dies in spite of every attention, and the narrator sees his funeral party on the way to the burial ground.

37. On the Strength of a Likeness

Hannasyde comes upto Simla where he meets Mrs. Landys-Haggert. She reminds him of Alice Chisane, who had once promised to be a sister to him, but married another man.

38. Wressley of the Foreign Office

Wressley falls for a flighty little thing called Tillie Venner who has an interest in his studies. He then writes the book *Native Rule in Central India*. His girl Wressley does not appreciate it. Now he is a broken man.

39. By Word of Mouth

'By Word of Mouth' is ghost story. It has an atmosphere of plausibility.

Dumoise, a civil surgeon loses his wife and takes some leave in the Hills. Ram Das, his servant declares that he met the deceased woman who gave him a message that her husband was to meet her at Nuddea the next month. When Dumoise comes back to his place, he is ordered to go to Nuddea to deal with an outbreak of cholera. He goes, but the cholera claims him there.

40. To be Filed for Reference

The narrator meets McIntosh Jellaludin, an Oxford man who has taken to drink and an Indian woman. He retains his interest in studies. McIntosh finally dies of pneumonia, leaving his book *The Book of McIntosh Jellaludin*, containing an account of the life and sins of Mother Maturin.

Unlike Ortheris, McIntosh *Jellaludin* does not repent and recover his social position. He has disappeared once and for all into the Indian underworld, taken a native wife, become a convert to Islam. By every Anglo-Indian standard he has failed utterly. And yet he has captured Kipling's imagination: the conversations between McIntosh and the reporter suggest in a curious way that two conflicting impulses in Kipling himself are debating against one another; McIntosh embodies that part of Kipling's mind for which the restraints of Anglo-Indian life were intolerably burdensome.

Kipling's first book of tales is really impressive. This is a man's book. There is nothing ordinary about them. The very scenes are strange, scenes of Anglo-Indian life, military and official; of native life; of the life of half-castes and Eurasians. The subjects in themselves would be a hindrance and a handicap to most authors, because the general reader is much averse to the study of Indian matters, and is baffled by *jhairuns*, and *khitmatgars*, and the rest of it. It may safely be said that *Plain Tales from the Hills* will teach more of India. Here is an unbroken field of actual romance, here are incidents as strange as befall in any city of dream and the incidents are true. Rupert Croft-Cooke in his book *Rudyard Kipling* observes, "Isolated from the rest of Kipling's work and re-read to-day the stories in *Plain Tales from the Hills* are impressive."

Plain Tales is not about ghosts or soldiers or natives or life at Simla; in so far as it has a subject, that subject is British India—as many aspects of British India as the young author's sensibility can encompass and control. The narrator of *Plain Tales* is a created fictional character who exists in and through the stories he tells. Sometimes he takes on substance as an 'I' who has more or less of a role to play in the action; at other times, he is closer to what Wayne Booth calls the 'implied author,' the person whose views, attitudes, sympathies, and moral standards we infer from the narrative itself. If Kipling were concerned only with delusion and disguise, the *Plain Tales* would conform to a pattern that has often been ascribed to them by critics: that is, the narrator-author, a cocksure young cynic, is using the short story as a vehicle to persuade his readers that he has plucked out the heart of the Anglo-Indian mystery. A number of the *Plain Tales*, especially the ones that deal with Mrs. Hauksbee and her circle, do fit this pattern.

Louis Cornell observes "The title of the series and the general drift of Kipling's prose experimentation suggest the kind of stories he had in mind at the beginning. Plain in style, realistic in intention, the tales were to be about people like the

Kiplings and their friends—civil servants and officers who could afford to spend their holidays at Simla or another of the principal hill-stations."

2. Wee Willie Winkie and Other Stories (1888)

The book contains *Under the Deodars* as the first section (part). It has the first six stories. The book has fourteen stories in all.

Andrew Lang comments, "On the whole, Mr. Kipling's *Under the Deodars* is more conventional and less interesting than his studies of native life. There is comparatively little variety in playing lawn-tennis with the Seventh Commandment. Mr. Kipling, in his preface, intimates that Anglo-Indian society has other and more seemly diversions. Any persons who wish to see the misery, the seamy, sorry side of irregular love affairs, may turn to 'The Hill of Illusion.' It is enough to convert a man or woman on the verge of guilt by reminding them that, after all, they will be no happier than they have been, and much less respectable. 'A Way-side Comedy' contains a tragedy almost impossible in its absurd and miserable complexity of relations. Only a very small and very remote Anglo-Indian station could have produced this comedy, or tolerated it.

1. The Education of Otis Yeere

This story is also the first one in the section *Under The Deodars*. Mrs. Hauksbee intends to start a salon, but Mrs. Mallowe suggests that it would be better to be an Influence; the former then takes up Otis Yeere, who dresses badly and has lost his ambitions. He improves under her tuition, but begins to flirt with her and has to be dismissed.

2. At the Pit's Mouth

This is the second story featuring a man, his wife and the Tertium Quid (a third something) called Frank. The wife has an affair with Frank. The wife rides with Frank and there is a tragic accident in a landslide. Frank is killed and the women become insane.

In his stronger Simla stories, Kipling reveals a moral bias, as it were, by default; he no longer tries to provide a hero.

3. A Wayside Comedy

Kashima's white population consisted of Boulte and his wife, Captain Kurrell, and Major and Mrs. Vansuythen. As only the Major refrains from flirting, some misunderstandings arise, but in the end the four have to resign themselves to some show of companionship on conventional lines as the Major, who really does not know what is going on, keeps up a burdensome geniality.

4. The Hill of Illusion

He and she (the former is called Guy) have agreed to go away together, but she withdraws. He suspects the influence of another man.

5. A Second Rate Woman

Mrs. Delville (the Dowd) enters Simla society; Bent (the Dancing Master) flirts with her until his wife and child appear. The latter goes down with diphtheria and is moved to Mrs. Hauksbee's house. The complaint becomes very serious, but the child is saved by the prompt and courageous action of Mrs. Delville, who had lost her own child in similar circumstances.

6. Only a Subaltern

Bobby Wick joins the Tyneside Tail Twisters in India and becomes a good and popular officer, even taking trouble with Private Dormer. When the latter goes down with cholera, Wick sits up all night with him, only to go down with the disease himself.

7. The Phantom Rickshaw

Kipling published the second section *The Phantom Rickshaw* as the book of stories once. It was included in *Wee Willie Winkie* later. Jack Pansay, returning to India by P. and O., forgets his fiancée, Miss Mannering, and flirts with another passenger Mrs. Keith Wessington. He tires, but she is infatuated and his neglect worries her into an early grave. Pansay has returned to Miss Mannering, but on the very day he intends to buy the ring, meets Mrs. Keith Wessington in her rickshaw with the *jhampanies* in their distinctive livery. She accosts him, but they ride right through what turns out to be a phantom. He meets it again on several occasions, and consults his doctor—who is sympathetic but incredulous—and prescribes for complaints of the stomach, brain and eyes. Although he seems to recover, the phantom reappears and his extraordinary conduct causes his prospective father-in-law to write a letter returning the ring and breaking off the engagement.

8. My Own True Ghost Story

The narrator, staying in a dak-bungalow, hears various noises in the night, indicating the arrival of other travelers and a game of billiards in a room where he knows there is no table. He learns in the morning that the bungalow had been a billiards-room when the railway was being built and that one of the engineers died during a game. There is a quite natural explanation of the phenomenon at the end.

9. The Strange Ride of Morrowbie Jukes

Jukes, outriding, stumbles into a village of the dead situated in a half-moon hollow of sand bordering a river. The inhabitants are those 'who should have died'; escape is prevented by the steep sandy slope, quicksands, and a guard-boat. Jukes is shown how to catch crows by Gunga Dass, a former telegraph operator whom he once knew, and there is a gruesome account of the life of these unfortunate people. Jukes is later saved by his servant Dunnoo who had followed the tracks of his pony across the sand.

The parallel being so close that one half suspects Kipling of having invented a human analogy to the myrmelcon. The abominable settlement of living dead men is so vividly described and discussed, that no one who possesses the happy gift of believing can fail to be persuaded of the truth of the tale. The character of Gunga Dass, a Deccanee Brahmin whom Jukes finds in this reeking village, and who, reduced to the bare elements of life, preserves a little, though exceedingly little of his old traditional obsequiousness, is an admirable study.

10. The Man Who would be King

The White Hussars are entertaining a Russian officer named Dirkovitch. Dinner is interrupted by shots and a limp heap of rags is brought in. It turns out to be Lieutenant Limmason, missing before Sebastopol, who has managed to escape from Siberia and find his way back to his old regiment.

A still higher place, however, one is inclined to claim for the daring invention of 'The Man who would be King.' This is a long story and it depends for its effect, not upon any epigrammatic surprise but on an imaginative effort brilliantly sustained through a detailed succession of events. Two ignorant and disreputable Englishmen, exiles from social life, determine to have done with the sordid struggle, and to close with a try for nothing less than empire. They are seen by the journalist who narrates the story to disappear northward from the Kumharsan Serai disguised as a mad priest and his servant starting to sell whirligigs to the Ameer of Kabul. Two years later there stumbles into the newspaper office a human creature bent into a circle, and moving his feet one over the other like a bear. This is the surviving adventurer, who, half dead and half dazed, is roused by doses of raw whisky into a condition which permits him to unravel the squalid and splendid chronicle of adventures beyond the utmost rim of mountains, adventures on the veritable throne of Kafiristan. The tale is recounted with great skill as from the lips of the dying king.

The Man Who Would be King, a longer and better work, was described by H.G. Wells as one of the finest stories in the world.

The telling of the story is very full and detailed, despite its teller's reduced condition and the tiresome wanderings of mind so caused.

11. Wee Willie Winkie

The first story in the book of the same name; tells of the exploits of Percival William Williams, how he found Lieutenant Brandis kissing Miss Allardyce and did not tell, and how he saved her from the Bad Men who would have kidnapped her when she willfully crossed the Border, having been told not to.

12. Baa Baa Black Sheep

The second story in *Wee Willie Winkie*, which tells of the two small children, Punch and Judy, who are brought home from India and placed in the care of Antirosa and Uncle Harry.

The Mrs. Squeers of the Rocklington lodgings, is a sub-Dickensian creature, tricked out with a few touches of reality, but mainly a survival of early literary hatreds. The boy Harry and the soft little sister of Punch are rather shadowy. But Punch lives with an intense vitality, and here, without any indiscretion, we may be sure that Kipling has looked inside his own heart and drawn from memory. Nothing in the autobiographies of their childhood by Tolstoi and Pierre Loti, nothing in R. L. Stevenson's 'Child's Garden of Verses,' is more valuable as a record of the development of childhood than the account of how Punch learned to read, moved by curiosity to know what the falchion was with which the German man split the Griffin open. Very nice, also, is the reference to the mysterious rune, called 'Sonny, my Soul' with which mama used to sing Punch to sleep.

The story is autobiographical, recalling Kipling's sad childhood memories at 'Lorne Lodge.' According to Louis Cornell, "Whatever its aesthetic merits, 'Baa Baa, Black sheep' provides an indispensable key to the attitudes and themes expressed in Kipling's fiction."

This story may be compared with Jean-Paul Sartre's 'Enfance d'un chef' W. W. Robson says, "Critics have used the story to 'explain' the alleged cruelty of Kipling and his tendency, springing from fear, to take the side of the bully. It would be just as easy to use it to account for Kipling's horror of religious bigotry, which appears everywhere in his work.

13. His Majesty the King

The child of estranged parents unwittingly prevents them parting and an attack of fever reconciles them whereby he enjoys their love.

14. The Drums of the Fore and Aft

Jakin and Lew, drummer-boys, accompany the regiment to a frontier war; the lack of seasoned soldiers brings about a shameful withdrawal in the face of the enemy. The boys strike up 'The British Grenadiers' on a drum and fife; this, together with the remarks of their officers, brings the regiment to attack with success. The boys are killed.

By far this is the most powerful and ingenious story, however, which Kipling has yet dedicated to a study of childhood. 'The Fore and Aft' is a nickname given in derision to a crack regiment, whose real title is 'The Fore and Fit,' in memory of a sudden calamity which befell them on a certain day in an Afghan pass, when if it had not been for two little blackguard drummer-boys, they would have been woefully cut to pieces, as they were routed, by a dashing troop of Ghazis. The two little heroes, who only conquer to die, are stunted children of fourteen and also the disgrace of the regiment. In their little souls, however, there bums what Mr. Pater would call a hard, gem-like flame of patriotism, and they are willing to undergo any privation.

Kingsley Amis observes, "*Wee Willie Winkie* consists first of pieces that might be called fancy tales from the hills about amours and adulteries at Simla and elsewhere. They lack the economy and force of the earlier stories, and are written in a cheaply urbane style that, together with the setting and subject-matter, might make the unversed reader mistake them for the work of Somerset Maugham on an off-day. Kipling saw—or his mother told him—that this sort of thing was not his forte and he never again attempted it."

3. Life's Handicap (1891)

Kipling called this book *Life's Handicap: Being Stories of Mine Own People*. The book has 27 stories published in 1891. The book helped him establish as a literary figure in London. These stories reflect his experience of India. The atmosphere of a group of horror stories permeates the collection as a whole, with its air of haunted lives.

1. The Incarnation of Krishna Mulvaney

This is the first story in *Life's Handicap*. Dearsley, in charge of a railway gang, 'raffles' a magnificent palanquin every week and the winner always gives it back to him. Mulvaney agrees to fight him for it and takes Ortheris and Learoyd with him. Dearsley chooses the latter and gets badly mauled. The winners hide their prize in the narrator's stable and Mulvaney eventually goes off to sell it, but cannot resist calling on Dearsley to mock him. Dearsley takes it quite well, gets him drunk, and puts him, palanquin and all, on a train for Benares. The priests there recognize it as belonging to a certain Maharanee and take it, with Mulvaney inside, to the temple where a Queens' praying is in progress. He is enchanted by the sight of the beautiful royal woman but manages to escape after taking money and a necklace off a priest. He eventually rejoins his friends and the narrator.

2. The Courting of Dinah Shadd

Mulvaney explains how he wooed and won his wife. He fell foul of old Mother Shehy, who cursed him and the girl.

According to Johnson the one story in the book, admirable from first to last, is 'The Courting of Dinah Shadd': the tragedy of his life, told by Mulvaney. The Irishman's story is told with perfect truth and pity: Kipling makes not one mistake in sentiment. But had Mulvaney's colonel told the story of his life, Kipling would have filled it with cheap jests and cynicisms, gall and bitterness. Lord Birkenheard thinks many critics consider the story to be one of Kipling's most perfect short stories.

3. On Greenhow Hill

In On Greenhow Hill the three soldiers, Mulvancey, Ortheris and Learoyd, are gossiping in the lull of an operation on the North-West Frontier, and Learoyd speaks of the memories of his Yorkshire boyhood. Here, again, Kipling is triumphant in recapturing atmosphere; the peaceful green valleys round Skipton, and the tragedy of Learoyd's passion for a dying woman, are in strident contrast to the harsh outcrops of rock and the whining bullets among which the story is unfolded.

Criticism was made of the accuracy of Learoyd's Yorkshire speech as compared to Mulvaney's Irish, which was frequently described as that of a stage Irishman, and the cockney words of Ortheris.

'On Greenhow Hill': This story is unusual in that the setting for the soldier's reminiscences, and his passion for a dying woman, is green Yorkshire valleys. The mood of *'The End of the Passage,'* in which Hummil, the victim of terrifying nightmares, is literally scared to death, is also felt in 'The Limitations of Pambe Serang.'

J. H. Fenwick observes, "The most successful of all the later soldier tales is indubitably 'On Greenhow Hill.' In many ways it is unique in the series, and attempts new objects. Nevertheless, one can see it as a natural extension of the *Soldiers Three* frame.

4. The Man Who Was

The White Hussars are entertaining a Russian officer named Dirkovitch. Dinner is interrupted by shots and a limp heap of rages is brought in. It turns out to be Lieutenant Limmason, missing before Sebastopol, who has managed to escape from Siberia and find his way back to his old regiment.

The story has all the marks of melodrama that made it so successful on the London stage with Beerbohm Tree in the lead. Yet there is nothing more probable than Russian spies in Peshawar in the eighties or torture in Russian prison camps, then. What seems to falsify it is the note of awe with which young Kipling recounts the splendours and traditions of this famous regiment's ceremonial. The East African administrator Lord Lugard's reaction, when he first read the story in 1894, is interesting, because he had known service in the Afghan War in 1880 and the Burmese War of 1886-7. he said, 'Kipling's knowledge of the barrack room is greater than that of the officers' mess.'

5. The Head of the District

The narrator has been disturbed in camp by a camel getting loose at night; other animals appear and discuss their various fears. They all take part in a magnificent Review before the Viceroy and the Emir of Afghanistan the next day. The poem 'Parade-Song of the Camp-Animals' follows.

In particular, the story has always been a cause of offence to liberal and Indian readers of Kipling.

Of course no-one would deny that Kipling vigorously beat the imperial drum: nor will anyone seek to contest the fact that a great number of his stories work within an implicit or explicit framework statement reiterating what might be described as the British Imperial Aptitude. Clearly Kipling's artistic inspiration emerges 'en politique.' But to say this as if it were all there is to be said: to see Kipling as 'the laureate of Joseph Chamberlain's designs,' as Mr Tindall does, is to see the surface pattern merely:—and sometimes not even that.

6. Without Benefit of Clergy

John Holden lives with a Muslim woman Ameera; a son, Tota, is born to them. The child dies, followed by his mother. Holden is called away to duty in a cholera-stricken district; his landlord tells him that as he does not wish to keep the house on he will sell it to the municipality and they will demolish it and build a road, so that no man will be able to tell where it stood.

According to Allan Sandison, "One of Kipling's best short stories—'Without Benefit of Clergy' derives its excellence from its intense awareness of, and sympathy with, the human context of this conflict. The brief little tragedy of Holden and Ameera is played out against a background not of marching feet and thudding rifle-butts, but of India's silent, malignant and jealous power which overarches everything and allows none to live save in the grace of its own inexorable law."

It is a story of an Indian woman, the 'Uncovenanted wife' of an English civilian and mother of his son, a story which gave the middle-aged critical admirers of his youth a sudden thrilling belief that there were deeper things in store. It is easy to sympathize with Maurice Baring when, as an old man, he described a certain passage in this story as containing the most beautiful words that Kipling ever wrote. We have usually looked in vain among Kipling's dazzling talents for signs of tenderness and compassion.

7. At the End of the Passage

The story is about hard work in bad conditions in India. Hummil, an assistant engineer, entertains Mottram, Lowndes, and Spurstow every week and at one such meeting he is unwell; but he will not go sick because Burkett, who would relieve him, would bring his wife and child to the post. The three men return the following Sunday to find their host dead, apparently from fear or great shock. It seems that Spurstow, the doctor, attempts to photograph the retina of his eyes and then breaks up his camera, but we are not told the result, which appears to be horrible.

Lord Birkenhead observes, "In 'At the End of the Passage' the Terrors of hallucination in the Indian heat are brilliantly explored, and as a study in the macabre the story is the equal of that other classical tale of horror, 'The Mark of the Beast,' which had produced such a feeling of scandalized agitation in the bosom of Andrew Lang."

8. The Mutiny of the Mavericks

Fenian Plotters in the United States send young Mulcahy to foment a mutiny in an Irish regiment in India. He has ample funds for beer, so nearly everybody joins; then the regiment is ordered on active service, which he had not bargained for. After unsuccessful attempts to get a certificate from the doctor, he goes forward and is finally killed by the Afghans.

9. The Mark of the Beast

Fleete, after dining with the narrator and Strickland, desecrates a temple, and a leper touches him. The next day he is ill with what appears to be a mixture of leprosy and hydrophobia. He is cured by the prompt and drastic action of Strickland, assisted by the narrator.

10. The Return of Imroy

Imray disappeared; Strickland later rented his bungalow and the narrator stayed with him and Tietjens, his Rampur bitch. She would not settle down in the bungalow, as there was an atmosphere of unrest. They hunt snakes in the roof, finding the body of the long-lost Imray, killed by his servant Bahadur

Khan, in the belief that he had cast the evil eye on his child. The servant steps on a karait and dies, thus avoiding being hanged.

11. Namgay Doola

The narrator meets the king of a country four miles square, on the road to Thibet. He complains that one of his subjects will not contribute to the revenue. The next day there is a logjam on the river, which is relieved by the delinquent, a red-headed, blue-eyed man named Namgay Doola. He is shown to be the son of an Irish solider who married a native woman, and is, on the recommendation of the narrator, renamed Patsay Doola and promoted to be chief of the army.

12. The Lang Men O' Larut

Esdras B. Longer, calling at Larut, bets that he is the longest man on the island. His host then introduces him to Jock Coan, Sandy Vowle, and Long Lammitter; Coan is the smallest at six feet five inches and Longer, who has intended to play his name on his card, surrenders. There is then some celebration.

13. Bertran and Bimi

The story is related by Hans Breitmann. A gruesome yarn of Bertran, a French naturalist, who tamed an orang-outang named Bimi and taught him to live almost like a man. When Bertran tells Breitmann that he is about to marry, the latter advises him to give the girl the stuffed figure of Bimi. Bertran laughs at this, but the ape understands; the wife is later found dead and Bertran kills Bimi after a dreadful fight in which he too dies.

14. Reingelder and the German Flag

Reingelder, together with Hans Breitmann, the narrator, is searching for orchids and coral snakes in Uruguay. The former hopes to find a snake known as the German Flag (so called because it is marked in the colours of the old Imperial German Ensign), and when one is brought to him, he handles it, despite Breitmann's warning, because Yates, an authority on these creatures, had written that it was not provided with poison-glands. He shut the book with a bang, nipped the snake, which promptly bit him twice. He died in great agony.

15. The Wandering Jew

John Hay inherits money and is obsessed with the notion that he will not live long to enjoy it. He knows that if you go round the world from west to east you 'gain a day' and thereupon starts on his travels. His heir (with the help of a doctor) devises a cure.

16. Through the Fire

Madu, a charcoal-burner, beats his wife, Athira, who runs away with a Sepoy named Suket Singh. Madu sends a curse; the woman falls sick and they return. Suket Singh shoots her on a pile of wood ready for burning, lights it and pulls the trigger with his toe in the classic manner.

17. The Finances of the Gods

Gobind tells of Shiv noticing a poor but very holy man near the steps of a temple, and asking Ganesh to do something for him. Ganesh promises that he shall receive a lakh of rupees in three days. He obtains the money by working on the avarice and fear of a money-lender who overheard.

18. The Amir's Homily

Abdur Rahman is dispensing justice and one who has stolen for hunger is brought before him. The Amir contends that the man stole 'for drink, for lust, for idleness,' and relates how he himself once worked as a coolie.

19. Jews in Shushan

Ephraim, with his family and some others, form the Jewish colony; two more, and they will be able to apply for a synagogue. Death reduces their numbers, the adopted boy runs away, and the remainder return sorrowfully to Calcutta.

20. The Limitations of Pambe Serang

Nurkeed eats the meal of Pambe Serang; the latter tries to kill him on several occasions, whereupon the former ships in another vessel. They later come together, when Pambe is ill with pneumonia and Nurkeed visits him. Pambe kills him, is nursed back to health, and hanged.

21. Little Tobrah

He is in court, accused of murdering his little sister by pushing her into a well; he is discharged for lack of evidence, and tells a harrowing story in the groom's quarters. The child was blind, and their parents were dead; as he said, 'It is better to die than to starve.'

22. Moti Guj—Mutineer

Deesa, Moti Guj's (Pearl Elephant) mahout, takes ten days' leave for a drinking-bout and tells the elephant he is to behave himself for that time. He is overdue from leave and the elephant will not work. There is trouble until Deesa returns and the elephant at once goes to work with him.

23. Bubbling Well Road

The narrator and his dog, Mr. Wardle, are out-hunting in the jungle and come across weird noises and an evil echo. A one-eyed priest shows them the way out.

24. 'The City of Dreadful Night'

The story gives a realistic picture of Lahore sweltering in intense heat.

25. Georgie Porgie

This is the fifth scene in *The Story of the Gadsbys*, set in the third week of their marriage.

26. Naboth

The narrator unwisely gives one rupee to Naboth, with permission to sell sweetmeats in the compound. Business prospers until he has a gut, a wife and family, and assistants.

27. The Dream of Duncan Parrenness

Parrenness, a dissolute young writer in the service of the East India Company at Calcutta, dreams that he meets his older self, who bargains with him, taking his trust in man and his faith in woman. Before he leaves, he places something in his hand. It is a piece of dry bread.

28. L'Envoi it is collected as 'The Woman' in *Soldiers Three*

Lionel Johnson observes, "The one great fault in Mr. Kipling's work is, not its brutality, nor its fondness for strong effects, but a certain taint of bad manners, from the literary point of view." He insists upon spicing his stories with an ill-flavoured kind of gossip, wholly irrelevant, and very offensive. For example: 'The Man Who Was,' an admirable story, full of that indefinable spirit, military patriotism and regimental pride, is spoilt by this pointless passage.

4. Soldiers Three (1892)

The book contains 13 stories, first published in 1888 alongside the booklets *Under the Deodars, The Phantom Rickshaw*, and *We Willie Winkie*. All these were later published in a two volume collection in 1892.

Kipling depicts the soldierly virtues necessary to sustain the Empire. It is for his creation of the daily life of the British fighting man and of an army on the alert against potential invaders from Afghanistan that the stories are chiefly admired. Through the taxing ordeals of action and drilling, Mulvaney, one of the 'soldiers three,' learns the stoical virtues. His rule-breaking individualism and imagination are the qualities which are central to the later *Stalky & Co.*

These stories evidence Kipling's cinematic vision as Hardy's epic drama *The Dynasts* does it so. The strongest ingredients are the atmosphere of the brooding landscape and the men's stoicism, companionship and ability to survive a tedious, emotionally cheerless routine.

The book has several episodes, mostly in dialogue form, collected in *Soldiers Three*, showing the devil-may-care Captain taking a wife, and the conflict between the claims of his family and the army.

1. The God from the Machine

This is the first story in the book. Mulvaney presents an elopement arranged to coincide with amateur theatricals. The story views military society and sees the corruption at bottom, but it is told from a distance: Mulvaney's involvement is negligible and the story itself slight.

2. Private Learoyd's Story

Learoyd exercises the terrier, Rip, belonging to the Colonel's wife. Mrs. DeSussa is attracted to the dog and offers to buy it. Learoyd and Ortheris disguise the canteen-sergeant's cur and sell it to the lady for three hundred and fifty rupees.

3. The Big Drunk Draf

The story is told by Mulvaney after he retired from the Army and took a job in India. He found a draft behaving badly, and so gave good advice and very able assistance to the young officer in charge.

4. The Solid Muldoon

Mulvaney tells how he was hanging about the married quarters when he was a young soldier, hoping to secure the favours of Annie Bragin, a Colour-Sergeant's wife. He finds another loiterer and the woman in a very distressed state; Bragin finds his wife and Mulvaney in a compromising situation, the men fight, and Bragin gets the worst of it. The other man reappears, to be recognized as Corporal Flahy, who lost his wife there three years ago, went mad and died of grief.

5. With the Main Guard

The narrator hears Mulvaney and his friends tell the story of the fight at Silver's Theatre, of O'Neil and the little officer-boy who was prevented from joining in the fighting by a sergeant whose mother is a tenant of his family. 'The Solid Muldoon' returns one to moral problems in a military setting, and though the corruption is less apparent than in 'The God from the Machine', the sadness underlying the story is deeper.

6. In the Matter of a Private

Losson torments Simmons until he runs amok and shoots his tormentor, escaping with a rifle and thirty rounds. He wounds an officer and Corporal Slane, who finally captures him. All Slane wants by way of reward is four battery horses to draw his wedding carriage. It is like a thesis story.

7. Black Jack

Mulvaney has been in trouble with Sergeant Mullins and, after pack-drill, has been walked off by Ortheris and Learoyd to recover his temper. He later tells the story of how Sergeant O'Hara was shot at by Private Vulmea. Mulvaney had overheard the plot whereby one of the men—chosen by the cards, the first on to be dealt Black Jack, the Ace of Spades—was to do the shooting, using Mulvaney's rifle so that he would be blamed for it. Mulvaney tampers with his rifle so that Vulmea is wounded instead of the Sergeant; the latter, although understanding the situation, treats it as an accident.

J. H. Fenwick observes, "'Black Jack' is the clearest example of the way in which Kipling can, by interweaving two tales or incidents, call on all the resources of this society which he has recreated. It is also the best example of the complex unity, both moral and aesthetic, that he can achieve by this sort of equipoise—by the elaborate structure of cross-references, parallels and contrasts between the frame and the central narrative."

8. Poor Dear Mamma

This is the title of the first section of *The Story of the Gadsbys*. The Captain, calling on Mrs. Threegan, meets her daughter Minnie and in a few weeks transfers his affection to her.

9. The World Without

This is the second part of 'The Story of the Gadsbys.' Gadsby's engagement has reached the Club, where the members discuss it, wondering how Mrs. Herriott will be discarded and how she will take it.

10. The Tents of Kedar

Gadsby sits next to an old flame, Mrs. Herriott, at dinner and has a quiet but agonizing scene about his engagement.

11. With any Amazement

Title taken from the Marriage Service in the Book of Common Prayer. This is about Gadsby's wedding.

12. The Garden of Eden

This is the fifth scene in 'The Story of the Gadsbys,' set in the third week of their marriage.

13. Fatima

The sixth item in 'The Story of the Gadsbys'; Mrs. Gadsby investigates her husband's professional life and is informed of several things it would have been better she did not know. It seems she is pregnant.

14. The Valley of the Shadow

This is the seventh scene in 'The Story of the Gadsbys.' The wife is seriously ill, but recovers thanks to the wise ayah and the doctor.

15. The Swelling of Jordan

This is the last scene in the 'The Story of the Gadsbys.' A son is born, and Gadsby decides to send in his papers and go home for the sake of his wife and the child.

16. 'L' Envoi collected as 'The Winners'

This is a cynical poem on the theme 'He travels the fastest who travels alone.'

17. Dray Wara Yow Dee

This is the first story in the series *In Black and White*, later collected in *Soldiers Three*. A Pathan accosts the narrator with a request that he buy almonds and raisins; the Sahib is an old acquaintance, so he explains that his wife has intrigued with one Daoud Shah, whom he intends to kill, as he has killed the woman. The story recounts his wanderings and the 'eternal triangle' from an Eastern viewpoint.

18. The Judgment of Dungara

This is the second story *In Black and White*. The Rev. Justus Krenk and his wife go to convert the Buria Kol, and start a small mission which is ruined by the high priest of Dungara, the local deity, who contrives to have the community clothed in garments made from a very irritating fibre. 'The Judgment of Dungara' is as good, in a comic and cynical manner. So is the tale of a sahib called 'Yankum Sahib.'

Just as disastrous is the result of the mission of Justus Krenk, Pastor of the Tübingen Mission to the people of the Berbulda Hills in 'The Judgement of Dungara.' This was written in 1888 before the Germans had acquired the satanic quality that they increasingly had for Kipling from 1890. They were seen as well-intentioned, plodding people. But their Mission in Berbula is a disaster as great as Dan and Peachey's kingdom. 'The chapel and school have long since fallen back into the jungle,' the story ends.

19. At Howli Thana

At Howli Thana is the third story in *In Black and White*. An ex-policeman begs for employment and tells how he came to leave the police. They had been sent to deal with some dacoits, but he came to terms with them. Their report-book and rifles are later missing, so they trump up a story which is to be supported by wounds of various kinds and return to headquarters where Yunkum Sahib (who rides a tricycle on occasion) hears their story and takes them into his bathroom, where lie the book and rifles which he himself had taken as they slept.

20. Gemini

Gemini is the fourth story *In Black and White*. Durga and Ram Dass quarrel and there is some confusion as they are very much alike.

'Gemini' might make a Radical Indophile laugh, and might teach him a good deal about his clients.

21. At Twenty-Two

'At Twenty-Two' is the fifth story in *In Black and White*. Janki Meah, a blind miner, saves a party of miners, including Kundoo, his wife's lover, from a flooded mine. Unda, the wife, elopes with Kundoo a week later.

22. In Flood Time

Is there no connection, then, between race and race, or between individuals of the same race in this northern corner of India, the Punjab? A chance contact may go deep, for the moment, as in 'In Floodtime,' where the hurrying Sahib is held up all night at a ford by rushing floodwater that even the elephants refuse to face. Here he listens to the old Moslem ford guard's tale. It is a grim enough story of his impious wooing of a Hindu girl and his coming to save her in another terrible flood of time past, riding his rival's floating body. In Flood Time is the sixth story of *In Black and White*. The old Keeper of the Barhwi Ford tells a sahib who is waiting for the flood to go down of the greatest flood he knew in thirty years. He used to swim the river to meet a Hindu widow and was carried away by the flood-waters, to be saved by the buoyancy of a body that turned out to be that of his rival for her love. Hardy's novel *The Return of the Native* has a similar theme.

'In Flood Time' is a little prose idyl of epical strength; there is something primitive in the adventure and something very sympathetic in the old warder of the ford who tells the tale.

23. The Sending of Dana Da

This is the seventh story in *In Black and White*. An Englishman who lapsed from a certain society that went in for magic of all kinds did a small service for Dana Da, who used to know the society; in gratitude the latter wishes to arrange a sending for him; accordingly, Lone Sahib, the man who was most bitter about the Englishman's lapse from the Tea-cup creed, is selected; he finds small kittens everywhere he goes. The Creed members are most interested in this when its laid before them; the explanation is both laughable and simple.

The 'Sending of Dana Da' is an Icelandic kind of miracle worked on esoteric Buddhists to their confusion and sorrow.

24. On the City Wall

Kipling achieves his most complex portrayal of native India in a story that has not been much discussed by critics — 'On the City Wall.' On the City Wall is the last story in *Soldiers Three*. Lalun, an enchanting courtesan, is, with her guests, attracted by a very old man who parades the ramparts of the fort. He is an old mutineer named Khem Singh who has been permitted to return from exile in Burma and is kept under light guard by the subaltern, who is interested in his stories. The narrator is unwittingly pressed into service to aid his escape during a riot, but the old man returns to his captivity after a week, disgusted with the present generation, who have forgotten him.

'On the City Wall' is one of the very best of the stories; the tale of conspiracy; riot, prison-breaking, organized by Lalun the Fair and Wali Dad, a young Mahommedan who was suffering acutely from Education of the English variety, and knew it. This Wali Dad is as clever a study as that of the Pathan horse thief; his modern melancholy, infidelity, *Welt-schmerz*, and all the rest of it, leave him at bottom as thorough a Moslem fanatic as ever yelled 'Ya Hasan! Ya Hussain!' How the British soldiers quell a multitude of yelling fanatics, without drawing a bayonet or firing a shot, is pleasant to read. And, at the end of the riot, there we find agnostic Wali Dad, 'shoeless, turbanless, and frothing at the mouth; the flesh on his chest bruised and bleeding from the vehemence with which he had smitten himself.' Wherefore we part from Wali Dad respecting him rather more than in his character of educated unbeliever; for the attitude and actions of the fanatic were more sincere than the sighs and sneers of the product.

The stories of this book *Soldiers Three* depict the soldiers, particularly in Lahore. Kipling has taken three widely different types of British soldier, a Yorkshire man, a Cockney, and a 'Paddy from Cork,' and in spite of the savagery of the first, the cynicism of the second, and the thrasonical complacency of the third, we can fully comprehend the attractions which their company is supposed to have offered to the narrator. Of a truth it must indeed have been better to sit out with Mulvaney than to dance many dances, if Mulvaney in the flesh was at all like his literary representation.

There have been men who learned Greek in their cradle, and Mr. Kipling was born with an insight into life. The knowledge of human feeling and human impulse he displays in *The Story of the Gadsbys* would be miraculous did we not reflect that it is intuitive: he probably knew as much at fifteen as he does at twenty-five. The book is intensely dramatic, and is packed with action and emotion. It has serious faults of diction which are all the more irritating to the reader because they might so easily have been avoided. Charles Whibley observes, "There is not one but lives and convinces the reader of his life. Captain Gadsby's explanation with Mrs. Herriott is done with amazing dexterity and with that impartial recognition of the facts that holds the scales of sympathy even.

J. H. Fenwick thinks with a smaller and even more coherent society, that of the private soldier, Kipling makes increasing use of the environment he treats. At no point does one find him suggesting that there is an answer to the problems raised by the conflict of this society and the individual. He observes, "This examination is carried out with great tact—owing to the relationship between the narrator and the three—and with great narrative skill in the handling of the three themselves as spokesmen." The stories in *Soldiers Three* were equations of a human and a social condition, one finding its expression through the other.

5. Many Inventions (1893)

Many Inventions is a collection of 14 stories, published in 1893. It includes six Indian tales, of which two concern characters who also appear in *Soldiers Three.* In 'His Private Honour' Ortheris's conduct is dictated by a code which transcends the army rule book. 'The Disturber of Traffic' is about the delusions and growing obsession of Dowse, a lighthouse keeper in the Java 'Straits; 'The Finest Story in the World' in which Charlie begins to recall moments of previous lives as a Roman galley slave and on a Viking ship; and 'The Record of Badalia Herodsfoot' is a realistic account of the heroine's struggle for survival in the London slums of the 1890s.

The collection *Many Inventions*, contains much of Kipling's most characteristic and most enduring work. George

Saintsbury says, "*Many Inventions* is not only good, but very good. I am inclined to think it, using words carefully, the best volume that Mr. Kipling has done. It is, of course, unequal; nobody could write fourteen different tales of the widest range of subject and style and not be unequal. Of course one reader will like this better than that, and another that better than this.

'To the True Romance' is said to be the Prelude to the book *Many Inventions.*

1. The Disturber of Traffic

This is the first story in the book. In this there is 'The Disturber of Traffic,' that humorous oddly realistic study of a lighthouse-keeper in the Dutch East Indies who is driven mad by watching the streakiness of the sea. Kipling writes,

> The streaks, they would run with the tides, north and south, twice a day, accordin' to them currents, and he'd lie down on the planking—it was a screw-pile Light—with his eyes to a crack and watch the water streaking through the piles just so quiet as hogwash. He said the only comfort he got was at slack water. Then the streaks in his head went round and round like a sampan in a tide-rip; but that was heaven, he said, to the other kind of streaks—the straight ones that looked like arrows on a wind-chart, but much more regular, and that was the trouble of it. No more he couldn't ever keep his eyes off the tides that ran up and down so strong, but as soon as ever he looked at the high hills standing all along Flores Strait for rest and comfort his eyes would be pulled down like to the nesty streaky water; and when they once got there he couldn't pull them away again till the tide changed. He told me all this himself, speaking just as thought he was talking of somebody else.

The narrator spends a night at a South Coast lighthouse where Fenwick, the Keeper, tells him of Dowse, who kept a lighthouse at the end of the Flores Straits. The currents run so swiftly that the water looks 'streaky' and Dowse gets the impression that the ships that use the Straits are the cause of it. He accordingly arranges light-buoys and so forth to give the appearance of wrecks in the channel, aided by Challong, the

Orang-Laut. He is eventually taken off the station, naked and mad, but recovers and becomes a wherry-man at Portsmouth, where the tides run crossways.

Angus Wilson suggests there is even a fear that Challong's (Caliban) animal side of nature, may play too large a part in the preoccupations of a Prospero, an artist, isolated as is Dowse, the Java Straits lighthouse-keeper. And yet, as we know, there is a desperate longing to escape not only from urban civilisation but from the civilising forces of the group, of the Square and so on. But not alone. It is a horrible and purposely puzzling tale, carefully told without clear definition.

2. A Conference of the Powers

The narrator is entertaining some Army friends at his chambers in London when Eustace Cleever, author of *As it Was in the Beginning*, enters: the boys compliment him on it and he questions them on their service in Burma, realizing, as they talk, that his life and outlook is somewhat narrow. They leave the narrator and go to a show, returning later singing a song from *The Gondoliers*.

3. My Lord the Elephant

Mulvaney tells how he came to be on the back of a mad elephant and the treatment that brought it back to its senses. Later, Malachi, the elephant, holds up a body of troops by refusing to move from a narrow pass. Mulvaney is in hospital nearby; his old friend recognizes him and is persuaded to cross a bridge out of the pass, whereby the situation is saved.

4. One View of the Question

This is a letter to Kazi Jamal-ud-Din at the Court of Rao Sahib of Jagesur, written by Shafiz Ullah Khan who is visiting Britain in his service. The letter recounts his activities, with many shrewd comments on local customs.

5. The Finest Story in the World

Charlie Mears, a bank-clerk, fancies he can write poetry; he has a splendid story in his head that he cannot get on paper but is able to explain it; it turns out to be a yarn of life in a Greek galley which he cannot possibly have read anywhere. The story becomes that of a Viking and the hero cannot remember how or where he obtained the information. The narrator discusses this with Grish Chunder, a Bengali law student in London, and they agree that he must be remembering previous existences.

'The Finest Story in the World' is said to have been aroused by his cousin Ambo Poynter's ineffectual search to express himself in poetry.

6. His Private Honor

Ouless, a recently joined lieutenant, tears Ortheris's tunic with his cane during drill. The latter shields him when questioned by Captain Brander and the two go out 'shooting' together and settle it with their fists; Ouless is then able to pay for repairs and finds his self-confidence.

7. A Matter of Fact

Keller, an American journalist, Zuyland, and the narrator see a monster of the deep in tropical waters. The American sees a 'scoop' and writes his story. The narrator tells him that he will not submit it when they eventually reach London. He does not.

The story is a crude poetic writing which we can call as S-F today. This is the death of the grotesque and blinded sea monster thrown up from the ocean's depths by an earthquake and wounded by a passing liner, and with it, the moving cry of misery that comes from its mate. The passage expresses Kipling's deep sense of pity with a clear force, that is impossible where he is concerned with human beings.

8. The Lost Legion

The Goorkhas and cavalry go out in the dark and wet to capture the Gulla Kutta Mullah. They are conscious of other troops in their rear and catch an Afghan who is terrified of 'the Ghost Regiment'. It seems that many years ago, during the Mutiny, the locals had hunted a disaffected regiment to death in these same hills for the sake of their arms and equipment.

9. In the Rukh

Dick Hatt, secretly married to a girl, leaves her at home and goes to a job in India. He works too hard, but cannot afford the fare to bring her out; a baby is born, and dies; the girl becomes entangled with another man. Hatt is then offered the promotion that would have solved his problems. He resigns and disappears.

10. Brugglesmith

The narrator dines aboard the Breslau and meets Brugglesmith, 'a crapulous ruffian.' They get adrift in the dinghy, are rescued by the River Police, and after further adventures meet a policeman known to the narrator in the Strand. In the end, the narrator wheels the old reprobate to Brook Green, Hammersmith, in the ambulance from St. Clement Danes, a covered vehicle rather like a large perambulator.

'Brugglesmith' is for instance, that crazy farce in which Kipling piled absurdity on absurdity till it seemed that he would rouse the London night about him in guffaws, in the legitimate forebear of 'The Bonds of Discipline.'

11. 'Love-o'-Women'

Raines shoots Mackie for playing about with his wife. Mulvaney remembers other affairs, including that of Larry Tighe, who was with him in the Black Tyrone. They were at Silver's Theatre, where Tighe tells of his reglets—drink no longer 'bites'—and his desire to get shot during the fighting. He comes through safely, but falls sick with locomotor ataxia (he is known as 'Love-o'-Women'). At Peshawar he meets a woman whom he calls 'Egypt'; he manages to get out of his litter and into her house, after some talk he dies in her arms. She shoots herself.

Here the title is a man's nickname. This excites incredulity: could you bring yourself to say, for instance, 'Have one on me, Love-o'-Women!' Kipling here indulges too in his favourite vice of over, mystification—old Love-o,'Women is a disappointed man, but we never find out quite what disappointed him. The climax, though melodramatic and improbable, touches our pity, and the opening is admittedly splendid, perhaps the most powerful he ever devised. It turns out, however to be the opening to one of his frame-narratives.

12. The Record of Badalia Herodsfoot

The scene of the story is the East End of London; Badalia is deserted by her brutal husband and interests herself in good works under the guidance of Sister Eva, the Rev. Eustace Hanna, and Brother Victor. Herodsfoot, tired of the woman he lives with, returns and demands money; she refuses to hand over the Mission funds, is badly knocked about, and dies, refusing to disclose that husband was responsible.

13. Judson and the Empire

Lieutenant Harrison Edward Judson ('Bai-Jove-Judson') takes a small gunboat which he commanded in a very able manner to join the Cape Station. The Admiral is impressed and leaves him in command; Judson finds a gunboat belonging to another Power up a certain river on the coast of Africa, is fired on without damage, and runs his opponent ashore. He then sees to the safety of a party of English adventurers and returns to the scene of his victory with the local Governor. The Admiral arrives in his flagship to assist, but finds that hostilities have ceased and a party begun. One of the most amusing of the naval stories, based on the exploits of Lieutenant F. W. Keary, commanding H. M. S. *Red-breast.*

14. The Children of the Zodiac

The young elephant had a nose like a boot and was interested to find out what the crocodile had for dinner. He was nearly the dinner, but the Bi-Coloured-Python-Rock-Snake helps him, whereby his nose is stretched into the trunk we know today.

'Envoy' is the verse collected as 'Anchor Song' at the end of the book.

Ruport Croft-Cooke observes, "'*Many Inventions* contains much of Kipling's most characteristic and most enduring work. He is no longer satisfied with the merely exciting, the merely bizarre or the merely comic. He is interested in people as people and not as chessmen moved to make a surprise ending or a clever twist in he plot."

6. The Jungle Book (1894)

The first *Jungle Book* was published in 1894 and the second in 1895. The sequence of stories about the boy Mowgli, accidentally thrust out of the human community into the jungle forms the core of these collections. The Cambridge Guide to literature adds: "'His growth from jungle boyhood to dominance over the animals, and his eventual return to human service as a forest ranger, provides the basic framework. The code of conduct in the animal world is severe and requires a high level of responsibility; this is demonstrated in 'Letting in the Jungle,' where retribution is brought on the village which sought to destroy Mowgli. In comparison with the jungle law and the stoic social duty of the animals, humanity is unruly and undignified.

The book is something like a Bilgungsroman. Myth can also be found therein—of the fallen Eden. Mowgli's transformation is like Paradise Lost. Likewise, 'The Miracle of Purun Bhagat' is about a man who has to adjust from western codes of conduct to the life of a Hindu holy man.

Rupert Croft-Cooke observes, "Kipling made what so many writers have desired and created a world of his own in which the laws of probability were of his own choosing. Swift, Butler, 'Anatole France, Cabell, Jatnes Stephens are but a few of the story-tellers who have demanded an escape from the tiresome inhibitions imposed by space and time and the common understanding of cause and effect. Kipling created a Jungle in which there was Law and even Order, in which the animals, while conscientiously retaining certain of the habits of their kind, spoke and loved and obeyed as humans."

1. Mowgli's Brothers

This is the first story in *The Jungle Book*. A baby is found and cared for by the wolves. He grows up with the pack, is educated by Baloo and Bagheera, and finally accepted as one of the Free People. The other Mowgli stories are: *Kaa's Hunting, 'Tiger! Tiger!', How Fear Came, Letting in the Jungle, The King's Ankus, Red Dog, The Spring Running,* and *In the Rukh.*

The story is followed by 'Hunting—Song of the Seconee Pack.'

2. Kaa's Hunting

In spite of warnings from Baloo, Mowgli talks to the Monkey People, who carry him off to their headquarters in a deserted city, the Cold Lairs. He manages to pass a message to his friends, who enlist the aid of Kaa and rescue him.

'Kaa's Hunting' contains one of the most horrible scenes in all Kipling's work—and that work contains many such. It is the picture of the Bandar Log monkeys swaying helplessly towards their doom in the great ruins of the King's palace in a hypnotic trance induced by the coiling and looping of Kaa, the python's body and his 'never stopping, low humming song."

The story is followed by 'Road—Song of the Bandar—Log.'

3. 'Tiger! Tiger!'

After the Red Flower incident at the Council Rock (*Mowgli's Brothers*) Mowgli makes his way to an Indian village where he meets Messua, who might well be his mother. He lives in the village and is set to mind a herd of buffaloes, where Grey Brother warns him that Shere Khan, the Lame Tiger, is going to waylay him. With the help of the wolves, the tiger is killed in a stampede. Mowgli is interrupted in his skinning by Buldeo and sets Akela to frighten him off. The villagers stone him away and he returns to the jungle, finding the Free People at the Council Rock, somewhat lawless for lack of a leader. The story is followed by 'Mowgli's Song.'

4. The White Seal

Kotick, born on the island of St. Paul in the Bering Sea, wishes to free his people from the sealers who kill thousands yearly, and spends seven years looking for suitable breeding grounds where men cannot come. He meets various creatures in his travels and finally Sea Cow leads him through a submarine tunnel to magnificent beaches to which he later leads the seals. The poem 'Lukannon' is the song of the seal-rookeries.

5. 'Rikki-Tikki-Tavi'

'Rikki-Tikki-Tavi' is the name of the mongoose who is the hero of it. He is washed out of his nest and found in the garden of a bungalow in Segowlee cantonment; revived, he makes friends with Teddy, the son of the occupier, and becomes a household pet. He has various adventures with Nag and Nagina, a pair of cobras, but manages to kill them with the help of Darzee the tailor-bird and his wife.

'Rikki Tikki Tavi' has rightly commanded some attention because the fight between the mongoose and the snake takes place in that clearly seen backyard bungalow compound which is Kipling's visual forte; but it is marred surely for modern readers by the whimsical intrusion of the human family.

'Darzee's Chaunt' is sung in honour of the above.

6. 'Toomai of the Elephants'

'Shiv and the Grasshopper' is the song Toomai's mother sang to the baby.

7. Her Majesty's Servants

The narrator has been disturbed in camp by a camel getting loose at night; other animals appear and discuss their various fears. They all take part in a magnificent Review before the Viceroy and the Emir of Afghanistan the next day.

'Parade-Song of the Camp-Animals' is at the end of 'Her Majesty's Servants.'

7. The Second Jungle Book (1895)

The Second Jungle Book has the following stories: How Fear Came, The Miracle of Purun Bhagat, Letting in the Jungle, The Undertakers, The King's Ankus, Quiquern, Red Dog and The Spring Running.

1. How Fear Came

This is the first story in *Second Jungle Book*. The story is about the early days in the Jungle before the animals learned to kill, and what happened when they did.

The Poem 'The Law of the Jungle' follows the story.

2. The Miracle of Purun Bhagat

Purun Dass, a high-caste Brahmin and Prime Minister of a Native State, relinquishes his office and assumes the garb of a Sunnyasi. He makes friends with the wild animals in his retreat in the Hills, and, one wild night, learns from them that a landslide is coming. He manages to warn the villagers who have fed him, but loses his own life.

'A Song of Kabir,' as a poem, follows the story.

3. Letting in the Jungle

Mowgli returns to the village to find his mother and father bound by the villagers, who hate them for being rich and suspect them of witchcraft. The boy releases them, directs them to a place of safety, and then calls on Hathi and his sons to help demolish the village and ruin the fields. The jungle soon takes over and it is difficult to believe that there was ever a village there at all.

'Mowgli's Song against People' is a poem in five verses at the end of the story.

4. The Undertakers

The Mugger of Mugger Ghaut, an old alligator, has terrorized a certain ford for forty years. Now a bridge has been built and he has enjoyed the workmen who fell from it. He discusses this and other matters with several animals—all old friends—and remembers the Mutiny when he was very well fed, but made a pass at an English child in a boat for sport. The child managed to withdraw his hands in time, while his mother opened fire with a revolver. The Engineer of the bridge shoots the Mugger and it is revealed in conversation that he was the child in question.

The poem 'A Ripple Song' follows.

5. The King's Ankus

Kaa and Mowgli revisit the Cold Lairs and find the treasure-house, guarded by an old white cobra; the boy takes away a jewel-studded elephant goad because he wishes to see it in the sunshine; when he learns its use he throws it away and goes to sleep. A villager picks it up and is killed by a Gond, who is himself killed by four men. They are found dead with the ankus beside them. Mowgli returns the ankus to the Treasure-House before it can cause any more killing.

The story is followed by the poem 'The Song of the Little Hunter.'

6. Quiquern

Kotuko, an Esquimau boy, has a puppy, and they grow up together. Famine comes on the tribe, the dog goes mad and runs away. The boy, half-mad himself with starvation, comes to the hut with a story of a *tornaq*, a woman-thing who promised to guide him to seal-holes. He goes, with the Girl from the North who was befriended by the tribe, and they see Quiquern, the two-headed monster, which turns out to be their own dog tangled up with another, both quite sane. They release them to seals, which they kill and take to the village. The boy and girl marry on their return home.

The story is followed by the song 'Angutivaun Taina' also called 'Song of the Returning Hunter.'

7. Red Dog

'Red Dog' was first called 'Good Hunting.' Won-tolla, the Lone Wolf, brings news of probable trouble with the dholes. Kaa advises Mowgli that they are most afraid of bees; a plan is concocted, and Mowgli lures the dholes to the Rocks and dives into the river where Kaa is waiting for him. The dholes are attacked by the bees, and also jump into the river to escape them. Those that survive the stream and the stings are decimated by the Pack.

'Chil's Song' is a song at the end of the story.

8. The Spring Running

This is the last story in the book. There is little or no plot; it is a picture of the influences that work in the jungle in spring-time that make Mowgli return to men.

The sequence of stories about the boy Mowgli, accidentally thrust put off the human community into the jungle, forms the core of these collections. His growth from jungle boyhood to dominance over the animals, and his eventual return to human service as a forest ran-ger, provide the basic framework. The code of conduct in the animal world is severe and requires a high level of responsibility.

Rupert Croft-Cooke observes, "And now Kipling made what so many writers have desired and created—a world of his own in which the laws of probability were of his own choosing. Swift, Butler, Anatole France, Cabell, James Stephens are but a few of the story-tellers who have demanded an escape from the tiresome inhibitions imposed by space and time and the common understanding of cause and effect. Kipling created a Jungle in which there was Law and even Order, in which the animals, while conscientiously retaining certain of the habits of their kind, spoke and loved and obeyed as humans."

There were precedents enough for this giving of logic and speech to the beasts, from Esop to Kenneth Grahame. But Kipling's is the most interesting of them all. With a human boy reared by wolves as his protagonist he makes the best of both worlds. Mowgli is Man and all our sympathy is with him.

8. Phantom Rickshaw (1898)

This book is not reissued afterwards. In fact it is clubbed with *Wee Willie Winkie.* The original book had just three long stories, My Own True Ghost Story, The Strange Ride of Morrowbie Jukes and The Man Who would be King. These stories are discussed in the other places.

9. The Day's Work (1898)

The Day's Work, containing the short stories written in Vermont, was published in 1898, and the high quality of these was the fruit of that sense of sudden accession of power which had come to him at a certain moment in America. Here we find two great stories of craftsmanship and machinery, 'The Bridge Builders' and 'The Ship that Found Herself,' which appeal even to those who are bored by this aspect of Kipling's art.

Soldiers Three, which was made up of earlier material,

came, as late as 1898 as *The Day's Work.* Though its stories are set in three continents, Kipling is here most fluent and at home, for he is writing of the daily labour of other men (and of animals and machines), a theme in which he always took delight. He has mastered each of them, down to the most abstruse technical detail, yet it is unfair to say that he parades his knowledge.

Lafcadio Hearn in his letter to Mitchell McDonald in 1898 observed of Kipling's greatness as a story writer with reference to this book:

> " ... Ah! I had almost forgotten. I *have Kiplin's* 'Day's Work' already. It is great-very great. Don't mistake him, even if he seems too colloquial at times. He is the greatest living English poet and English story-teller. Never in this world will I be able to write one page to compare with a page of his. He makes me feel so small, that after reading him I wonder why I am such an ass as to write at all."

1. The Bridge-Builders

This is the first story in *The Day's Work*, in which is mentioned the book's theme which gives its title and significance—'Stand by the day's work and wait instructions.' Findlayson and his assistant have nearly finished their bridge over the Ganges when they receive warning of approaching floods and hasten to secure everything. Findlayson eats nothing in his desire to get the work done, so Peroo, one of his native assistants, gives him some opium. The two get adrift in a boat, are carried downstream, and land on an island, where they hear the gods discussing the bridge. They are rescued in the morning and find the bridge still standing.

Thus the engineer, Findlayson, wins through, but only after agonies, and, in any case, we are aware that Findlayson's bridge is a particular bridge and the mud flat where he suffers his drugged dream of the Gods is a particular mud flat; and that both will pass in time as do all mud flats and bridges. Lord Birkenhead adds that "The bridge is the emblem of the stabilizing effect of European civilization on India, and the story ends with Findlayson, delirious on a river island, imagining that, the animals round him are a *punchayet* or meeting of the Indian gods."

2. A Walking Delegate

The horses on a Vermont farm (USA) are visited by a strange horse who has never done an honest day's work in his life and attempts to stir up discontent amongst Tedder, Gabler, Deacon, Rod and Rick, Nip and Tuck, Muldoon, Tweezy, Marcus Aurelius Antoninus and some others. He does not succeed.

3. The Ship that Found Herself

The *Dimbula*, a newly-launched cargo-vessel, is on her maiden voyage and is not yet 'shaken down.' Various parts of her structure discuss their job until they find out how it is done and speak in one voice as their ship. Buchanan, the Chief Engineer, the Captain, and Miss Frazier, the owner's daughter are the chief human characters.

This is an allegory. If an organisation- a State, for instance- is to be worth its place in the world, all the bits in that organisation have to do their separate work in the best way they can and not mind if their toes are trodden on, because that is inevitable.

According to Lord Birkenhead "There is symbolism, too, in 'The Ship that Found Herself.' As the skipper of the *Dimbula* explained to the owner's daughter, the vessel had yet 'to find herself.' All the parts of the ship must learn to work together until they become a true whole, as in any human society man must learn to work, sometimes to yield and compromise, to resolve conflicting strains, so that the whole society may survive and become strong. And so, in this superbly wrought story, all the component parts of the vessel talk and sing in their struggle with the elements, and at last achieve harmony as they are riveted together by the sea in perfect unison."

4. The Tomb of His Ancestors

John Chinn goes to India to join the regiment of which his father had been Colonel, in the Cantonments where he himself had been born. The boy's grandfather, John Chinn the First, had brought the Bhils under some subjection and they believe, with Bukta, a senior native officer who knew Chinn as a baby, that he is a reincarnation of his grandfather; the more so as he has a birthmark, many well remembered mannerisms of his father, and is also fever-proof. Later there is trouble with the wilder members of the tribe who object to being vaccinated, and a rumour that Chinn the First has taken to leaving his grave in the hills and riding about the countryside on a Clouded Tiger. The Colonel grants Chinn leave to go 'shooting,' and he and Bukta clear up the vaccination trouble, the boy spends the night at the tomb (without Bukta) and shoots the Clouded Tiger. So all ends happily with Bukta expressing the hope that the boy will soon marry and have a son to carry on the line.

5. The Devil and the Deep Sea

The Haliotis, a pearl-poacher, is shelled by a foreign gunboat and the engine-room wrecked. She is arrested and towed to an out-of-the-way harbour and the crew are sent up-country. Some eight months later they are ordered to be returned, and as it will be two months before they can get a passage, Wardrop suggests they live in their ship. They manage to effect repairs and steam away, scuttling her in the mouth of a harbour, where, it is to be supposed, she will wreck the gunboat on its next call.

6. William the Conqueror, I and II

John Martyn of the Indian Police is sent with Scott to assist Sir James Hawkins o' famine-relief. Lady Hawkins and Miss Martyn (William or Bill) go as well. The work progresses; Scott travels with grain-carts collecting refugee children whom he feeds on goats-milk, while William looks after others in camp. The famine is finally brought under control, Scott and the girl realize their love for each other, and it appears that a wedding is in the offing.

7.—007

Kipling also produced at this time two stories in which engines are given an independent life, or rather a life dependent upon each other, to serve, in each case, as an allegory for human society. These two stories are praised highly by engineers, sailors and railway men. Kipling's story of American locomotives, '007,' works well; and for ships' engineers, his dialogue between the machine parts of a steamship, 'The Ship That Found Herself,' is a delight.

In this a new engine appears in an American railway-yard, where its appearance is criticized by some of the others and a switching (shunting) engine named Pony gives advice and encouragement. In the end, 007's first serious run is to take a breakdown-gang to the scene of a wreck, the engine of which (the Mogul) had been most unpleasant in his manner.

8. The Maltese Cat

This is widely understood to be the best polo story ever written. The Cat is the leading pony in the Skidars' team in a match against the Archangels; Lutyens is his owner and rider.

Lord Birkenhead thinks Kipling has written here what is probably the finest description of a game in the English language. It is an animal story of which the polo pony, the Maltese Cat, is the hero, and is told so brilliantly that even readers ignorant of the game are held spellbound by the Cat's tactics, and the terse instructions he gives to the other ponies, for Maltese Cat is the real captain of the side rather than the ostensible one.

9. Bread upon the Waters

The narrator dines with McPhee and his wife and hears the story of the salvaging of the *Breslau*, from which ship he had been dismissed because he would not agree to an impossible schedule. He is taken on by McRimmon (the Blind Devil) in his ship the *Kite*, which is sent in the wake of the Grotkau, the latter being loaded with a valuable cargo in spite of a seven-inch crack in her shaft. Naturally, the shaft cracks in the Irish Sea and the crew are rescued by a mail-ship. The *Kite*, owing to McRimmon's planning, is handy to take her in tow as a derelict—McPhee takes a leading part in this—and get her into Plymouth. McPhee draws £25,000 as his share of the salvage-money.

10. An Error in the Fourth Dimension

Wilton Sargent, son of Merton Sargent, an American railway magnate, settles in England. Coached by friends and servants he becomes more English until he tells his butler to stop a train so he can get to London in a hurry. This causes trouble with the railway company, who think him mad when he offers to buy the line. He returns to New York.

'An Error in the Fourth Dimension' is a story which he wrote while at Tisbury on a visit to his parents in 1894. This story has been much disliked as cruel. And, at first sight, it seems a needlessly ruthless crushing of a pleasant butterfly.

The story throws light on Kipling's disquietude at his own position in America. Like Wilton Sargent, he was driven out of his ill-chosen Eden, though, unlike Wilton, he never perhaps truly settled down in his native paradise.

11. My Sunday at Home

The narrator meets Emory, an American doctor, in a train to Plymouth. He is delighted with the English countryside; when the train stops at Framlynghame Admiral—a very small station—the guard goes to each carriage reading a telegram to the effect that a gentleman has taken a bottle of poison by mistake. Emory at once dashes on to the platform with his bag and administers an emetic to a drunken navvy who happens to be there, not realizing that the gentleman in question is at Woking. The train continues, but the narrator stays to see the fun. The remainder of the story is concerned with the wrath of the navvy and how the narrator helped the doctor to escape.

12. The Brushwood Boy

This is the last story in *The Day's Work*. George Cottar dreams of a certain girl from his childhood; on his return home on leave from the Army in India he finds her as a guest in his own home. Miriam Lacy des not know him until he tells her when they are out riding.

Kipling has written a novel with this title and both—the story and the novel—have similar themes.

Rupert Croft-Cooke observes, "Though its stories are set in three continents, Kipling is here most fluent and at home, for he is writing of the daily labour of other men (and of animals and machines), a theme in which he always took delight. He has mastered each of them, down to the most abstruse technical detail, yet it is unfair to say that he parades his knowledge. He writes as one expert to another, with a cheerful assumption of his reader's interest and understanding, in much the same way as he assumers the reader's sympathy for empire-building."

10. Stalky & Co (1899)

The book begins with a verse called 'A School Song.' It is a prelude to the book. Lord Birkenhead says, "Whathever he may have been doing in his earlier stories, in *Stalky and Co.* Kipling was presenting actual people, many of whom must have been still alive. This gives the book a special interest."

Stalky & Co is a collection of nine stories, first published in 1899. Five other Stalky tales appeared in separate collections; the 14 tales were brought together in *The Complete Stalky* & Co. (1929). Kipling drew on his boyhood experiences at the United Services College at Westward Ho! in Devon, a school founded by retired army officers largely to fit its pupils for an army career.

Stalky & Co. is a fantasy and a celebration. In Steven Marcus's words, "It is an idealized recollection and re-creation of Kipling's experience at school. It celebrates a period of life and a way of life, or culture. The period of life is what was once called boyhood." Ian Hay observes, "We have many to choose from *Stalky*, for instance. *Stalky* has come in for a shower of abuse from certain quarters. He hits the sentimentalist hard. We are told that the book is vulgar, that the famous trio are 'little beasts.' Still, Mr. Kipling never touches any subject which he does not adorn, and in *Stalky* he brings out vividly some of the salient features of modern school life. He has drawn masters as they have never been drawn before: the portraits may be cruel, biased, not sufficiently representative; but how they live!"

1. In Ambush

This is the first story in *Stalky & Co.* The boys are smoking on the edge of the cliff—Colonel Dabnney's land—and see his keeper take a shot at a fox. McTurk is so incensed that he takes the others up to the house to report it to the Colonel; the keeper returns to his lobster-pots and the boys are given the freedom of the estate. Prout, King, and Foxy·trail them on suspicion of drinking and breaking bounds, only to be caught by Dabney, who thinks they are poachers. The boys are brought before the Head who beats them and they revenge themselves on King and Prout by repeating, in their hearing, some of Dabney's that they overheard.

2. Slaves of the Lamp, pt. i (and the ii)

The boys are turned out of their study by king; Stalky 'tweaks' the carrier Rabbits-Eggs, with his catapult from the window of No. 5. The carrier believes King in the room below to be responsible and practically wrecks it with stones (and a little help from Beetle who happened to \be in there). Pt. ii is the last story in the same book, and takes place some years later when the friends are on leave from India at the Infant's house; they hear the story of how Stalky, on the Frontier, repeats the Rabbits-Eggs/King manoeuvre from a fort where he is in danger of being trapped, and plays the Khye-Kheen against the Malots, which enables him to withdraw. The song 'Arrah, Patsy, mind the baby' runs through both parts of the story.

3. An Unsavoury Interlude

King makes offensive remarks about the cleanliness of some of Prout's boys. Stalky and his friends resent being called 'Stinkers' and introduce a dead cat into the flooring so that they may live up to their nicknames. Richards, the odd-job man who takes up the floor and discovers the corpse, does not disclose to authority the fact that it obviously did not get there of its own accord as he, too, resents the unfounded accusations.

4. The Impressionists

The masters decide that they are to be turned out of their study for cribbing. They create havoc in the form-room and are eventually permitted to return to the study for the sake of peace and quiet. They are beaten by the Head, which would appear to be an injustice, but they accept it as well deserved.

5. The Moral Reformers

Gillett visits No. 5 and tells them that there is bullying in the Coll. His hint leads them to find the culprits—Sefton and Campbell—and subject them to some real bullying.

6. A Little Prep

A day-boy gets diphtheria and bounds are curtailed. The Head is not seen for a day or two, but finds Stalky and his friends smoking in a field; they are ordered back for a caning. An old boy, Duncan, is killed in a frontier war; Crandall, who recovered his body, is in the Old Boys' team at the annual rugger-match and is persuaded to tell of his experiences. Stalky finds that the Head has sucked the infection out of major's throat and asks Crandall his opinion of a man who would do such a thing, which is 'It's about the bravest thing a man can do. . .' The school is given 'Prep' on last night—an unheard-of thing—and it is rather noisy; Stalky and his two friends then spread the news of the Head's brave act, so that when he appears to bring his boys to order he is greeted with ceaseless cheering. He intends to beat the whole school the next day, but gives up after a while, as those awaiting execution continue to cheer. So the term ends.

7. The Flag of their Country

A visit to the Coll. by General Collinson leads to the formation of an unpopular cadet-corps only suffered because it is a good way of learning drill. Mr. Raymond Martin, M. P., addresses the boys, tramples on their traditions and personal views, and presents them with a Union Flag for the corps, which is promptly disbanded.

8. The Last Term

Beetle is editor of the Magazine; they find exam. Papers in the printing-office and 'edit' them, which causes confusion in the classroom. There is further trouble when Stalky arranges for

Mary Yeo, an attractive girl in a dairy, to kiss Tulke, an unpopular prefect.

Stalky and Co. has a certain kindred with *Tom Brown's Schooldays*, but although it is a supremely 'healthy' book it did foresee the days when boys would be treated in fiction as human beings.

In *Stalky & Co.* he conveniently brought home the lesson, by constantly overriding the prevailing English public-school ethics, which derived ultimately from the great influence of Thomas Arnold's reforms at Rugby School in the early years of Victoria's reign. A mature boy (and the Stalky trio were in fact, as they are in fiction, strangely mature, or, more truly, like boyish men rather than boys) will not accept the ruling of his life by repeated rotes, whether 'pijaws' from the padre, or talks about house honour from the housemaster, or pep talks on the team spirit from the prefects. Within the framework of what the school demands, which we learn from the last story in the book is what service for the Empire (and, indeed, what the preservation of civilised society) demands, though the boys always deflate it in their everyday life to some practical demand like getting through exams, a man or a boy has every right to use any weapon in order to learn what life is really like and to find out how he is best fitted to live.

Later Short Stories

Kipling settled at Bateman's in 1902, and from then till his death in 1936 his output in fiction consisted of six books of short stories—*Just So Stories* (1902), *Puck of Pook's Hill* (1902), *Traffics and Discoveries* (1904), *Actions and Reactions* (1909), *A Diversity of Creatures* (1917), *Land and Sea Tales for Scouts and Guides* (1923), *Debits and Credits* (1926) and *Limits and Renewals* (1932).

Let's know that all these later tales (though the earliest of them must go back to Kim's time) are what Kipling called 'pummiced ivory-smooth,' but never over-written. He does not hesitate and search for words or visibly form his phrases as Pater did. He is always- at ease, unhurried but never distracted from his theme. He seems to have been content to become an

Elder Craftsman. No longer audible is the confident chuckle of the early stories, the air of "I can do it, you just watch." His stories, on the contrary, open quietly now, sometimes slowly, and go steadily forward to their riotous climax.

11. Just So Stories (1902)

This is the only book for which Kipling supplied his own illustrations. It was written to be read aloud by adults to children. The interplay between the human and the animal worlds in the first seven stories is a simpler and more playful device than in the earlier *Jungle Book*. The language made 'appropriate' for the animals veers between the childlike and the diction of a grown-up world. An element of teasing is most obviously apparent in such stories as 'How the Leopard Got Its Spots,' where Kipling travesties the Darwinian notion of evolutionary progression; the humour can satisfy both children and adults.

An anonymous reviewer in the *Athenaeum* observed in 1902 that, The *Just So Stories*, in which Mr. Kipling appears both as author and illustrator, should regain the favour which he has lost in some quarters by indifferent verse. Mr. Kipling is, at his best, the most inspired teller of tales that we have; he understands young folk as few writers do, and better than other mysteries which he has attempted to tackle with expert haste. The result is that several of these stories-for instance those concerning the invention of letter-writing and of the alphabet by the daughter of a cave-dweller, the independence of the domestic cat, the reason for the elephant's trunk-are perfect, told once for all so that other tellers need not hope to compete. The stories being for younger folk than the *Jungle Books*, deal a good deal in what is pure nonsense to the child, and clever fooling with ornate words and phrases to the adult-such writing, in fact, as the catalogues of remedies in Kingsley's *Water Babies*.

1. For Little Children

This is the first story in the book and it ends with 'How the Whale got his Throat.'

2. How the Camel Got His Hump

This is the second story in the book. The camel shirked his share of the work and said 'Humph' once too often.

The poem 'The Camel's hump is an ugly lump' follows.

3. How the Rhinoceros Got His Skin

Strorks, the Rhinoceros, steals a cake which Peston-jee Bomonjee had made ... When the former had removed his skin to go bathing the latter filed it with stale cake-crumbs. Strorks was so irritated that he rubbed his skin full of folds.

The poem 'The Uninhabited Island' follows.

4. How the Leopard Got His Spots

Spots, the leopard, is of a plain color (without spots) and he hunts with an Ethiopian named Sambo who is not black. The other animals have grown so like their surroundings that these two cannot find them and are likely to starve. Sambo therefore blackens his skin and then makes finer marks all over Spots so that they, too, can blend into their backgrounds.

5. The Elephant's Child

The young elephant had a nose like a boot and was interested to find out what the crocodile had for dinner. He was nearly the dinner, but the Bi-Colored –Python-Rock-Snake helps him, whereby his nose is stretched into the trunk we know today.

The poem 'I keep six honest serving-men' follows.

6. The Sing-Song of Old Man Kangaroo

Boomer, the Kangaroo with four legs of about equal size, goes to the gods and asks to be made different from the other animals. Little God Nqa and Middle God Nquing tell him to go away, but Big God Nquong sets Yellow Dog Dingo to chase him all over Australia until his hind legs had grown so much that he was indeed different from the other animals.

The poem 'This is mouth-filing Song' follows.

7. The Beginning of the Armadilloes

The tortoise teaches the hedgehog to swim, the latter returns the compliment and teaches the tortoise to curl up, so that the young jaguar is unable to eat them. He tells his mother that he has found a new animal whose name he does not know; she advises him to call it an armadillo.

The poem 'I've never sailed the Amazon' follows.

8. How the First Letter was written

Tegumai breaks his spear, and his daughter Taffy sends a picture-letter home in the hands of a Tewara, or Stranger-man, who happened to be passing. The letter is misunderstood at home and the Tewara comes in for some rough treatment until all is later settled happily.

The poem 'There runs a road by Merrow Down' follows.

9. How the Alphabet was made

This story is a sequel to 'How the First Letter was Written,' telling of the efforts of Tegumai and his daughter Taffy to prevent another misunderstanding.

The poem 'Of all the Tribe of Tegumai' follows.

10. The Crab that Played with the Sea

Pan Amma the Crab will not obey the Son of Adam, and so hides in Pusat Tasek and causes trouble when he floods the beaches and rivers by going out to look for food. The Eldest Magician reduces the Crab to the size we know him, and as the Man suggests that it will be a weary task to paddle the canoe home, the Magician tells the Fisherman of the Moon to pull the sea with his line twice daily forever, which was the beginning of the tides. There are alternative titles.

The poem 'China-going P. and O.'s' follows.

11. The Cat that Walked by Himself

The story is about Adam and Eve in the Garden of Eden, their expulsion, the birth of their children, and how the Mole spied on them, thereby losing his eyesight.

The poem 'Pussy can sit by the fire and sing' **follows.**

12. The Butterfly that Stamped

This is the last of the *Just So Stories*. The story is about how King Solomon intervened in a quarrel between a butterfly and his wife and thus reduced his own importunate wives to peace. He prepared a meal for all the animals in the world which is eaten by Small Porgies.

Angus Wilson observes, "But each of the seven is a triumph in the special art of communicating with young children. Kipling had glimpsed the Camel's Arabian desert and the Rhinoceros's Arabian sea shore from a ship; he had touched upon the Kangaroo's Australia; he had sailed in the Whale's ocean; he had 'never sailed the Amazon ... never reached Brazil ... 'Oh, I'd love to roll to Rio. Some day before I'm old,' he was sixty-one when he eventually got there in 1927; but the South African veldt and rain forest, and the Limpopo he had seen and felt. This is why the Leopard and the Elephant are the most visual of all *The Just So Stories*. It was an artistic gain from the South African years if a small one."

12. Puck of Pook's Hill (1902)

This book has 10 stories and accompanying poems, published in 1906. The stories were intended for both adults and children. *The Cambridge Guide to Literature* has this to say: The meeting of two children, Dan and Una (loosely modeled on Kipling's own children), with the nature spirit Puck provides the framework for tales reaching back in English history, past the Normans and Saxons to the Roman invaders. Much show individuals who are able to illuminate their historical predicaments, such as the centurion, Parnesius, whose unorthodox handling of his Imperial duties—in cooperating with the Picts—shows an insight which is absent from the higher echelons of the declining Roman Empire. The stories also point to the capacity of civilization to renew itself."

Lord Birkenhead is of the opinion, "The book consists of a sequence of short stories in which the children Dan and Una are entertained by the return of people from history and legend who meet them in their own secret corners of their Sussex home, always introduced by the very English sprite Puck, 'alias Robin Good-fellow,' alias 'Nick o' Lincoln,' alias 'Lob-Lie-by-the-

Fire,' the last survivor in England of those whom mortals call Fairies."

A sequel to the collection, *Reward and Fairies* (1910), followed a similar format. Both volumes contain some of Kipling's best-known verse. In the latter volume particularly, 'A St. Helena's Lullaby,' 'The Way through the Woods' and 'If' have been much admired.

'Puck's Song' is the first song in the book.

1. Weland's Sword

This is the first story in the book. Dan and Una are acting a version of *A Midsummer Night's Dream* in a meadow near their home when Puck appears; he promises to show them Old England, and commences with the story of Weland and how he made a magic sword for Hugh the Novice who had released him from his servitude by making a farmer thank him for shoeing his horse and wishing him well. Weland leaves England, Puck seeing him go as he saw him arrive. The children naturally wish to know what happens to Hugh and the sword, but magic provides their memories of the story by Oak, Ash, and Thorn, so that when they see their father they only remember acting their play and going to sleep. Kipling and his children played this game once. The character of Weland is very well described in the book. For ex,

> He looked down at the horse's feet, and saw the new shoes fastened as only Weland knew how to fasten 'em. (Weland had a way of turning down the nails that folks called the Smith's Clinch.)
>
> The Yellow Man, whose name was Kitai, had with him a brown box. In the box was a blue bowl with red marks upon the rim, and within the bowl, hanging from a fine thread, was a piece of iron no thicker than that grass stem, and as long, maybe, as my spur, but straight. In this iron, said Witta, abode and Evil Spirit which Kitai, the Yellow Man, had brought by Art Magic out of his own country that lay three years' journey southward. The Evil Spirit strove day and night to return to his country, and therefore, look you, the iron needle pointed continually to the South.

The poem 'A Tree Song' follows.

2. Young Men at the Manor

Dan and Una meet Sir Richard Dalyngridge, who tells them of his part in the Battle of Hastings, how Hugh of Dallington saved his life, and how he settled down on his Manor. The poems 'Sir Richard's Song' and 'Harp Song of the Dane Women' follow.

3. The Knight of the Joyous Venture

Dan and Una hear how Sir Richard and Hugh went to sea with Witta, of their adventures in Africa, and their return home with the treasure. The story is preceded by 'Harp Song of the Dane Women' and followed by 'Thorkild's Song.'

4. Old Men at Pevensey

Gilbert de Aquila is now Warden of Pevensey Castle; Sir Richard and Hugh see they are not wanted at their manors, and so they come to live with him and look after the gold. Trouble is brewing between Robert of Normandy and Henry of England; Fulke, a double agent, is unmasked by de Aquila, who keeps his son as a hostage and remains in charge of the Gate of England. The poems 'The Runes on Weland's Sword' and 'Cities and Thrones and Powers' follow.

5. A Centurion of the Thirtieth

Dan and Una meet Parnesius, a Roman Centurion, and hear of his military activities in Britain.

The poem 'A British-Roman Song' follows.

6. On the Green Wall

Dan and Una meet Parnesius again; he tells them of his march from the South to the Great Wall, where he meets Pertinax, and how they make friends with Allo, a leader of the Picts. Maximus comes to take more troops for his war in Gaul, leaving the two young men north of the Wall with Allo where they meet him, on the understanding that he will meet them again the next day and proclaim them Captains of the Wall. The poem 'A Song to Mithras' follows.

7. The Winged Hats

Parnesius meets Dan and Una; they hear how he and Pertinax were made Captains of the Wall, how the Norsemen heard of the death of Maximus, and how they fought hard until relief came.

The poems 'A Pict Song' and 'Prophet have honor all over the Earth' colleted as 'Prophets at Home' follow.

8. Hal o' the Draft

Dan and old Springett meet Hal, who tells of his restoration of the ancient church of St. Barnabas, how he became friendly with Cabot, and how everything went wrong with their work; the former could not proceed with the restoration and the latter could not get his guns from a local foundry until they accidentally find the locals are up to the neck in gun-running. Sir John Pelham, a magistrate, puts things right and all ends happily. Hal also appears in *The Wrong Thing*.

The poems 'A Smuggler's Song,' 'The Bee Boy's Song,' 'Dymchurch Flit,' 'A Three-Part Song' and'Song of the Fifth River' follow.

9. The Treasure and the Law

This is the last story in the book. Dan and Una meet Kadmiel, a Jew from Spain, who knew England in the days of King John. He tells them of Elias of Bury and the finding and final disposal of the treasure that De Aquila and Sir Richard Dalyngridge hid in the tidal well at Pevensey.

The poem 'The Children's Song' follow.

Alfred Noyse says, "In *Puck of Pook's Hill* we suspect that Mr. Kipling has for the first time dug through the silt of modern Imperialism. He has gone back to the old ground-works and seen the inscription upon them. The scheme of the book is simple. Some children meet Puck, the fairy, who introduces them in separate, yet connected stories to Romans, Normans, Saxons, Picts and Englishmen from different periods of English history; and the chief of these characters tell their own stories-grim, humorous and pathetic, in a manner illustrating the respective period of each; and on each successive period one seems to find inscribed *After me cometh a Builder*! We know no book in the guise of fiction that gives the pageant of our history with such breadth and nobility of feeling, and with so sure and easy a touch. There are few passages in modem fiction more beautiful than that which describes the chivalry of a Norman to a conquered Saxon woman, whom he falls in love with, and eventually, though at first she rails against him as an enemy, wins and weds. There are· few passages in modern fiction more stoically grand than the farewell letter of the doomed Caesar to his two young captains on the Great Wall."

Kipling's last collection of stories, *Limits and Renewals,* was published in April 1932, but although he continued to write, his mind was becoming increasingly engrossed in politics.

Dan and Una are again present in each episode: indeed each of Kipling's children was given a personal story in *Rewards and Fairies*; John's is a tale of craftsmanship set in a builder's yard, *The Wrong Thing*, while in Elsie's story, the delightful *Marklake Witches*, the narration takes place against the background of a lesson in cow-milking, a true fact in Elsie's life and is written in the manner of Jane Austen, whom Kipling so deeply revered.

Lord Birkenhead thinks "Kipling is an intuitive historian, but generations of children have come to see through his eyes the moving pageant of England's story. In the *Puck* stories one sees Hal Dawes 'dear, dear land,' the long process of change—the God of the Knife, the Roman soldier, the Norman knight, the Renaissance craftsman."

But although the children are taken in these books on a breathless journey through time, and many characters from the past are brought before them in the familiar woods, we are conscious that Kipling's real intention is to leave in our minds an impression of the endless continuity of English life, the persistence of the land and its people through war and disaster. He had cast his mind back and tried to explore everything in her history that had contributed to this strength the 'Glory of the Garden'—that he saw all round him. And for this reason it has been rightly said that the real hero of the two books is not

Puck, not Dan nor Une, not the Roman Centurion nor the Norman knight—but old Hobden, the hedger who knows all the lore of the valley and the stream, and, the list of his forebears stretching deep into bygone centuries, seems to symbolize the spirit of the place, brooding over it and filling his creator with humility:

> His dead are in the churchyard—thirty generations laid.
> Their names were old in history when Domesday Book was made
> And the passion and the piety and the prowess of his line
> Have seeded, rooted, fruited in some land the Law calls mine.

Kipling's books—*Puck of Pook's Hill* and its sequel *Rewards and Fairies*—are quite touching. He himself wrote afterwards of these two books: "'I worked the material in three or four overlaid tints and textures, which might or might not reveal themselves according to the shifting light of sex, youth and experience. It was like working lacquer and mother o' pearl, a natural combination, into the same scheme as niello and grisaille, and trying not to let the joins show.'"

13. Traffics and Discoveries (1904)

This book has 11 stories and 11 poems (a story with a poem, succeeding it), published in 1904. The stories range in subject matter from the supernatural to the Boer War.

Kingsley Amis observes, "The two collections of stories, *Traffics and Discoveries* and *Actions and Reactions*, can be considered together: both are mixed bags. At the top of the list come three tales of the supernatural, not the savage or horrific supernatural as we meet it in some of the Indian pieces, but something gentle and elegiac."

1. The Captive

The story is also titled as 'From the Masjid-al-Aqsa of Sayyid Ahmed.' Here the poet meets a prisoner who does not rail against his captivity.

For the rest, 'The Captive' has been highly praised, but here we are confronted with all the growing faults of Kipling's later work—over-technical language, too elaborate a framework of narration—and there is none of the compensating depth that makes the best of his later stories so fine.

2. The Bonds of Discipline

Pyecroft relates the story of the French spy, M. de C., who calls himself Antonio, and stows away in H.M.S. *Archimandrite*, and the extraordinary show that is put on for his benefit. The poem 'The Runners' follows. The poem speaks about a Sahibs' War; how there might have been another Mutiny in India if things had gone differently in the Boer War.

3. A Sahibs' War

The narrator is in South Africa during the Boer War and meets Umr Singh, a trooper of the 141st Punjab Cavalry, who is more than he seems. The narrator sorts out some little difficulty and then hears the story of how Captain Walter Decies Corbyn—Kurban Sahib—obtains leave from his duties in India and manages to see some service in South Africa. They meet Sikandar Khan who becomes their cook, and then join up with the Australians, where Corbyn is killed in a white-flag incident. The Indians decide that this is no war for them, as it is fought in an unfamiliar manner. They pray for the repose of Corbyn's soul and return home.

It is typical that the most fully seen story of the war, 'The Way That He Took,' should peter out as a boy's story, a simple account of a military ruse to avoid ambush. Yet, in the more adult Boer War stories, the vision is seldom there.

4. 'Their Lawful Occasions' pt. i. and ii

The narrator is to sail on manoeuvres with the Red Fleet; he meets Pyecroft, who is disguised, and accompanies him to his vessel, Torpedo-Boat No. 267. The commanding officer, Lieutenant Morshed (Moorshed), is not at first anxious to take a passenger, but is persuaded. 267 has been left behind by the fleet with somewhat ambiguous orders, but Moorshed is determined to strike a blow for his side and disguises his vessel to resemble a destroyer. Pyecroft bluffs an unsuspecting officer to part with a copy of the Red Fleet's secret signals, and they proceed to Tor Bay where they find H.M.S. *Cryptic* and *Devolution* at anchor repairing defects. In the dark and fog it is an easy matter to row alongside and stencil Moorshed's initials in several places on each ship's side and claim to have put them out of action. This is another of the very funny naval stories, with wonderful word-pictures of the sea and remarkable insight into the sailor.

'The King's Task' is a song of the Saxons and their wars, after which those who returned made mock of ancient custom. It can be construed as a plea to the new King, Edward VII, to reform the Army at the end of the Boer War.

5. The Comprehension of Private Copper

Copper is taken by a Boer but turns the tables and takes him prisoner. There is much topical talk.

The same floating Indian memories are even more out of place in 'The Comprehension of Private Copper.' Here the Transvaal burgher who captures Copper and tortures him is given a chi-chi accent, a dark complexion and a plover's-egg eye so that we are forced to conclude that his father who settled in the Transvaal was a Eurasian rather than an Afrikaner. And this, in fact, undoes Kipling's propaganda against the treacherous rich Boer farmers. The only reason for this muddle seems to be the desire to provide Private Copper with memories of his Indian service, for his captor's broken Eurasian chi-chi accent, as he taunts him, recalls an incident at a regimental dance in Umballa, the main military cantonment in the Punjab.

6. Steam Tactics

The story begins with the poem 'The Necessitarian.'

Here a policeman trying to enforce the speed limit is kidnapped and left at night in a park where the owner keeps wild animals at large.

The narrator, out in his steam-car meets Pyecroft and Hinchcliffe and invites them to join him. Although the latter had rejoiced that he would not see a steam-engine until his leave was up, he is at once interested in the 'land-crabbing steam pinnace,' which he examines with great interest and also drives. They are then stopped by a policeman in plain clothes, who charges them with breaking the speed-limit. He has no written authority so they decoy him aboard and drive off, intending to drop him somewhere a long way from home. The car breaks down, another motorist, turns up, stops to inquire the trouble, and transfers everybody except the two chauffeurs, who are left to effect repairs, to his own car and the trip continues through Sussex and Kent, until the unfortunate policeman is dropped in Sir William Gardner's Park and left with kangaroo, heaver, and zebra.

7. Wireless

The story begins with the poem 'Kaspar's song in 'Vada.' Mr. Cashell, a chemist in a South Coast town, permits his nephew to experiment with wireless in a room at the back of the shop and the narrator is invited to attend. He meets John Shaynor, the chemist's assistant, who suffers from consumption. The latter goes out in the bitter cold night with his sweetheart, Fanny Brand, and on his return the narrator gives him a dose of 'cordial' not unlike that mixed by Culpeper. Under the influence of this the young man goes into a trance and writes extracts from the poems of Keats; in the meantime messages are coming through on the wireless but the narrator is too interested in Shaynor to pay any attention to this.

8. The Army of a Dream, p-i, and ii

The narrator dreams of a time when military service has become a national obligation gladly undertaken by all ranks and spends some time with one of the hearing about their activities and witnessing exercise.

'The Army of a Dream,' a long, two-part account of a dream in which Kipling spends an afternoon with the recruiting section and the citizen army on manoeuvres of an ideal England which has accepted military service as an integral part of national life.

9. They

In the story, 'They,' the blind, childless woman speaks of how she has been laughed at. The narrator comments, 'I was silent reviewing that inexhaustible matter—the more than inherited (since it is carefully taught) brutality of the Christian people, beside which the here heathendom of the West Coast Nigger is clean and restrained.

The earliest story that announces this new world of Kipling's is 'They,' published in August 1904, nearly two years after the move. When one says that this story reveals much of Kipling's desperate mourning for his dead Josephine; and that it expresses to the full his almost mystical love of children; and that it does both in the form of an enigmatic account of the psychical phenomenon of dead children returned to a beautiful old house and garden to assuage their parents' grief; and that it was published in the year of the knockout Success of *Peter Pan* on the West End of London stage; the reader may expect the worst. Yet 'They' has little of the whimsy.

'They—which hints at Kipling's feelings for his daughter Josephine, who died as a child in 1899—describes the narrator's visits to an otherworldly house where he finds elusive but charming children.

It is one of the first stories in the distinctively 'late' manner and it is convenient to open discussion of the later Kipling with a work so totally different from the conventional account of him. But the first thing to be noticed about 'They' is that the part played by the ghostly children and the blind childless woman whose love draws them to the beautiful house she has made for them, has nothing to do with a ghost-story strumming on the nerves. The mode of the tale is nearer to 'Burnt Norton' than to 'The Turn of the Screw.'

Lord Birkenhead comments, "They is an allegory deriving from his un-assuaged grief at Josephine's death, its background the fruit of his own experiences driving about Sussex in search of a house."

10. Mrs. Bathurst

The story begins with the poem 'From Lyden's 'Irenius.'

Kipling produced only one post-war story laid in South Africa. It has been highly praised. This is the famous 'Mrs Bathurst' which has aroused as much puzzle-solving among his devotees as the unfinished *Edwin Drood* has among Dickensians. But, although important work which breaks new ground is often likely to puzzle the most sensitive and perspicacious readers, puzzle in itself is no merit in literature. Admirers of Kipling have understandably but mistakenly seized on the difficulty of not knowing what Kipling really means in 'Mrs Bathurst' in order to insist that he too can be 'difficult' like authors so admired by highbrows. But the difficulty of Mrs Bathurst is of little interest, for, in the last resort, the story is empty.

'Mrs. Bathurst' has a strong element of unexplained mystery, but not of the supernatural, in its account of the effect that Mrs. Bathurst, a New Zealand hotel-keeper, has on Vickery, a naval warrant-officer. Vickery's desertion and violent death in a thunderstorm is unexplained and tantalizingly. The story associates Mrs. Bathurst with the terrible retribution of an otherwise random universe.

W. W. Robson observes, "'Mrs. Bathurst' is one of the earliest of Kipling's experiments in indirect or suppressed narrative, and its experimental character might make that explanation plausible."

11. Below the Mill Dam

'Our Fathers Also' is a poem in the beginning. It is a delightful catalogue of the herbs used in times when 'Half their remedies cured you dead,' which finishes with a plea for hearts as stout.

'Below the Mill Dam' is the last story in the book. The Spirit of the Mill—Robert's Mill, in use since the Conquest—and others discuss the arrival of Felden, an engineer called in by Madden to install electricity.

With the new century, first in *Traffics and Discoveries* (1904), Kipling normally prefaced or followed (sometimes both) his stories when they were collected, with poems, often written quite separately and often themselves in Kipling's later years more or less painfully obscure. Sometimes this is a happy conjunction, giving extra meaning or clarity to the story and poem, sometimes it makes for a crossword-puzzle obscurity, more flattering to the ingenuity of the reader than really enriching of the works; sometimes it produces difficulty which unsophisticated Kipling devotees love to ponder, but which is surely due to lack of any worthwhile relationship. Occasionally the juxtaposition throws light upon the author as much as upon his work.

14. Actions and Reactions (1909)

This book is not reissued afterwards and some of its good stories are published in new editions. The original version has the following stories: An Inhabitation Enforced, Garm—a Hostage, The Mother Hive, With the Night Mail, A Deal in Cotton, The Puzzler, Lottle Foxes and The House Surgeon.

1. An Habitation Enforced

In the first story George Chapin, American millionaire, had a breakdown and travels with his wife Sophie. They are eventually recommended to stay in a remote English village, where they lodge with Cloke and his wife at Rocketts. Their ramblings about the countryside bring them to a magnificent old house, Friars Pardon, which they buy and renovate. They then discover that Mrs. Chapin's ancestors were formerly owners of the estate –the locals have already found this out-and they are taken up by the neighboring landowners. When their son is born Chapin realizes that he has come to stay.

This story is autobiographical. As we know, the Kiplings settled down in Vermont (in the USA) for four years and because of Kipling's quarrel with his brother-in-law, they came back to England.

Angus Wilson observes, "Alas with all its excellencies of scene and background characters, 'An Habitation Enforced' doesn't convince. The healing of Mr and Mrs Chapin seems improbable, their discontented return to Brown's Hotel after a few days, much more likely."

According to Lord Birkenhead Kipling's newly discovered love of England was revealed again in the story *An Habitation*

Enforced, in which his usual hostile attitude to Americans is reversed.

An Habitation Enforced: In three stories he told of a man, or a man and wife, learning their way to the heart of an English country home—'An Habitation Enforced,' 'My Son's Wife' and 'Beauty Spots.'

The story is followed by the poem 'The Recall.'

2. Garm –a Hostage

Ortheris has been in trouble and is put straight by the narrator, to whom he gives Garm, a fine bull-terrier. Ortheris comes to see the dog secretly, and then goes to the hills on sick-leave, whereupon they both pine. A happy reunion is arranged when the narrator himself goes on leave. The story ends with the poem 'The Power of the Dog.'

3. The Mother Hive

This is a politico-economic parable set in a colony of bees that is invaded by the wax-moth.

To a great extent this is true of Kipling's later political fable, 'The Mother Hive.' Here the menace to the British Imperial civilisation is not so much Tory old guardism as it had been when Balfour ruled in 1902. The new enemies were progressivism, liberal individualism, pacifism, cosmopolitanism, egalitarianism, little Englandism, class division—all the elements in the Liberal Government's rule that worked against a cohesive, well-armed Empire ready both physically and psychologically to resist the growing German menace to the English world-civilizing mission. Kipling attacked the Balfourists in 'Below the Mill Down."

This corrupting enemy is represented in the fable by the Wax Moth a deadly progressive female who enters the beehive, and, laying the eggs, sets up an internal rot. Here she was safe, for young bees will tolerate any sort of stranger. It is the susceptibility of the young to new ideas that allows the progressivist Wax Moth to spread her deadly eggs.

Critics think 'The Mother Hive' is a fable in which Kipling's hatred of Socialism, and of a society in which he thought men were paid to do nothing and exonerated from their sins, is driven home, and is yet another example of the preoccupation with England's defence which he had expressed at the same period in 'The Dykes.'

The story is followed by 'The Bees and the Flies.'

4. With the Night Mail

The narrator accompanies Purnall and Hodgson in Postal Packet No. 162 from London to Quebec in A.D. 2000. There are extracts and advertisements from the *Monthly Report* of the Aerial Board of Control.

In the twenties, when the reaction to the Great War was at its height, such utterances were dismissed as bad faith. Kipling can be charged with Bottomley-like bad faith; but I think that he can be charged with an excited sincerity that is near to the point of no return. As such, it is often repulsive. And it continued after the war and towards all kinds of Germans.

The poem 'The Four Angels' follows.

5. A Deal in Cotton

An infant entertains house-party which includes Stalky,. Strickland, and his son, the latter being home on sick-leave from Africa where he is Assistant Commissioner at Dupe. He is interested in growing cotton, and the account of how he obtained £200 from Ibn Makarrah, a slave-trader, to gather with the labor that would enable him to begin, is related by Imam Din.

The poem 'The New Knighthood' follows.

6. The Puzzler

'The Puzzler,' an extravaganza in which the Lord Chief Justice with a stump-leg barrel-organ strapped to his shoulder joins an Italian organ-grinder in chasing a monkey through a strange house, the owner and his wife arriving while the hunt is in progress in the bedrooms.

Penfentenyou and the narrator witness an experiment carried out by Lundie, Tomling, and Loman, who are trying to make an organ-grinder's monkey climb a 'Monkey-Puzzle' tree in the garden of an empty house. The new occupiers and the moving –men catch them in the act, and they are only saved by the intervention of Penfentenyou. This is one of the funniest of the stores. The narrative is in the middle rank of Kipling's humorous tales.

The poem 'The Puzzler' follows.

7. Little Foxes

This is sub-titled as 'A Tale of the Gihon Hunt.' The Governor of a province (Dongola?) finds he has foxes and sends home for a few couple of hounds; Baker, the Inspector, is Whip and he is Master. He settles a few land-cases when earths are not stopped and finds the Hunt a good way of governing his territory. Baker, on leave, tells the story of the Hunt to four M.F.H.s and another man, who turns out to be a most unpleasant M.P. named Lethabie Groombride who is somewhat misled by the tall stories and eventually appears in the territory on a one-man fact-finding mission. He learns a certain native word from Baker which he uses to the inhabitants with devastating consequences; and retires in confusion.

The poem 'Gallio's Song' follows.

8. The House Surgeon

This is the last story in the book. The narrator meets L. Maxwell M'Leod, a retired fur merchant, and spends a weekend at Holmescraft, the latter's house. It is not exactly haunted, but there is a 'something.' The narrator agrees to help clear it up and sees Baxter, solicitor and cousin to the Misses Moultrie, the vendors. It turns out that M'Leod had insisted on a guarantee that nobody had died in the house; this is given, but another sister had fallen from her bedroom window and died just underneath it in circumstances that indicated suicide but turn out to be accident. When all this emerges peace returns to the house. Kingsley Amis calls it "a powerful macabre tale."

In *Something of Myself* Kipling describes his home at Torquay, outwardly large and bright but inwardly burdened with a 'brooding spirit of deep, deep despondency.' It cannot be doubted that in 'The House Surgeon' he gave point to this.

The poem 'The Rabbi's Song' follows.

15. Rewards and Fairies (1910)

Kipling's next book *Rewards and Fairies* which is a sequel to *Puck of Pook's Hill* volume, has a fine introduction by the author. These stories are in a framework. Kipling's biographer Lord Birkenhead comments: "These were the days of 'sequels' and Kipling had already written a *Second Jungle Book* after the first, Stevenson had written *Catriona to Kidnapped*, Barrie, unfortunately, *Tommy and Grizel* to *Sentimental Tommy*, and Haggard and Doyle had followed the fashion-a fashion which is at the moment unpopular among writers of large successful books. When *Puck of Pook's Hill* (1906) caught the public imagination it was followed in 1910 by *Rewards and Fairies*."

It can be said that the whole sequence is a clear expression of Kipling's love for England. But it is not quite the love of an Englishman for his homeland which is expressed here, that inarticulate nostalgia which becomes embarrassing in words. It is the love of a man who has first heard the name from a distant country and has come to know his beloved after he has reached manhood. Someone has pointed out that the best descriptions of London have been written by provincials who had never taken the capital for granted but in childhood had heard of it with awe and in boyhood had longed chiefly to get to it.

1. Cold Iron

The story begins with the poem 'A Charm.'

This is the first story in the above. Puck tells Dan and Una of the Boy adopted by Sir Huon and Lady Esclairmonde, and how he was kept from touching Cold Iron for some years until, finding a slave-ring that Thor had made. He accepted his destiny.

2. Gloriana

Dan and Una meet Queen Elizabeth I, who tells them of 'Admiral Boy' and 'Vice –Admiral Babe,' two young men who fought the Spaniards on her behalf and gladly went to their deaths at her bidding. The poems 'The Looking –Glass' and 'A Truthful Song' follow.

3. The Wrong Thing

Dan is making a boat in Springett's workshop; Hal o' the Draft appears and tells the rigiano the quarrel with Benedetto, his draft of certain decorative work for a ship, and his knighthood. The quarrel is made up and he is punished by his master for doing bad work. The poems 'King Henry VII and the Shipurights' and 'The Way through the Woods' follow.

4. Marklake Witches

Una is learning to milk and finds a girl watching her. She turns out to be Philadelphia Buck-steed, suffering from consumption, who tells her of the village in Napoleonic times. The poems 'Brookland Road' and 'The Run of the Downs' follow.

5. The Knife and the Naked Chalk

Dan and Una meet Dudeney, the old shepherd on the Downs, and then come across Tyr and Puck; they hear the story of how Tyr obtained for his people the knives which enabled them to master the wolf. The story is preceded by 'The Run of the Downs' and followed by 'Song of the Men's Side.'

6. Brother Square–Toes

Puck introduces Dan and Una to Pharaoh Lee, a smuggler who went to North America and saw George Washington. The story is followed by the poems 'If———,' 'A St. Helena Lullaby,' 'Poor Honest Men' and 'Eddi's Service.'

7. The Conversion of St. Wilfrid

Dan and Una meet Wilfrid, saint of Sussex and Archbishop of York, in St. Barnabas' Church. He tells them how he came to convert the men of Sussex and went fishing with Meon, was wrecked and saved; how Meon adhered to the faith of his fathers in the face of great danger but was later converted after he had in some measure converted Wilfrid. The story is followed by the poems 'Song of the Red War –Boat,' 'An Astrologers' Song,' 'A Doctor of Medicine,' 'Our Fathers of Old' and 'The Thousand of Man.'

8. Simple Simon

Dan and Una are watching some woodmen carting away a tree intended to form the keel of a fishing-boat and meet Simon Cheyneys, shipbuilder of Rye, and a former boy on Francis Drake's vessel. He is injured in a fight with the Spaniards and is obliged to stay ashore; he becomes a burgess of Rye and he and his aunt are able to provide logistic support for Drake at the time of the Armada. The story is followed by the poems 'Frankie's Trade' and 'The Ballad of Minepit Shaw.'

9. The Tree of Justice

This is the last story in the book. Sir Richard tells Dan and Una of the great hunt that De Aquila held for King Henry and how an old, broken-down pilgrim turned out to be King Harold, who should have died at Senlac, and how moved Henry was at seeing Hugh kneel to his rightful king.

The poem 'A Carol' follows.

16. A Diversty of Creatures (1917)

This small book of Kipling's stories published in 1917 has some interesting stories like The Village That Voted the Earth Was Flat, Regulus, As Easy as ABC, Transportation and others. He has never shown himself a greater master of the art of storytelling, never combined creative imagination with more triumphant realism, or handled his own English prose with more ease, economy, and certainty of effect.

Lord Birkenhead comments, "We have already seen how in *A Diversity of Creatures* Kipling launched successfully into science-fiction, and as usual there is a wide variety in this collection—a new note with the beautiful drug addict of 'In the Same Boat,' violent and revengeful mirth in 'The Village that Voted the Earth was Flat,' and at the end the story that brought brick-bats showering on Kipling for sadism, cruelty and vindictive hatred of the Germans—'Mary Postgate.'"

1. As Easy as A.B.C

This is the first story in the book. It is a fantasy of the future that has, in many respects, come true. It is a S-F story.

How we have a picture of the world in 2065, when under the benevolent technological rule of the Aerial Board of Control, a small group of experts from many countries (including Japan)—no Anglo-Saxon, or racial, or even colour purity in this ideal society—an era of world contentment and prosperity has been established in which wars have been eliminated, and longevity and physical health generally established in great degree by scientific control of the birth rate as well as of the other aspects of life.

Democracy, the last of history's tyrannies, has been eliminated. As McDonough's Song, the accompanying poem, says:

Holy State or Holy King—
Or Holy People's Will—.
Have no truck with the senseless thing.
Order the guns and kill.

Because democracy has meant the rule of the crowd and the end of privileged individualism, it has been outlawed by a world that has suffered too much from it tyranny.

The members of the Aerial Board of Control are brought in to help authority and are only able to restore order by using the dread ray that brings human activity to a stop. As for the recidivist democrats, they find their place carrying out their antics of voting and speech-making on the London music-halls.

Angus Wilson observes, "It is hard to convey, in summary, the power and tension of the story's dramatic events, which are, of course, heightened by Kipling's own pessimistic view of humanity that lies behind it. But the real subtlety of the story comes not from the narrative alone but from two other aspects."

It is a futuristic fantasy. Here Kipling like Lawrence, hates democracy because it encourages crowds and invades privacy.

2. Friendly Brook

Two woodmen working on a hedge discuss the doings of their neighbors- especially Jim Wickenden and his adopted daughter, whose father arrived unexpectedly and was later found drowned in the brook. The poem 'The Land' follows.

3. In the Same Boat

Conroy and Miss Henschil suffer from 'nerves' and delusions; Dr. Gilbert sends them on a train journey together as a cure. Nurse Blaber looks after and her suggestions help them to rehabilitation. The poem 'Helen all Alone' follows.

Kipling's imperialism is found in 'In the Same Boat' and 'The Dog Hervey. But, in both cases, the psychic element is so irrelevant or so metamorphosed into an appearance of medical psychiatry that its use as a solution or a means of identification of the source of the ill obscures and weakens otherwise interesting situations.

4. The Honours of War

Stalky, the infant, and Beetle have another reunion, and meet Bobby Trivett and Eames, two subalterns who are concerned in a rag with another, Wontner. The poem 'The Children' follows.

5. The Dog Hervey

A weird story about a squinting dog and a girl whose father used to patch up drunken young men; how the dog appeared to one of them long after he had left the place, and how he met Moira Sichliffe again. The poem 'The Comforters' follows.

6. The Village that voted the Earth was Flat

Some motorists are fined for exceeding the speed-limit and treated badly in court. The Press and the Theatre combine in an ample revenge on the magistrate responsible, Sir Thornas Ingell, Bart., M.P. In parts, it is one of the funniest of the stories. The poem 'The Press' follows.

This story was the last comic fling before Armageddon broke out, it is also a piece of violent farce at a time when Kipling's political speeches and intentions had, like those of most of his associates, reached a point of hysteria which threatened violence. The promise of Home Rule for Ireland, made by the Liberal leaders to the Southern Irish politicians, on whom, after 1910, their parliamentary majority depended, brought the Right Wing to a point of frenzy.

Croft-Cooke says, "No other English writer has attempted sheer farce on this scale, so that the superlatives which suggest themselves are scarcely necessary. Starting simply, with a conscious platitude ('Our drive till then had been quite a success'), it goes forward with an awful inevitability through a series of wild imbecilities till the noise of its rhapsodic foolery fills the world. It is, incidentally, a tale of vengeance—not for some serious crime, but for stupidity and malice, and Kipling takes care to have the reader on the side of the avengers, and to give him the incidental pleasure of seeing that vengeance magnificently fulfilled.

7. In the Presence

This story is about how four Goorkhas took their turn at the Lying-in-State of King Edward VII and how a Sikh brought the story back to his regiment in India. The poem 'Jobson's Amen' follows.

8. Regulus

This is a Stalky story collected in *A Diversity of Creatures* and *The Complete Stalky & Co.* Horace's Ode is translated and applied. Winton lets a mouse loose in class, gets an imposition, and is beaten by Mullins. The poem 'A Translation' follows.

9. The Edge of the Evening

Zigler meets the narrator, takes him to the country house he has rented from Lord Marshalton (formerly Captain Mankeltow), and tells the story of the death of two spies who landed in an aircraft.

The poem 'Rebirth' follows.

10. The Horse Marines

The narrator lands at Southampton to find that his car has four new tyres. Leggatt will not explain, so they drive to Portsmouth and call on Pyecroft at his uncle's shop. There he hears the story of how a rocking-horse was exhibited to the Army and what happened thereafter. The story is preceded by what purports to be an extract from a daily paper about the issue of mechanical horses to the Army and followed by 'The Legend of Mirth,' 'My Son's Wife,' 'The Floods' and 'The Fabulists.'

11. The Vortex

Penfen-tenyou, Lingnam, the Agent-General, and the narrator go motoring and have some amusing adventures when they cause a boy on a bicycle to drop several boxes of bees. There is a political moral, but it is still a very funny story.

'The Vortex' is a grand piece of nonsense between a bore and a swarm of bees.

The story is followed by 'The Song of Seven Cities' and 'Sweet and Garnished.'

12. Mary Postgate

In this story Mary, Miss Fowler's companion brings up her orphan nephew Wyndham Fowler. He is killed in training with the Royal Flying Corps and she burns his belonging when she dies beside the German airman who has bombed the village. He begs in broken English and French for a doctor. But she says, 'Nein. Ich habe der todt Kinder gesehn.'

The story is deeply shocking. It is true that the overall psychological tragedy of the story, unlike 'Swept and Garnished' transcends its propaganda. In the last resort, Kipling is aware with deep pity of the waste of a human life that can only be brought to some sense of exhilaration by a cruel act of vengeance. And he prepares this sense of the waste of Mary Postgate's life most carefully. She is that extinct creature a genteel middle-aged spinster without money reduced to being a paid lady-companion to a wealthy old woman.

In Lord Birkenhead's view, Something more must be said of this story, which was called by Stannley Baldwin's son, Oliver, 'the wickedest story ever written.' It cannot be questioned that in writing 'Mary Postgate' Kipling not only invited trouble, but positively entreated it. Nor can we doubt that he had by this time a murderous hatred of the Germans for the havoc they had brought into the world, for their love of war, their hideous massacres of French women and children, and their barbarous sack of Louvain."

The poem 'The Beginnings' follows.

17. Debits and Credits (1916)

Brander Matthews observes, "It is pleasant to welcome this new collection of Rudyard Kipling's short stories in *Debits and Credits* the first in ten years; and it is pleasant to know that his popularity is attested by the steady sale of his many volumes."

Lord Birknhead thinks, "Rudyard's deterioration of health was accompanied by a change in his manner of writing. The collections *Debits and Credits*, published in 1926, and *Limits and Renewals*, in 1932, contained stories which puzzled many of his readers, for they were dark, involuted, and sometimes agonizing—stories which if, in the words of a critic, they had been 'the work of a young and unknown writer the average editor might have condemned as ridiculously obscure, or dismissed as perversely morbid.'"

1. The Enemies to Each Other

The story is about Adam and Eve in the Garden of Eden, their expulsion, the birth of their children, and how the Mole spied on them, thereby losing his eyesight.

The poem 'The Changelings' follows.

2. Sea Constables

Portson, Maddingham, Tegg, and Winchmore are dining at the Carvoitz; the story of a certain neutral captain and his ship, suspected of supplying German submarines with oil-fuel, is related. To begin with it has a lively frame for its telling. Four naval officers, three of them war-time officers who have been rich city men, assemble for luncheon at a very smart West End of London restaurant. They are in civilian clothes, and, as they eat and drink with rare satisfaction through a gourmet meal, they are watched with disgust by a foreign millionaire and a foreign actress. She sings, 'Sons of the Empire, Go Forward!' at the Palemseum. 'It makes the aunties weep,' says one of the officers. 'Now what's the matter with those four dubs yonder joining the British Army or doing something?' asks the actress of the millionaire she is lunching with.

It is obvious that these rich foreigners, who so easily comment on apparent British shirking, are American neutrals. And, when the four men begin to exchange accounts of the various dangerous activities they have been carrying out in terrible conditions, defending England's shores, it is, at last, to a story of the pursuit and defeat of a neutral ship, carrying oil for the enemy.

The poems 'The Vineyard,' 'Banquet Night,' 'In the Interests of the Brethren' and 'To the Companions' follow.

3. The United Idolaters

Stalky and his friends are at the Coll. Brownell, an unpopular temporary master, arrives in place of Macrea who has had a climbing accident in Switzerland; the boys are taken with the idea of the Tar-Baby in Uncle Remus and make one, parading with it and a tortoise—painted in the colours of King's house—to represent Terrapin. There is a near-riot, followed by the usual punishments, but all ends happily when Brownell goes and Macrea returns. The poems 'The Centaurs' and 'Late Came the God' follow.

4. The Wish House

'The Wish House' is another story, pitiful and harrowing, in which Kipling enshrines that belief in a sublime love and readiness for sacrifice which he believed to be the ultimate compassion, the supreme emotion of which a human being is capable, in a setting of witchcraft and occultism. It is written in his most spare and sinewy prose, the horror accentuated by the matter-of-factness, the fabular and the actual cunningly blended, and the whole pierced by shafts of horrible realism.

It is the story of a woman who, for love, has taken upon herself, by a pact in witchcraft, the agony of another person—the worthless man who has deserted her. The clues are provided more generously than usual in the poem preceding the story, 'Late Came the God,' in which the agony of cancer

> Daily renewed and nightly pursued through her soul to her flesh-Mornings of memory, noontides of agony, midnights unslaked for her,
>
> Till the stones of the streets of her Hells and her Paradise ached for her. ...
>
> And she builded an Altar and served by the light of her Vision-
>
> Alone, without hope of regard or reward, but uncowed,
>
> Resolute, selfless, divine.
>
> These things she did in Love's honour ...
>
> What is a God beside Woman? Dust and Derision!

Mrs. Fettley calls on her old friend Mrs. Ashcroft for tea and a talk about old times, old lovers, and old doings. The latter has a bad leg-cancer—which started when she took all Harry Mockler's ills upon herself by saying her wish through the door of no. 14, Wadloes Road.

It is probably Kipling's most successful single story; certainly his best story in the psychological fashion that so many recent critics, mistakenly take for the necessary sign of maturity in fiction.

There is much in 'The Wish House' that would repay analysis; T. S. Eliot, while praising it, has called it 'hard and obscure,' and in a fuller treatment of the story due consideration should certainly be given to the use of the symbolism of cancer which recurs, some would say obsessively, in Kipling's later work.

The poems 'Rahere' and 'The Survival' follow.

5. The Janeites

This is one of the Masonic series; Brother Burges is on duty at 'Faith and Works, 5837', E.C., for a Saturday afternoon clean-up; some old friends reappear and new ones are introduced, including Humberstall, who rejoined his battery in France after being blown up; as he is slightly 'affected' he is given the job of mess-waiter. He is initiated into a secret society built round Jane Austen and her books and survives another bombardment. His possession of the 'pass words' gets him into a hospital-train and so home to his hairdressing. Anthony, who acts as a chorus throughout the story, is to marry his sister. The poems 'Jane's Marriage' and 'The Portent' follow.

6. The Prophet and the Country

The narrator, motoring in the Midlands, gets mixed up with cattle and licence-control in a market-town. Later his car breaks down and a strange vehicle stops to help. The driver is a real-estate man named Tarworth from Omaha with strong views on Prohibition which he proposes to air in a film. The story is preceded by 'The Portent' and followed by 'Gow's Watch.'

Kipling disliked England as much as America (for its dislike of his imperialism) in his last years. In the story, we find an American of Nebraska having shot a film that way. But he does not want to show it as he is afraid. Kipling meets the American and hears his story when stranded at night on the Great North Road. The concept of the man's movie attack on his own people is amusingly told.

Europe, save for France, was hardly more satisfactory than the United Sates. Kipling was closely associated with Rider Haggard in the short-lived Liberty League, intended to alert England to the dangers of Bolshevism.

The episode is chiefly memorable for the humorous verse in the *Daily Herald* in March 1920;

Every Bolsh is a blackguard
Said Kipling to Haggard
That's just what I say
Said the author of 'They'
I agree, I agree
Said the author of 'She.'

The menace of Soviet Russia was much in Kipling's mind all through these last years. It is surely part of the danger against which he counselled in his famous 1935 speech to the Society of St George, which is usually held to be a warning entirely devoted to Germany and Hitler.

7. The Bull that Thought

The narrator is motoring in France and visits the Camargue, where there is a stretch of road suitable for a speed trial. He meets Andre Voiron, a local magnate who comes along as well, later providing a bottle of magnificent champagne; over this he tells the story of a very intelligent bull who anticipated his antagonist's actions and killed several people and animals. In the bull-ring he shamed the matador Villa-marti and played up to old Chisto, finally leaving with the latter's arm round his neck. The poems 'Alnaschar and the Oxen' and 'Gipsy Vans' follow.

8. A Madonna of the Trenches

Of all the stories of Kipling's 'late' manner 'A Madonna of the Trenches' is the most brilliantly written. Like several others, it was set in the Masonic Lodge of Instruction, and like 'The Wish House' is a story of sublime love.

The heading is from Les Noyades by Swinburne. Another Masonic story of 'Faith and Works 5837', E.C., in which young Strangwick tells how he saw the ghost of his Aunt Bella Armine in the trenches at the time that she died in London. Bella's husband appears unexpectedly at the end to take the boy home. The poem 'Gipsy Vans' follows.

'A Madonna of the Trenches' is one of a number of stories Kipling wrote after the war, imagining that the ritual and fellowship of freemasonry might be the proper means to cure the war's mental and nervous casualties. They are all, including 'The Madonna of the Trenches' which is the best. Here his fellowship with doctors is expressed as strongly as in the other group of purely medical healing stories. But there is also a very lively and sympathetic concern with tradesmen—grocers, tobacconists, apothecaries, and hairdressers—an affectionate and admiring feeling for the petit-bourgeois world.

The story speaks about man's survival after death and man's life-long enduring passions.

9. The Propagation of Knowledge

Stalky and his friends are studying English literature; Beetle discovers *Curiosities of Literature* and strange Baconian heresies which he passes on to the others, who use them in a test and in the Army Exam., the latter being conducted by one Hume of Balliol and Sutton, who congratulate King on his open-mindedness. King is very annoyed and has to be soothed by Gillett, who knows of the plot but does not disclose it to King. The story is preceded by 'The Birthright' and followed by 'The Legend of Truth.'

10. A Friend of the Family

This story is told by Bevin in the Lodge. One Hickmer an Australian soldier from the outback, makes friends with Bert Vigors during the 1914 war and hears of his family troubles. Bert is killed and Hickmer takes revenge on the Margetts who took over his father's business and does a good turn for Bevin. The poem 'We and They' follows.

11. On the Gate

This is a tale of 1916. Death and St. Peter are discussing the effect of the war on their staffs; admission to Heaven is regulated by a Civil Service, naturally, very over-worked. Various souls come up for admission, some still in their uniform covered with the mud of Flanders. The poems 'The Supports' and 'Untimely' follow.

But Jesus's plea for forgiveness of his enemies is certainly a central point of Kipling's later thinking. His son John's death surely turned him to this, for it first becomes central in 'On the Gate.' But the same allegory of judgement of sorrows is repeated in 'Uncovenanted Mercies.' The earlier story is cast in a witty-serious satire upon bureaucracy; the later one, making the Judgement Seat a railway station, is more a satire upon what we should now call social workers.

12. The Eye of Allah

John Otho, better known as John of Burgos, is an artist who illuminates manuscripts; when in England he works in St

Illod's the Abbot's scriptorium. He goes to Spain where his mistress dies in childbed and he returns to the monastery with various drugs, colors, and a cornelian necklace for the Abbot's lady, Anne of Norton. He also produces a primitive microscope which he demonstrates to Roger of Salerno, Roger Bacon, and Thomas. The Abbot saw a similar one when he was a prisoner of the Saracens. They all appreciate that it would be of great service to the sick, but the Abbot destroys it as they would be burned for heresy if it became known to the Church. The story is proceeded by 'Untimely' and followed by 'The Last Ode.'

'The Eye of Allah' is a kind of science fiction. A forerunner of the microscope turns up in a thirteenth-century English monastery and is destroyed on purpose as too likely to attract charges of diabolism. The monastic setting displays Kipling's grasp of detail—detail of processes as well as of appearances—at its very best.

Lord Birkenhead adds, "*The Eye of Allah* is on one level a story about what happens to a group of people in a mediaeval monastery; on another level it is a story about a premature discovery (the microscope); on a third it is about the impact of the Renaissance on the mediaeval world picture; on a fourth about the attitude of the artist, the physician, and the philosopher to science, and on the fifth about four aspects of civilization personified as the artist, the scientist, the philosopher, and the Church dignitary and statesman, and illustrated by confronting them with an emblem of the new science: the microscope."

13. The Gardener

Kipling's other story of the war is for many of his admires his finest work. This is the fourteenth and last story in the book. Helen Turrell brings home the infant son of her late brother with an elaborate explanation of how and why she has taken charge of the child. Michael grows up in time to join the army and dies at Ypres. She goes to see his grave in Hagenzeele Third after the Armistice and the suspicion that the dead boy is in fact her son is confirmed by one working in the cemetery whom she supposes to be the gardener.

Lord Birkenhead is of the opinion that, Equally memorable, and with a theme that uplifts rather than harrows, is 'The Gardener,' which Kipling placed at the end of *Debits and Credits* with the object of drawing particular attention to it. Like 'The Wish House' it is a story of compassion, and like 'The Bull that Thought' appears at first glance a clear and straightforward one: of an un-married mother who loses her son in the war and visits his grave in a war cemetery, being shown its position by one of the gardeners.

But it may be said that, though 'The Gardener' is one of Kipling's best stories, it is hardly typical of him. And, indeed, it may well be that Kipling's best stories are not his most representative.

The story is followed by 'The Burden.'

18. Limits and Renewals (1932)

1. Dayspring Mishandled

Graydon ran the Fictional Supply Syndicate and employed many young writers, including Manallace, who loved Vidal Benzaguen's mother, and the unpleasant Castorley who proposed to her and was refused. He inherited wealth and gave up 'hack-writing' for 'literature.' Manallace made steady progress while Castorley became a critic and an expert on Chaucer. A fragment of a new 'Canterbury Tale' is found in the U.S.A. which Castorley pronounces to be genuine, although, unknown to him, Manallace had forged it. The former is knighted but dies before the latter has made up his mind to disclose it to him. Lady Castroley obviously has her eye on the doctor, Gleeag. The story is followed by 'Gertrude's Prayer.'

'Dayspring Mishandled' is the story of a Stalky joke that misfires, a picture of a life wasted in hoarded-up hatred and complicated revenge. It is a new and significant extra twist in Kipling's concern for forgiveness in his last years. Lord Birkenhead thinks in 'Dayspring Mishandled' Kipling has threaded a gloomy labyrinth of treachery, disease and death.

This is a 'revenge' story of a savage feud between a genuine and a spurious bibliophile in which literary forgery takes place

(Kipling typically going so far as to forge a mediaeval manuscript himself before writing the story).

2. The Woman in His Life

'The Woman in His Life,' a sentimental dog story, begins with a harming description of a nervous break.

John Marden sets up an engineering firm with Burnea and other ex-servicemen after the 1914 war. It is successful, but he has a period of great depression brought on by overwork and his experiences underground in the war. Shingle, his servant, gets him Dinah, an Aberdeen terrier puppy, who assists his recovery. They go to stay in the country with Shingle's sister; Dinah is lost, Marden and Jock, a collie, find her trapped underground, get her out and back to the cottage where Marden collapses. He is better after a bath and a rest and is able to return to work. The story is preceded by 'Dinah in Heaven,' and followed by 'Four –Feet.'

Kipling's emptiness was in part filled by studying the Aberdeen terriers he kept at Bateman's. He attempted, alas, to write a whole book out of this—*Thy Servant a Dog*.

3. The Tie

The story begins with the poem 'The Totem.' The narrator, although a man of some age, is a junior officer in the Army in 1915. The food in the mess is dreadful until the contractor, one Morrison Haylock, falls into their hands. He is wearing tie of a school that some of them attended, and is bullied as if they were all small boys again. He then castigates the mess-steward and from that instant the food is superb.

4. The Church that was at Antioch

Valens, a young Roman follower of Mithras, is sent by his widowed mother to Antioch, where his uncle, Lucius Sergius, is Prefect of Police. He meets Paul, Peter and Barnabas and does a good turn to their church. He is later stabbed and dies, asking his uncle to forgive his assailants because they did not know what they were doing. The poem 'The Disciple' follows.

'The Church That Was at Antioch' is a delight to read.

5. Aunt Ellen

The narrator lunched with Miss Gillon (known as Aunt Ellen) near Grantham and agreed to deliver an eiderdown in which various articles were wrapped to an old servant-Prescott- whose birthday was the next day. The bundle traveled better on the back of the car, but after dinner in a college of a university town it became detached and was run over by Phil, an undergraduate, who thought it was a woman. The story develops into an imitation film; a young constable and Phil are covered with feathers; so that on arrival at Cadogan Gardens the latter is not recognized by Doris, the girl he has come to meet. The story begins with the poem 'The Playmate,' and is followed by 'Naaman's Song.'

6. A Naval Mutiny

The story begins with the poem 'The Coiner.' Admiral Lord Heatleigh goes to Bermuda to convalesce after bronchitis and meets an old shipmate, Winter Vergil, who does not recognize him. They get yarning. And Heatleigh hears about the two cruisers who landed parrots for target practice and the trouble that ensued, how their owners came to blows, and how old Vergil sorted it out.

7. The Debt

William, six-year-old son of the doctor of the gaol, is left with his ayah while his parents are out playing tennis, but 132 (a prisoner) and Mahmud Ali the sewing-man are looking after him. It is the time of King George V's illness and 132 tells how the King was inspecting War Cemeteries in France just after the 1914 war in very cold weather and told a general to put on his British Warm; the General said that he owed his life to the King, and 132 maintained that for that reason the King would recover from his illness.

The poem 'Akbar's Bridge' follows.

8. The Manner of Men

Baeticus comes into Mareilles in his wheat-ship and meets Quabil, the Port Inspector, and some others. The story of St.

Paul's ship-wreck on Malta is related. The poem 'At His Execution' follows.

9. Unprofessional

Harries comes into money and provides his friend Vaughan with a nursing-home in Sloane Street, where Ackerman and Loftie also take a hand, with the assistance of Frost. One of their patients is a Mrs. Berners, who later becomes a housekeeper after she has had treatment. They are carrying out research into cancer on very original lines and appear to have some success when Mrs. Berners suddenly relapses and starts behaving in the same manner as the mice with which they are experimenting: she is not only convinced that she is to die but seems to wish to, there and then. She again recovers, with careful treatment, and it seems that she and Frost have an understanding. There are many references in Bodelsen and Tompkins.

'Unprofessional' is based on cancer and suicide: the theme of cancer is again to be found 'In The Eye of Allah' and 'The Wish House,' while 'A Madonna of the Trenches' is a story of cancer and suicide in a setting of shell-shocked hysteria and ghostly visitation.

The poem 'The Threshold' follows.

11. Beauty Sports

Walter Gravell, a chemist, and his son James (Jemmy) have a busybody—Major Kniveat—for a neighbour. Gravell senior adds chemicals to a dell adjoining the road to encourage plants; the trees lopped by the council with Kniveat assisting, the wall is damaged, and parties of trippers picnic there. A mysterious complaint—Bloody Measles—affects a thousand or so thereafter; Angelique, a pet pig, also appears to have contracted it. Kniveat, deceived by greasepaint, accuses the Gravells of concealing the diseased creature, only to find the paint washed off when he goes to have another look at her. The spectators think he is drunk, and he thus loses any hopes he has of further influence in the village. The story is preceded by the poem 'Neighbours' and followed by 'The Expert.'

12. The Miracle of Saint Jubanus

The narrator, in search of stained glass, meets an old priest in a village in the Auvergne and hears how laughter cured a boy who had returned from the 1914 war in a depressed mental state, and how Falloux, a freethinker, an umbrella, and two acolytes assisted. The story is preceded by the poem 'The Cure' and followed by 'Song of Seventy Horses.'

13. The Tender Achilles

The narrator and his host Keede forgather with Sir Thomas Horringe at his rooms in Wimpole Street after a St. Peggoty's dinner. The story of Wilkett and the 1914 war is told, how he suffered from remorse after operating on wounded soldiers for a considerable time under great pressure; a small wound on his own foot gives trouble and he is discharged. His mother takes him to the seaside but Belton wants him for St. Peggoty's and sends Keede and Horringe after him. It is agreed between them that his foot is tubercular and required an operation. This is done and it later emerges that the foot was not tubercular, but a woman in the laboratory changed the slides over. Belton points out that such carelessness would not have happened had Wilkett been at the hospital in his proper job. Anyway, he is cured of his delusions and it seems to be understood that he will return to take charge of the Laboratory—quite unaware that the woman loves him and mixed up the slides on purpose. The story is preceded by the poem 'Hymn to Physical Pain' and followed by 'The Penalty.'

14. Uncovenanted Mercies

Azrael, Gabriel, and the Archangel of the English discuss a man and a woman under test for the Ultimate Breaking Strain and we see what happens when they meet.

The poem 'Azrael's Count' follows.

Later Stories

Kipling (or his publishers) collected and selected many groups of stories and published them at various places and times.

Kipling has himself suggested his own process to other writers:

> This leads me to the Higher Editing. Take of well-ground Indian Ink as much as suffices and a camel-hair brush propropionate to the interspaces of your lines. In an auspicious hour, read your final draft and consider faithfully every paragraph, sentence and word, blacking out where requisite. Let it lie by to drain as long as possible. At the end of that time, re-read and you should find that it will bear a second shorting. Finally, read it aloud alone and at leisure. Maybe a shade more brushwork will then indicate or impose itself. If not, praise Allah and let it go, and 'when thou hast done, repent not.' The shorter the tale, the longer the brushwork and, normally, the shorter the lie-by, and *vice versa*. The longer the tale, the less brush but the longer lie-by. I have had tales by me for three or five years which shortened themselves almost yearly.

All these later tales (though the earliest of them must go back to Kim's time) are what Kipling called 'pummiced ivory-smooth,' but never over-written. Rupert Croft-Cocke observes that Kipling's later stories deal with an idea rather than with a plot. They are abstract and philosophical

Except for one story, rather unsubstantial compared with its predecessors, the soldiers three have disappeared, alas, and in their place is Mr. Pyecroft of the Royal Navy (Kipling had been on naval exercises with the Home Fleet). Pyecroft is a joy and Kipling's contemporary readers must have learnt to anticipate with relish the outrageous events which followed his every appearance. But they missed Mulvaney, Learoyd and Ortheris and looked in vain for their reappearance with Private Copper in South Africa, and never knew quite the same frank friendship with any of the later reappearing characters. Kipling's later stories followed the course of his own later life.

W. W. Robson thinks of Kipling's later stories. According to him, "Kipling's theory of art, furthermore, was 'classical' and 'impersonal.' He believed in inspiration—the Daemon—but he thought of it as something coming from outside, not generated by the conflicts within: in his story 'Wireless' he works out as a sort of sustained metaphor the likeness between wireless telegraphy (then a novelty) and the temporary invasion by

Keats's genius of the soul of a consumptive chemist's assistant. He asked his critics to 'seek not to question other than | The books I leave behind.' Yet no author is more strongly personal than Kipling. For one of the peculiarities of Kipling's art in his short stories is that, while showing obvious variety and range, it does not in any obvious sense show *development*. Kipling's supreme achievements in prose fiction seem to be those in which his genius as a fabulist and myth-maker is felt to be shaping the story without detriment to the author's true and sensitive perceptions of actual human beings, 'They' and 'Mrs. Bathurst' and 'The Wish House,' 'Mary Postgate' and 'The Gardener' exemplify this power of the short story to suggest the *distillation* of a human life, the rendering of its essence as latent within a momentary situation, or an anecdote, or an episode."

Some of the later books of Kipling's stories are as follows:

19. Collected Dog Stories

This was published in ___. G. L. Stampa illustrated these stories. The book has the following short stories.

1. Private Learoyd's Story

This story has already appeared in *Soldiers Three.*

2. Germ—Hostage

This dog story has appeared in *Actions and Reactions*. The poem 'The Power of the Dog' follows the story. In fact, it elaborates the theme of the story.

3. Quiquern

This dog story has appeared in *The Second Jungle Book.*

4. The Dog Harvey

This dog story has appeared in *A Diversity of Creatures.*

5. The Woman in his Life

This dog story has appeared in *Limits and Renewals.*

6. 'Dinah in Heaven'

This is about a little bitch who waited in Heaven until her owner arrived.

7. 'Thy Servant a Dog'

The first story in the book of the same name. Boots, a black Aberdeen terrier, meets Slippers, another, in the Park. This introduces their master and mistress, who eventually marry. The whole party moves to the country where a son (Smallest) is born. There are various activities with Kitchen Cat, Cookie, add the hounds and so forth, all told in simple language.

8. The Great Play Hunt

This is the second story in *The Servant A Dog*. Boots continues his account of life with Smallest, now called Digby, and his family. The boy was anxious to hunt, but was considered too young for the current season, so Slippers, Ravager and Tags, the lame fox, arrange a run for him which is a great success.

9. Toby Dog

A dog in a Punch and Judy show and the last story in *The Servant A Dog*. He belongs to Dirty Man, who performs a show in Digby's bedroom at Flat-in-town where the boy is recovering from an operation on his tonsils. It is the end of the season for Punch and Judy, so Toby feigns illness and the kind-hearted family send him off to The Place with James. Boots and Slippers return there later; Toby is frightened by a shot-gun, but shows the others how well he can kill rats. Ravager, the old hound, is ailing; in spite of Moore's protests, Upstart is to go to a show at Peterborough; Toby discusses this with the other dogs and arranges a scheme whereby Upstart is discredited. Ravager dies that night with his friend Boots keeping him company and is buried next day. Boots cannot understand this and tries to dig him up until Adar, herself in tears, prevents him. That is the end of Boots' stories.

10. The Supplication of the Black Aberdeen

In this a dog begs his master not to avert the light of his countenance.

11. His Apologies

This is the story of a dog from eight weeks to old age.

12. A Sea Do

Admiral Lord Heatleigh, Vergil, and others are sailing in the old sloop while the Commander (Heatleigh's nephew) spins them the yarn of Malachi, a dog he had in a destroyer during the 1914 war.

20. Land and Sea Tales

The book begins with a preface to all to whom this little book may mean.

1. Winning the Victoria Cross

The first story in *Land and Sea Tales* gives an account of the origin of the decoration and tells how many brave men won it.

2. The Way that He Took

In the second story a captain of Mounted Infantry meets a nursing sister of a hospital train who tells him of her young days in South Africa, and how she was taught never to go home the way she came out. Months later he is sent to reconnoiter a position the Boers seems to be leaving but where they have arranged an ambush. He sees what has happened and, remembering Sister Margaret, returns by a different route, reporting the ambush to his commanding officer, who does not believe him.

3. An Unqualified Pilot

This is the third story in the book. Young Jim, son of Martin Tervor, a Hugli pilot, is interested in his father's job, spends a lot of his spare time on and about the river, and wishes to become a pilot himself. His friend Pedro introduces him to Erh-Tze, master of a junk who wants a cheap pilot. And the boy takes the unwieldy vessel safely down by following first his father and then McEwan, who are taking other vessels out. The boy is beaten by the former when he reaches the pilot-cutter and then accepted as a pupil by the latter. The story is followed by the poem 'The Junk and the Dhow,' the poem about ship-building.

4. His Gift

William Glasse Sawyer, a fat Boy Scout in the Pelican Troop, is useless at everything until Mr. Marsh teaches him cooking. The story is followed by the poem 'Prologue to the Master-Cook's Tale.'

5. A Flight of Fact

H.M.S. *Gardenia* (Lt. H. R. Duckett) returns to harbour and berths between *Phlox* (Lt. Commander Jerry Martlett) and *Stephanotis* (Lt. Augustus Holwell Rayne, 'the Damper'), ready for a boiler clean. The two latter go on board for a drink and a yarn. It turns out that Duckett's Acting-Sub has a cousin named Baxter who was flying in All the Pelungas (which Martlett knew as a Midshipman) and had to make a forced landing. After some trouble he and his observer were received kindly by the inhabitants and spent a very merry time until they returned to their ship. After some professional conversation with Coxswain, Duckett goes on leave.

6. The Burning of the 'Sarah Sands'

This is a story of heroism at sea. The 54th Regiment went to India in 1857 in the *Sarah Sands*, which caught fire; the troops extinguish it and sail the ship to Mauritius; they re-embark in the *Clarendon*, where a worse disaster befalls them—they run out of tobacco. They are replenished by an American ship which refuses payment on learning who they are. The Commander-in-Chief praised the regiment in a General Order. The story is followed by the poem 'The Last Lap.'

7. The Parable of Boy Jones

Jones is taken to see the village Rifle Club and thinks that there in nothing in it. He takes a shot and breaks a window in the miniature range. He is then taken over to the open range where things are explained to him, whereby he is converted to the necessity of being 'ready' and is later found learning to shoot in the miniature range. The story is followed by the poem 'A Departure.'

8. The Bold Aprentice

Young Ottley was apprenticed to the D.I.R.; his father, a pensioned driver, is anxious for him to get on; the boy is inclined to waste his time, but Olaf Swanson, a top-link driver and Mason, insists on giving him a copy of his classic book *The Art of Road-Locos Repair* and seeing that he learns it. The boy responds and Swanson uses his influence to have him made a sergeant in his company; he is on his way to a rifle match when the train breaks down in pouring rain. He is able to deal with the damage and drive the train to Serai Rajgara Junction where Swanson is waiting with the Down Mail, very angry at the delay. He is, however, delighted that his teaching has borne fruit and sees that Ottley gets a job as a driver. The story is followed by the poem 'The Nurses.'

9. The Son of His Father

Little Adam, son of Strickland and his wife, is beaten in front of his ayah, considers he has lost his honour, and would have thrown himself into a well had he not been prevented. Later, on the way to Dalhousie, he sees an opportunity to work a hoax on his father, whereby several people are arrested for the drunken foolishness of a stupid groom. The child feels that he has had an ample revenge on his father and thus squared the account.

10. An English School

This story tells of the United Service College and its surroundings, how the Head had been a master at Haileybury, how the prefects were allowed to smoke pipes, and gives some account of the lawful and unlawful goings-on. The germs of *Staley & Co.* are here set forth. The story is followed by 'A Counting-Out Song.'

21. Sea Warfare

This book is typical in its containing stories and poems. 'The Fringes of the Fleet' is the first chapter in *Sea Warfare*. This book has many sketches like 'Submarines,' 'Patrols,' 'Tales of the Trade,' 'Some Work in the Baltic,' 'Business in the Sea of Marmora,' 'Ravages and Repairs,' 'My Boy Jack,' 'Stories of the Battle,' 'The Night Hunt,' 'The Meaning of 'Joss,' 'The Minds of Men' and many verses.

22. Soldier Tales

Many stories of this collection like 'With the Night Mail' appeared in different books like *Soldiers Three*. 'The drums of the Fore and Aft' appeared in *Wee Willie Winkie*. 'The Man Who Was,' 'The Courting of Dinah Shadd' and 'The Incarnation of Krishna Malvany' appeared in *Life's Handicap*. 'The Taking of Lungtangpen' and 'The Madness of Private Other' appeared in *Plain Tales from the Hills*.

23. The Complete Staley & Co

This book has stories like 'The United Idolaters,' 'Regulus' and 'The Propagation of Knowledge' and these stories appeared in different books as the stories of *Soldiers Tales*.

24. Thy Servant A Dog

This small book has certain stories like 'Thy Servant a Dog,' 'The Great Play Hunt' and 'Toby Dog,' which have appeared elsewhere.

25. Abaft the Funnel

This is a book of short stories /sketches by Kipling.

1. Erastasius of the 'Whanghao'

This is the first story in the book. A tailless Japanese cat falls down a ventilator.

2. Her Little Responsibility

An outcast tells of his emigration to America and his downfall following the marriage of the English girl to whom he was engaged.

3. A Menagerie Abroad

The captain of the Madura caps the tale of a monkey that chased a man until he committed suicide with a yarn of a giraffe that got loose during a trip.

4. A Smoke of Manila

The story of the capture of nine men in the act of robbing a warehouse. The smoke of a Manila cigar betrayed the leader.

5. The Red Lamp

In this the narrator asleep on the forecastle dreams of collusion.

6. The Shadow of His Hand

Lot Vermilyea fought Dougherty for his daughter's hand; the old man was so delighted at being beaten that he had to fight him almost daily.

7. A Little More Beef

The story tells of life and death on a cattle-ranch in the west.

8. The History of a Fall

This is a skit apparently literally translated from the French. Sir Cyril Wollobie is a great man in Simla, but not so important when encountered on a bus in London when he has retired.

9. Griffiths the Safe Man

A Man travels in Japan with another who believed in locking everything in his baggage.

10. It!

This is a tale of sea-sickness in the China Sea.

11. A Fallen Idol

This is about how Trivey lost his title of Monumental Liar of the club because his tallest yarn was true.

12. New Brooms

This is about the difficulty of preventing disease and famine in India owing to the ignorance of the people and the Government's desire to respect the liberty of the subject.

13. Tiglath Pileser

This is the name of several Assyrian kings who ruled about 1120-727 B.C., and the thirteenth story in the book. Staveley sells the narrator an utter brute of a horse, which has a passion for breaking up carriages.

14. The Likes o' Us

The narrator finds Gunner Barnabas dealing with Private Shacklock, who is too drunk to be trusted with a shot-gun.

15. His Brother's Keeper

Revel of the Canal Department tells of his experiences preventing Stovey from committing suicide.

16. 'Lleipner,' Late 'Thurinda'

Jale, owner of Thurinda, is killed while riding another horse. He leaves the mare to the man who picks him up, but she is thereafter haunted by the grey horse that killed Jale.

17. A Supplementary Chapter

Trewinnard allows Mrs. Reiver to obtain undue influence over him, which brings him departmentally in conflict with Hatchett. Mrs. Mallow gets him out of trouble.

18. Chautauquaed

The Professor takes the narrator to Chautauqua, a large summer school founded by John H. Vincent and Lewis Miller for the instruction of Sunday-school teachers. Postgraduate courses are also available. The establishment consists of many cottages and an Assembly Hall on a lakeside site of some 165 acres. Kipling does not approve of it, but makes quite an amusing story of his visit.

19. The Bow Flume Cable-Car

This story is a sketch of life in a mining district in the US.

20. In Partibus

The author complains of the vice, climate, and general corruption of London and longs for India again.

21. Letters on Leave

Two letters addressed to an Army officer in Assam—John McHail—on the author's experiences in England.

22. The Adoration of the Mage

This is a story of a cab-ride in a London fog.

23. A Death in the Camp

The narrator hears of the death of Strangeways in his own house with his own people about him and compares it with those he knows of in India, where young men die suddenly, alone and with no provision for their families.

24. A Really Good Time

The narrator is in London and the intellectuals cannot make up their minds where to place him—is he of the Neo-Gynekalistic school or not?

25. On Exhibition

This is a story of an English literary circle. The author is the lion of the afternoon—in the absence of a bigger man.

26. The Three Young Men

In this sketch the author meets various precious young men who affect an interest in French novelists.

27. My Great and Only

The narrator wrote a music-hall song with the chorus 'And that's what the girl told the soldier!' It was a great success. Part of it is quoted in 'Love-o' Women.'

28. 'The Betrayal of Confidence'

The narrator is visited by a would-be dramatist who expects financial assistance.

26. The Man Who Would be King and Other Stories

This book has numerous stories like The Strange Ride of Morrowbie Jukes, The Phantom Rickshaw, Gemini, At Twenty-Two, The Education of Otese Yerees, The Hill of Illusion, Dray Wara You Dee, The Judgment of Dungara, With the Main Guard, In Flood Time, Only a Subaltern, Baa Baa, Black Sheep, At the Pit's Mouth, Black Jack, On the City Wall and The Man Who would be King. These stories have appeared in other books.

27. Kipling's Uncollected Stories

Kipling published many stories, and some of them appeared in magazines and they were left uncollected. A few of them appear to be sketches just. The following are some of these unpublished materials.

1. My First Adventure

It is a splendid combination of Poe-like delirium and of Burne-Jones-like humour, in which a schoolboy, walking in delirious sleep, saves an old countryman from drowning and is taken by the old man for a ghost.

2. Bisesa

So Bisesa's room looked out through the grated window into the narrow dark gully where the sun never came and where the buffaloes wallowed in the blue slime. She was a widow about fifteen years old. A young Sahib Trejago, wanders aimlessly and hears her singing. Bisesa was an endless delight to him. She was as ignorant as a bird; and her distorted versions of the rumours from the outside world that had reached her amused Trejago almost as much as her lisping attempts to pronounce his name—'Christopher.'

3. The Infant

The British had a threat from Russia. A phrase in one of Lockwood's letters home to England in 1885 may stand for the general mood of the whites, 'We are all agog about the prospect of war with Russia,' and it was certainly no jingo. How much the Russian menace to India continued to seem real may be judged by Le Gallienne's comment in his hostile book of 1900 about Kipling's work, 'When India belongs to Russia, no one will understand Kipling.' This story relates to the event.

4. The Boy

In fact, the few stories of officers that are really telling deal not with decent, ordinary, brave chaps like the infant and Bobby Wick, but with the misfits: with 'The Boy,' the subaltern who takes reprimands and set backs seriously and commits suicide, 'The Worm,' the over-mothered pretty boy is the butt of the mess. The Senior Subaltern meant no harm; but his chaff was coarse and he didn't quite understand where to stop.

5. Mrs Hauksbee Sits It Out

This story speaks about Mrs Hauksbee. In a pleasant little comedy which she devises, she enlists the Viceroy to distract a snobbish, disapproving aunt from her niece's happy courtship by asking her to be on a Dress Reform Committee. Louis Cornell adds, "She is a brilliant creation: mischievous, intelligent, fascinating, she is the embodiment of the spell that Simla cast over the young Kipling."

6. The Man's Wife

Kipling wrote many stories about Simla. 'The Man's Wife' is about a temporarily insane woman, swinging round the corners, with her eyes and her mouth open, and her head like the head of a Medusa.'

7. The Bride's Progress

But Benares visit was not without its imaginative effect. One aspect had an ephemeral life as a story for the *Pioneer* in 1888, later to be the only good story included in the suppressed volume, *The Smith Administration* of 1891. It is a pity that it was suppressed, for it is one of Kipling's most telling blows at a group of people he detested for their insufficient concern for India—the globe-trotters as we should say now.

8. The Outsider

'The Outsider' never gets beyond the point that a rector's son with private means makes a bad officer, while Thrupp, the vulgar trader from the South African mining Rand, makes a good private. The Regular Army in South Africa, in fact, is useless, the volunteers are the relevant men. This is an attack upon the English upper-middle class.

9. My Son's Wife

Kipling carried the map of Kim's journey in his mind exactly as he carried his map of Mowgli's jungle. In this he was in his good work like William Golding at his best, say in *The Inheritors.*

10. The Friendly Brook

Yet Kipling's real success with Sussex (apart from the high triumph of the Puck stories) came in 1914 with 'The Friendly Brook,' a story of Sussex farm life that has no external irrelevancies. Its opening of two men hedging has the only symbolic overtones, where the uncared-for hedge has grown 'all manner of trees' that suggests, but lightly, the anarchy.

11. Swept and Garnished

This is the story of Frau Ebermann's visitation in her comfortable Berlin flat by the spectres of five little Belgian children. It is the least horrible of the trio. It appeared early in 1915, hot-foot upon the terrible stories of the atrocities in Belgium, and is the most superficially propagandist. Yet it is a well-organised short tale. Frau Ebermann is affected by flue and five Belgian refugee children are killed by troops in her dream.

12. Beauty Spots

But 'Beauty Spots' and another farce of the same period, 'Aunt Ellen' have another purpose than attacking the village. The true hero of 'Beauty Spots' is the self-made man's son, who avenges his father by means of a practical joke involving a pig.

13. Proofs of Holy Writ

This is a dreadful conversation piece between Shakespeare and Ben Jonson on the translation of a few verses of Isaiah. The two elder poets discuss the latest proofs of the *Authorised Version of the Bible* sent down to them from the supposed authors at Hampton Court for their correction.

14. The Mark of Solomon

Kipling is quite as contemptuous of those English who suppose that they can acquire Indian culture equally superficially, as we see in a very funny *Pioneer* story of May 1888—'The Mark of Solomon,' in which he takes a Mrs Ringdove to an Indian village play so that she may get ideas for her oriental amateur production to be performed soon at a hill station. Her bewilderment at the heroine with a slight moustache and the Sudanese slave with his boy wife, whose jokes the gallery so adore, is beautifully told and makes this one of his un-reprinted Indian pieces that deserves to be placed in the collected canon of his work.

5

Rudyard Kipling's Poetry

Rudyard Kipling was a great English poet. He was the poet of the British Empire. He was a great balladeer. Some of his major collections are *Departmental Ditties* (1886), *Barrack-Room and Other Verses* (1890); *The Seven Seas* (1896); *The Five Nations* (1903) and *The Years Between* (1919).

Kipling as the Ballad Laureate of the Empire

Kipling began to write poetry in 1876 at his age of 11. He became world famous with the Nobel Prize 60 years later. Today he is respected for his poetry as well as short stories. He is remembered for a host of his poems like 'The Recessional,' 'Gunga Din,' 'Mandalay,' 'The Land,' 'Danny Deever,' 'The Mary Gloster' and for such quotable lines as these from 'The Ladies':

> ... The Colonel's Lady and Judy O'Grady
> Are sisters under their skins!

Edward Dowden observes, "The inescapable fact remains that if poetry is memorable speech, Kipling had the gift, used it, and was loved for it. He was the latest and the most prolific of the popular poets and perhaps the last in the 20th century. His popularity came from his felicitous handling of the lolloping and hence memorable meters of anapest and dactyl, his wide range of novel, picturesque material, and his clear distinction in each poem between right and wrong. Kipling ought to be pleased with the acoustic properties of the world; his voice fills the building. To have something to say, no doubt, helps a voice to carry far; people cease from chatter and look up; and Kipling, especially perhaps in his verse, has things to say; he says them in no halting or hesitating manner, but 'after the use of the English,' as he has himself described that use, 'in straight-flung words and few.'"

The sources of Kipling's style are the ballad, the music-hall song, and the psalms. The last gives him the long, prophetic line in which he sent home the dispatches in verse from the outskirts of the British Empire. Much more of his verse is accompanied by the choruses which perform the same iterative function. The ballads, of which 'Sestina of the Tramp-Royal' is typical, are among his simplest and best though not most memorable verse, such as the quietly noble ballad stanzas of 'The Veterans,' written for 'the gathering of survivors of the Indian Mutiny' in 1907, or the gentle raillery of 'The Three-Decker.' Many poems depend on prologues and epilogues set in italics which bring the poem round to a repetition of the opening lines, again for emphasis. The most characteristic feature of his verse is its introduction not so much of clichés like 'the White Man's Burden' in a poem of that title (addressed with considerable foresight to America) but of foreign terms. There are too many of these in the Indian section; but a large number of poems stemming from the South African war, the larger number celebrating British regiments use native and military terms easily, such as *kopje* and *voorlooper* in 'Two Kopjes.' The worst feature of the verse is the hackneyed cockney that his private soldiers speak; this dialect sounds better in prose.

Kipling's verse has affected the whole world. He is aptly called the ballad-laureate of the British Empire. He is a music-hall singer as if addressing a vulgar crowd in the vulgar tones which they expect for the coin they pay.

Kipling sometimes twangs the banjo; and with its tinka-tinka-tinka-tink he has not done ignobly; as a satirist he has with it 'jeered the fatted soul of things'; he has with it gallantly mocked defeat, and sung the song of lost endeavor. But he has also touched the solemn organ-stops, and it is precisely to such a poem as 'Recessional,' with its old prophetic strain, its warning against vain idols, and folly, and carnal pride, that the deepest response of the English race is made.

A curious feature of Kipling's work is that he published in a unique form, most of his books combining stories and poems, sometimes with the same titles, such as 'The Benefactors.' Both are so related in *Puck of Pook's Hill*, which contains ten stories and sixteen poems that it is a moot point whether his poems can be considered apart from the stories they illustrate or the events they celebrate.

Kipling's range of material was in facts, but not in ideas and ideals. The occupations of the folk heroes of his ballads, from the water-carrier in 'Gunga Din' to the ships' engineer in 'McAndrew's Hymn' to the Viceroy of India in 'One Viceroy Resigns: Lord Dufferin to Lord Lands-downe,' are exalted as the cogs of Empire, without his realizing, as George Orwell later pointed out, that an empire exists to preserve and extend an imbalance of trade.

Kipling wrote of the British life overseas, and also the Eastern life as none did it splendidly earlier. It is also with Kipling's Imperialism. This is not a flourish of rhetoric, nor intoxication with a doctrinaire theory, but is rather a gathering up of his myriad observations into an ideal unity. It has its origin in 'the little things a fellow cares about'; it clings much to kinship and to comradeship; it rises to civic loyalty and pride:

Surely in toil or fray
Under an alien sky,
Comfort it is to say:
'Of no mean city am I.'

The Master Plot observes, "This imperialism passes from the city to the birth-land, knit by closet ties of sonship to the mother-country; it includes the shepherd on his hill, the ploughman drawing his furrow, the miner delving the ore, the white sails and long smoke trails on all the seas, where the swift shuttles of the great loom ply backward and forward; it embraces finally the whole congeries of thought and dream and deed which, below the North Star, the Southern Cross, make up the majestic unity of Empire, of which unity the flag serves as emblem; and at every stage of development the emotions are fed by sights, by sounds, by the very scents of East and West, of land-breeze and sea-breeze, by all brave memories and all tender associations." Kipling loves his people yet chiding the mob and inept leaders as in 'The Islanders.' who blamed when the balance of trade was not in favor of England after World War I.

Kipling was born and bred on the British frontier where the issues were simplified, and his poems show his continual interest not only in India but also in South Africa, Canada, Australia, and New Zealand, as in 'The Parting of the Columns' and 'The Song of the Cities,' stanzas on sixteen capitals of the Empire in four continents; he responded to the stimulus at the margin of Empire but found the heart of it, London, too sophisticated for his abilities and too preoccupied to heed his strident warnings. Kipling was an aggressive poet, known for both racism and imperialism and orientlists think that his sense of the right and wrong is based on the external (not ethical). Kipling was always conscious of the greater mass of Empire behind him whether he was confronting the Indian or the English native, and the greater is always to be imposed on the lesser; he sings the greatness of Empire in many poems.

Kipling was a friend of the then American President Teddy Roosevelt and he addressed the following poem to him for the sake of defending the Anglo-American banner:

He made his clarion call to America:

Take up the White Man's Burden-
Send forth the best ye breed—
Go bind your sons to exile
To serve your captives' need;
To wait in heavy harness
On fluttered folks and wild –
Your new caught sullen peoples,
Half devil and half child.

Take up the White Man's Burden—
No iron rule of kings,

But toil of serf and sweeper—
The tale of common things.

The ports ye shall not enter,
The roads ye shall not tread;
Go, make them with your living,
And mark them with your dead!

'The White Man's Burden' speaks of the other great trust of preserving the voice that gave us Mowgli and Kim and the Puck stories and of ordering it into a voice of art, not an empty self-indulgent gipsy song.

Of course, Kipling meant every word of his Imperial beliefs and gave most of his surface active life to them, but that the excess of the tensions they produced, his political frenzy in the years 1900-1914, can only be fully understood if one grasps that his fear of anarchy of foreign tyranny, his hopes of a sane, ordered *Pax Britannica*, a *Pax Anglo-Saxonica*, or, at last, a *Pax Franco-Britannica* were also a reflection of the deep inner struggle between the anarchic, romantic childlike force of his creative impulse and the ordered, complex, at times almost self-defeating pressure of the craft he imposed upon it.

Kipling's métier was light journalistic verse; it became awkwardly and strenuously didactic when he used it as a vehicle for the urgent lessons he was trying to teach the English before it was too late, and his chief enemy was apathy and ignorance about the enormous area and population under the control of a ruling race on a small and distant island. If the authority of the knowledge he claimed turned to bullying, the sense of inescapable service was often elevated to sacrifice; he rejoices when a British Army Sergeant, 'Whatishisname,' reforms the Egyptian Army or when, as in 'Two Kopjes,' the British Army at last learns how to fight the Boer. Kipling weeps for the young men sent abroad untrained and forgotten, as in his commemoration of the veterans of the charge of the Light Brigade in 'The Last of the Light Brigade.' His greatest success was 'The Absent Minded Beggar,' set to music and making over a quarter million pounds for the relief of the dependents of the

British Tommy. This poem, which was recited on stage and music hall and in drawing-rooms all over the country, is an extraordinary reflection of Kipling's abiding concern for the decent treatment of Learoyd, Mulvaney and Ortheris, perhaps, with its acccent on the cockney Tommy, especially for Ortheris. It is, of course, a recruiting song. And also in its famous lines-

> Cook's son—Duke's son—son of a belted Earl—
> Son of a Lambeth publican—it's all the same today!

Several of his best poems illuminate that craft: 'The Story of Ung,' the dissatisfied Neolithic cave painter; 'The Conundrum of the Workshops,' in which the Devil insists, 'Is it Art?'; the famous 'nine and sixty ways of constructing tribal lays' in 'In the Neolithic Age.'

Lockwood Kipling published Kipling's early verse as *Schoolboy Lyric* in 1881. These poems are derivative and not so famous. 'An Echo' reflects that of Browning's craft of versification. The first stanza is as follows,

> Let the fruit ripen one by one
> On the sunny wall;
> who is it suffers. What harm is done?
> None at all.

Other poems are 'Ave Imperatrix' and the sonnet 'Discovery.' The former speaks of Kipling's early imperialist moods so brilliantly. The sonnet is as follows :

> We found him in the woodlands, she and I.
> Dead was our teacher of the silver tongue.
> Dead, whom we thought so strong he could not die,
> Dead with no sorrow loosed, with bow unstrung.
> And round the great grey blade that all men dread
> There crept the waxen white convolvulus,
> And the keen edge that once fell hard on us,
> Was blunt and notched, and rusted yellow red,

And he our master, the unconquered one,
Lay in the nettles of the forest place
With dreadful open eyes, and changeless face
Turned upward staring at the noonday sun.
Then we two bent above our old dead King:
And set the dry baked earth above the thing.

Westward Ho!

In September 1884 Kipling was a little uneasy because of the spread of cholera in Lahore. In such bleak times, he would visit the famous Shalimar Gardens, and he would remember Tennyson's description of the garden of the Princess Ida by moonlight. His book of parodies *Echoes* appeared in August 1884. Trix was also its collaborator. He sent a copy of this little book to Aunt Edith with the inscription:

Though the *Englishman* deride it,
Though the captious *Statesman* chide it,
Your dear judgment shall decide it
Yours alone.
For the good that in each line is,
From the title page to Finis
Is your own.

On the copy given to his mother he wrote 'To the Mater from Ruddy, August 22nd 1884.' *Echoes* was to acquire a high scarcity value : a correspondent informed the author that having bought a copy from the penny tray in a bookshop, he forgot it for seventeen years, selling it in 1929 for £328. Aided by a building society, he bought a house with the proceeds and called it "Echoes."

Departmental Ditties (1888)

Kipling's debut was made in a volume of verse, called *Departmental Ditties,* which continued to enjoy considerable popularity and has frequently been reprinted.

Kipling's first book *Departmental Ditties* was well received. It had three impressions soon. It reflected the thoughts and feelings of actual men and women. The poems are about the Anglo-Indian community: This is not an attractive society, however. These people, particularly in Simla, flirt and intrigue in their small, but real ways. An example is the Mayfair matron, playing her musical pawns at her matinees.

Sir William Hunter, a well-known Indian civil servant and chronicler thinks that though Kipling's people are few, and his society small, it is quite alive and kicking. He writes, "It is a curious little world to which he introduces us. The few English men of letters who have passed a portion of their lives in India, from Philip Francis to Macaulay, and the still rarer stray scholar from foreign parts, like Csoma de Koros, who has sojourned there, seem to have found Anglo-Indian society sometimes bizarre, and more often intolerably dull. It is this weariness of uncongenial social surroundings which gives to Sir Alfred Lyall's poems their note of peculiar pathos. In spite of the brilliance of his own career, India is ever to him the Land of Regrets. The merry little people who flirt through Mr. Kipling's ditties look out on the scene with altogether different eyes."

Thus Mr. Potiphar Gubbins, the hero of one poem, gets hoisted over the heads of his brother engineer by the fascinations of his wife—an attractive and a complaisant young person who, for reasons of her own, has married Potiphar, although he is 'coarse as a chimpanzee.' Another piece relates how Mr. Sleary, an impecunious subaltern secretly engaged to a lady in England, obtains an appointment by proposing to the daughter of an Indian official. Having secured the post, he frightens his fiancée Number Two out of the engagement by pretending to have epileptic fits, then nobly marries fiancée Number One, and lives with her happily ever after on the produce of his fraud.

In the story of Uriah, an officer is dispatched to Quetta and dies there, in order that his wife may more freely amuse herself at Simla with the senior who got him sent out of the way. But Kipling handles each situation with a light touch and a gay malice, which make it difficult to be quite sure whether he sincerely admires his pretty marionettes, or whether he is not inwardly chafing and raging at the people among whom he is condemned to live. He very calmly expounds the scheme of creation in his curious Anglo-Indian world.

The opens with the prelude:

I have eaten your bread and salt.
I have drunk your water and wine.
The deaths ye died I have watched beside,
And the lives ye led were mine.

Andrew Lang who reviewed the book for the *Longman's Magazine* admired the book and its satirist poet. He appreciated the poems 'Who shall doubt the sacred hid,' and the tale of Jones and the tale in 'In Spring-time.' In the first, Kipling satirizes the white people as if monkeys governing India. Look at this:

'Who shall doubt' the secret hid
Under Cheops' pyramid
Was that the contractor 'did'
Cheops out of several millions?

Or that Joseph's sudden rise
To Comptroller of Supplies,
Was a fraud of monstrous size
On King Pharaoh's civilians?

Here we learn how Ahasuerus Jenkins, merely because he 'had a tenor voice of super Santley tone,' became a power in the state.

The tale of Jones who left his newly-wedded wife and went to the Hurrom Hills above the Afghan border had the irritation, because his tales (letters) were read by General Bangs,

With damnatory dash and dot he'd heliographed his wife
Some interesting details of the General's private life.

Still another one is the tale in the poem 'In Spring-time.' The first stanza speaks of the Englishman's nostalgia:

> My garden blazes brightly with the rose-bush and the peach,
>
> And the *koil* sings above it, in the *siris* by the well,
>
> From the creeper-covered trellis comes the squirrel's chattering speech,
>
> And the blue jay screams and flutters where the cheery *sat-bhai* dwell.
>
> But the rose has lost its fragrance, and the *koil's* note is strange;
>
> I am sick of endless sunshine, sick of blossom-burdened bough.
>
> Give me back the leafless woodlands where the winds of Springtime range—
>
> Give me back one day in England, for it's Spring in England now!

Andrew Lang thinks, "On the whole, these are melancholy ditties."

Barrack-Room Ballads and Other Verses (1892)

This is a collection of Kipling's poems, published in 1892. The book has some of the poet's best poems. Influenced by Robert Browning, Kipling uses the dramatic monologue; Irish and Scottish accents are heard as well as comic Cockney dialect. The popular traditions of the ballad and street-song help give the speakers representative rather than individualized voices. The rhythms of the hymn tune or, in 'Mandalay,' the music-hall song can be felt. Looking beneath the patriotic surface of poems like 'The Widow at Windsor,' recent criticism has begun to acknowledge the satirical force and originality of Kipling's depiction of the harsh life of the ill-paid common soldier.

First the book had two divisions, exposing the good and the bad of versification. Kipling's poetry is true and fine. The other verses of the title are said to be rhetorical and less true.

These poems are written in the dialect of the common

soldier, of Tommy Atkins. They speak of Wordsworth's 'Happy Warrier.' As Smollett in prose and Dibdin in verse wrote of the Army, Kipling wrote of the army of the British empire. There are twenty of these ballads; and there can hardly be said to be one failure among them, although two or three are of marked inferiority to the rest, and although the greater number look poor by the side of the four or five masterpieces. The most noticeable thing about them, on a first reading, is their swinging, marching music. The accents and best of the verse fall true and full, like the rhythmical tramp of men's feet. Take such rhythms and measures as,

> For it was—'Belts, belts, belts, an' that's one for you!'
> An' it was—'Belts, belts, belts, an' that's done for you!'

Or as

> When first under fire, an' you're wishful to duck,
> Don't look nor take 'eed at the man that is struck,
> Be thankful you're livin,' and trust to your luck,
> And march to your front like a soldier.
> Front, front, front, like a soldier,
> Front, front, front, like a soldier,
> Front, front, front, like a soldier,
> So-older of the Queen!

Or, best of all, as

> On the road to Mandalay,
> Where the old Flotilla lay;
> Can't you 'ear their paddles chunkin' from Rangoon to Mandalay?
> On the road to Mandalay,
> Where the flyin' fishes play,
> An' the dawn comes up like thunder outer china crost the bay!

These ballads deal with a few marked incidents, experiences, and emotions from the private soldier's point of view; some general and unlocalised, but most peculiar to military life in the East.

Tommy Atkins is presented to the ordinary reader, with no apologies and with no adornments. For example, look at it,

> We aren't no thin re 'eroes, nor we aren't no blackguards too,
>
> But single men in barracks, most remarkable like you.

He sings: in a genial and, at the same time, an acute expostulation with the people, who exalt him in war but despise him in peace.

Kipling's description of the 'Fuzzy-Wuzzy,' the Soudanese is as follows:

> So 'ere's to you, Fuzzy-Wuzzy, at your 'ome in the Soudan;
>
> You're a pore benighted 'eathen, but a first-class fightin' man;
>
> An' 'ere's to you, Fuzzy-Wuzzy, with your 'ayrick 'ead of 'air –
>
> You big black boundin' begger—for you broke a British square!

The most poetical is his description of 'Danny Deever,' the one hanged for shooting a comrade:

> 'Is cot was right-'and cot to mine,' said Files-on-Parade.
>
> 'E's sleepin' out an' far to-night,' the Colour-Sergeant said.
>
> 'I've drunk 'is beer a score o' times,' said Files-on-Parade.
>
> 'E's drinkin' bitter beer alone,' the Colour-Sergeant said.

And perhaps the most winning of them all is 'Mandalay': the Burmese girl and her lover, the British soldier, his sickness and disgust at London and England after those old times in the East,

I'm learnin' 'ere in London what the ten-year soldier tells,
'If you've 'eard the East a-callin,' you won't never 'eed naught else'

which would seem to be the experience of Mr. Kipling also.

These ballads give a picture of life and character more estimable and praiseworthy for many rugged virtues of generosity, endurance, heartiness, and simplicity, than are the lives and characters of many 'gentlemen of England, who stay at home at ease.'

Kipling's 'Other Verses' of the book are less pleasant for reading. Their rhetorical energy is splendid. At times they ring true to nature; but for the most part they are spasmodic, ranting, overstrained. For example, the volume opens with a poem to the praise of one whose death Kipling has an especial right to lament, while all lovers of literature have also their regrets. It imagines the great dead in a Valhalla of the windiest sort. There, beyond the farthest ways of sun, or comet, or star, or 'star-dust,' 'live such as fought, and sailed, and ruled, and loved, and made our world.' There 'they sit at wine with the Maidens Nine and the Gods of the Elder Days'; and

'Tis theirs to sweep through the ringing deep where Azrael's outposts are,
Or buffet a path through the Pit's red wrath when God goes out to war
Or hang with the reckless Seraphim on the rim of a red-maned star.

There 'they whistle the Devil to make them sport who know that sin is vain;' but that is not all:

And ofttimes cometh our wise Lord God, master of every trade,
And tells them tales of His daily toil of Edens newly made;
And they rise to their feet as He passes by gentlemen unafraid.
It is a Paradise, an Elysium, a Valhalla, of 'the Strong Men.'

In some of the finest pieces Kipling is a prey to the grandiose aspect of things. 'The English Flag' in which the Winks of the World witness to England's greatness, is grievously spoiled by exaggeration of tone. Of the remaining poems, far the best are 'The Ballad of East and West,' a thing to stir the blood like a trumpet; the 'Conundrum of the Workshops,' a charming satire upon critics and criticism; and the ballads of the 'Clampherdown' and the 'Bolivar.'

> 'The Ballad of East and West' begins thus majestically:
>
> Oh, East is East, and West is West and never the twain shall meet,
>
> Till Earth and Sky stand presently at God's great Judgment Seat;
>
> But there is neither East nor West, Border, nor Breed, nor Birth,
>
> When two strong men stand face to face, though they come from the ends of the earth!
>
> This poem is quite shaking.

Oscar Wilde writes of this about the book: "Of late years, however, Mr. Kipling has put forward, in a great variety of directions essays in verse which deserve much higher consideration. He has indulged the habit of prefixing to his prose stories fragments of poems which must be his own, for there is nobody else to claim them. Some of these are as vivid and tantalizing as the tiny bits we possess of lost Greek tragedians." He quotes a 'barrack-room ballad' used to introduce the story of 'The Madness of Private Ortheris':

> Oh! where would I be when my froat was dry?
>
> Oh! where would I be when the bullets fly?
>
> Oh! where would I be when I come to die?
>
> Why,
>
> Somewheres anigh my chum,
>
> If' 'e's liquor 'e'll give me some,
>
> If I'm dying 'e'll 'old my 'ead,
>
> An' 'e'll write 'em 'ome when 'I'm dead.

God send us a trusty chum!

Author Quiller—Couch observes: "For the *Barrack Room* volume does indeed contain verse for which 'splendid' is the only term—so radiantly it glitters with incrustations of barbaric words. It has genius in it, of course, in the grim effectiveness." He quotes the poem 'Danny Deever':

'What's that so black agin the sun?' said Files-on-Parade.

'It's Danny fightin' ard for life,' the Colour-Sergeant said.

'What's that that whimpers over 'ead?' said Files-on-Parade.

'It's Danny's soul that's passin' now,' the Colour-Sergeant said.

For they're done with danny Deever, you can 'ear the quickstep play,

The Regiment's in column, an' they're marchin' us away;

Ho! The young recruits are shakin', an' they'll want their beer today,

After hangin' Danny Deever in the mornin'!

and in the simple solemnity of the refrain,

Ford, ford, ford o'Kabul river.

Ford o'Kabul river in the dark!

In every line of 'East and West'—in almost every line of 'The English Flag,' and throughout in the stirring 'Envoi,' a poem that takes you by the heart and shakes you. But the first reflection to which this volume gives rise is that which Mr. Henley once made upon Dickens. W. D. Howells once said, "In the new *Barrack-Room Ballads* here, there is, to be sure, nothing with the peculiar thrill of 'Danny Deever,' nothing with the peculiar homesick, heartsick touch of 'Mandalay,' but there are other things as moving and as true, with a plunge of tragedy into depths which were not sounded before, however the surface was troubled." The *Ballads* thus introduced are twenty-one in number, of which the majority are descriptive of whatever is basest and most brutal in the character of the

British mercenary. One deals, naturally enough, with the want of sympathy shown in public-houses to Tommy Atkins in time of peace, as contrasted with the enthusiasm for him in time of war; another, entitled 'Cells,' begins as follows:

> I've a head like a concertina: I've a tongue like
> a button-stick:
> I've a mouth like an old potato, and I'm more than
> a little sick.
> But I've had my fun with the Corp'ral's Guard: I've
> made the cinders fly,
> And I'm here in the Clink for a thundering drink
> and blacking the Corp'ral's eye;

it is, in fact, the glorification of the familiar episode of 'drunk and resisting the guard.' In an equally sublime spirit is conceived the ballad 'Loot,' beginning:

> If you've ever stole a pheasant-egg be'ind the keeper's back
> If you've ever snigged the washin' from a line;
> If you've ever crammed a gander in your bloomin' aversack,
> You will understand this little song of mine;

and the verses are indeed, with their brutal violence and their hideous refrain, only too sadly understandable. Worse still, in its horrible savagery, is the piece called 'Belts,' which is the apotheosis of the soldier who uses his belt in drunken fury to assault civilians in the streets, and which has this agreeable refrain:

> But it was: 'Belts, belts, belts, an' that's one for you!'
> An' it was 'Belts, belts, belts, an' that's done for you!'
> O buckle an' tongue
> Was the song that we sung
> From Harrison's down to the Park!

Sir Arthur Quiller-Couch observes, "For the *Barrack Room* volume does indeed contain verse for which 'splendid' is the only term-so radiantly it glitters with incrustations of barbaric words. It has genius in it, of course, in the grim effectiveness (for instance) of 'Danny Deever'.

Kingsley Amis observes "*The Barrack Room Ballads* were a quite new venture, indeed without precedent (or descendant) in English poetry as regards both style and content. The Cockney dialect and the heavy rhythms of the music, hall song were used for serious purposes, and the life of the common soldier furnished the themes: parades, women, action, beer, leave, natives, officers, NCOs, sun, cholera, cells, discharge. Out of these conventionally unpromising elements Kipling produced among others the most harrowing poem in our language ('Danny Deever') and a love lyric ('Mandalay') unique for what a critic in 1900 called its 'wonderful transmuting use of the commonest material.' A powerful underlying message of the ballads is that freedom, order, and learning and everything we call civilization depends in the last resort on the activities of a few score thousand commonplace, ignorant, vulgar, violent men whom it is all too easy to despise."

Critics say that the success of the book was immediate. The book became as popular as Shakespeare's plays. Before the end of the century the poems were being recited or sung in music-halls and at smoking-concerns.

The Seven Seas (1896)

Charles Eliot Norton of Harvard observed of this book: "But in spite of omissions and inclusions alike to be regretted, *The Seven Seas* contains a notable addition to the small treasury of enduring English verse, an addition sufficient to establish Mr. Kipling's right to take place in the honorable body of those English poets who have done England service in strengthening the foundations of her influence and of her fame. The dominant tone of his verse is indeed the patriotic; and it is the tone of the new patriotism, that of imperial England, which holds as one all parts of her wide-stretched empire, and binds them close in the indissoluble bond of common motherhood, and with the ties of common convictions, principles, and aims, derived from teachings and traditions of the motherland, and expressed in the best verse of her poets. It is this passionate, moral, imperial patriotism that inspires the first poem in the book, 'The Song of the English,' and which recurs again and again through its pages."

'The Song of the English' is one of the best songs set to music. It speaks of the Englishman's empire and his greatness:

> Fair is our lot. Oh! Goodly is our heritage!
> (Humble ye, my people, and be fearful in your mirth!)
> For the Lord our God most High,
> He hath made the deep as dry,
> He hath smote for us a pathway to the ends of all the earth!
> Yea, though we sinned—and our rulers went from righteousness—
> Deep in all dishonour though we stained our garments' hem.
> Oh! Be ye not dismayed,
> Though we stumbled and we strayed,
> We were led by evil counselors—the Lord shall deal with them!

The passion for the sea, the mastery of its terrors, the confident but distrustful familiarity with it of the English seaman, have never had such expression as Kipling has given to them here. From his splendid paean of 'The English Flag'-'What is the flag of England, winds of the world declare,' to 'The Song of the English'-

> We have fed out sea for a thousand years,
> And she calls us, still unfed,
> Though there's never a wave of all her waves
> But marks our English dead.

Kipling's imagination, dwells with vivifying emotion on the heroic combat-now victories, now defeats of his race with the winds and the waves from which they draw their strength. All that belongs to the story of man upon the sea- the line-of-battle ship, the merchantman, the tramp steamer, the derelict, the little cargo-boats, the lighthouse, the bell-buoy-has its part in his verse of human experience.

Such a poem as 'McAndrew's Hymn' is a masterpiece of realism in its clear insight into real significance of common things, and in its magnificent expression of it. Here Kipling is at his best, revealing the admirable quality of his imaginative vision and obeying the true command of his genius.

THE FIVE NATIONS (1903)

This book appears to be a series of verse sketches. The poems deal with a variety of themes regarding Kipling's globe-trotting. The major themes are his obsession with India, his rambling about British imperialism and the Boer war in South Africa and the hegemony of the West everywhere in the world. He also speaks of man's duties.

Let us analyses Kipling's myriad poems about South Africa and its Boer war that maddened the English people at the close of the 19th century. It maddened Kipling more so. His poem 'Bridge-Guard in a Karroo' is verse describing the feelings of the sentries on the bridges during the Boer War. 'Dirge of Dead Sisters' is in praise of the nurses who died in the Boer War. 'M. I' is a splendid ballad of the Boer War, telling of a soldier who has become an expert soldier. 'Columns' speaks of the same war. 'Half Ballad of Waterwal' is about a captive's experience in the war. 'The Parting of the Columns' is about a parting platoon of soldiers. 'Piet' is about soldier's admiration for Boer's bravery. 'The Return' speaks of a soldier's wider experience after this. 'Stellenbosch' is a song of the war; any particularly incompetent generals were sent to Stellenbosch, capital of the district of the same name, about thirty miles east of Cape Town, where they would be unable to do much damage at the remount depot. 'Two Kupjes' is about fieldwork in the war. 'The Settler' is lines on the end of the Boer War. It speaks about the importance of dwelling in peace and tilling the land. 'The Truce of the Boer' warns of Russian's threat. 'South Africa' is a verse on the anniversary of Majuba Hill. 'General Joubert' is a general tribute to the Boer leader who died in March 1900. 'The

Burial' is verses on Cecil Rhodes, the founder of Rhodesia who died in 1902.

In 'The Islanders' the poet castigates his countrymen for their folly in permitting the Army and Navy to be incapable of completing the campaigner in South Africa without the help of strong contingents from the empire, and warns them to be careful.

'The Bell Buoy' is a musing about a bell. 'The Broken Men' is a lament of those who have left England for good reason. 'Buddha at Kamakura' is verses forming chapter headings in Kim. 'Cruisers' speaks of man's duties. 'The Destroyers' is a verse on the dangerous crafts. 'The Dykes' is a song of sea-defenses and it has patriotic feelings. 'Et Dona Ferentes' speaks of nations. 'The Explorer' is a ballad of the man who does not believe 'There's no use in going further' and finds rich land beyond the ranges. 'The Fact of the Young Man' is a song of those who must 'go away from here to Canada, the Baltic, the Far-East etc. 'Our Lady of the Snows' is a tribute to Canada.

'The Old Men' is a cry of those who live long and endure. 'The Palace' is a parable of a kingly builder who began a palace, only to find the remains of another, uncompleted, at lower level. He carved the legend he found there on his own uncompleted work. 'The Wage Slave' criticizes those who work only for wages. 'White Horses' is a song of the sea. 'The Young Queen' is about the inauguration of the Commonwealth of Australia in January 1901.

In 'The Peace of Dives,' Dives, the rich man is recalled from Hal and brings peace to the world. He says no nation may make war as each is indebted to the other. He then waits for the Devil to upset matters. 'The Pharugh and the Sergeant' is about the rise of the Egyptian Army with the help of British non-commissioned officers, personified as Sergeant Whatisname. In 'The Sea and the Hills' the seamen love their sea as Hillmen love their hills. 'The Second Voyage is Settler' is an allegory of settled matrimony. 'The Song of the Wise children' speaks of people yearning to leave the fogs of the UK and return to their own peace. 'Sussex' is a stirring tribute to the beautiful country in which the poet chose to live:

God gives all men all earth to love,
But since man's heart is small,
Ordains for each one spot shall prove
Beloved over all.
Each to his choice, and I rejoice
The lot has fallen to me
In a fair ground—in a fair ground—
Yea. Sussex by the sea.

'The White Man's Burden' is a famous poem setting forth the responsibility the European has for those who have not had his advantages. Loot at the first stanza:

Take up the White Man's burden—
Send forth the best ye breed—
Go bind your sons to exile
To serve your catpives' need;
To wait in heavy harness
On fluttered folk and wild—
Your new-caught, sullen peoples,
Half devil and half child

In 'A Recessional' the poet did not appreciate the art of a certain actress whom his son adored. Both the poet and the actress lost their sons in the 1914 war, but she continued to charm her audiences even though her heart was breaking. The poet changes his opinion, recalling how she used to delight his son and others on their rare spells of leave. Look at the poet's outburst:

God of our fathers, known of old,
Lord of our far-flung battle-line,
Beneath whose awful Hand we hold
Dominion over palm and pine—
Lord God of hosts, be with us yet,
Lest we forget—lest we forget!

The book *The Five Nations* has another section of poems called 'Service Songs.' 'Boots' speaks of marching. 'Chant Pagan' speaks of a British Soldier after Boer War, finding England too small and his duties too trivial. He returns to South Africa for a job. On the other hand, 'Lichtenberg' is about a soldier's nostalgia for his country England. 'The Married Man' speaks about a householder.

The Years Between

This is Kipling's last book of light verses. The poems are about many themes that beset the poet in his last years.

One predominant theme of the verses is about the World War I. 'The Benefactors' as a poem speaks of soldier's mind in the war. 'The Choice' is the poem on the entry of the US into the World War I. 'A Dead King' is a tribute to King Edward VII. 'A Death Bed' is a gruesome verse on the various ways men die in war. 'The Declaration of London' treats the theme of Edward VII's coronation. 'En-do' is about the deaths in World War I. So is the case with 'Epitaphs of the war.'

'For All We Have and Are' calls upon the people for World War I. The poet admires France in 'France.' In 'Gehazi' the poet indicts the Liberal Rufus Isaacs. 'Gethsemane' is a characteristic verse on World War I. look at it:

The Garden called Gethsemane
In Picardy it was,
And there the people came to see
The English soldiers pass.
We used to pass—we used to pass
Or halt, as it might be,
And ship our masks in case of gas
Beyond Gethsemane

The Garden called Gethsemane
It held a pretty lass,
But all the time she talked to me

I prayed my cup might pass.
The officer sat on the chair,
The men lay on the grass,
And all the time we halted there
I prayed my cup might pass.

It didn't pass— It didn't pass—
It didn't pass from me.
I drank it when we met the gas
Beyond Gethesmane.

So is the case with 'The Holy War.' 'The Houses' speaks of England's good relations with its Dominions. 'Justice' is a prayer for peace after World War I. 'The Irish Guards' praises that Irish guards. Kipling wrote a verse on Lord Roberts on his death. 'Mesopotamia' is a lament for those who died in that war in 1917. In 'My Boy Jack' the poet consoles a mother whose son is lost in World War I. Even the poem 'A Nativity' has a similar theme. 'The Outlaws' is a bitter verse on those responsible for the World War I. 'The Question' is about America's attitude towards World War I. 'The Rowers' speaks of Germany which wanted England to help her collect tax from Venezuela. 'Russia to the Pacifists' is a harsh criticism on Englanders who do not understand themselves. 'A Song at Cock-Crow' is lines on St. Peter's denial of Our Lord applied in 1918.

'A Song in Storm' is a naval poem of 1914-18 with chorus 'The game is more than the player of the game, 'The ship is more than the crew.' 'The Song of the Lathes' speaks of a woman who lost her husband and son in World War I. 'Things and the Man' is lines on Joseph Chamberlain. 'Ulster' is about Ireland. 'The Verdicts' is on the battle of Jutland. 'The Veterans' is about the survivors of the Indian Mutiny 1857. 'The Virginity' speaks of stability.

'The Craftsman' speaks about the origin of Shakespeare's plays. 'Dedication' as verse compares his verse to pearls and rubies. 'The Female of the Species' is about woman who is deadlier than men. 'The Hyaenas' speaks of those animals, who eat dead animals. 'Mary's Son' is a verse about man-sea relations. 'Natural Theology' speaks of the saying 'As was the Sowing, so the reaping. . .' 'The Oldest Song' is lines on an inconstant lover. 'A Pilgrim's Way' is about good life. 'The Pro-Consults' speaks of those who labor for the posterity. 'The Song of Martha' speaks of two classes of people: those who work and those who simply consume it.

What Kipling did was he attacked inefficiency and novelty and glorified the difficult work of the laboring few. For his mass he used the British Empire at its apogee; his individual hero is 'Thomas Atkins,' the British soldier to whom he formally dedicated *Barrack-Room Ballads* and, in spirit, all his work.

Kipling is known for his craftsmanship. How he wrote verse we do not know, but we enjoy reading them. Simply he wrote them very well. His language, style, folk imagery drawn from various sources, musical touch and the like are superb. Kipling had the pride of his craft. G.K. Chesterton observes: "... The first and fairest thing to stay about Kipling is that he has borne a brilliant part in recovering the lost provinces of poetry. He has not been frightened by that brutal materialistic air which clings only to words; he has pierced through to the romantic, imaginative matter of the things themselves. He has perceived the significance and philosophy of steam and of slang. Steam may be, if you like, a dirty by-product of science. Slang may be, if you like, a dirty by-product of language. But at least he has been among the few who saw the divine parentage of these things, and knew that where there is smoke there is fire-that is, that wherever there is the foulest of things, there also is the purest. Above all, he has had something to say, a definite view of things to utter, and that always means that a man is fearless and faces everything. For the moment we have a view of the universe, we possess it."

T.S. Eliot who edited Kipling's verse with admiration said: "Mr. Kipling is a laureate without laurels. He is neglected celebrity. The arrival of a new book of his verse is not likely to stir the slightest ripple on the surface of our conversational intelligentsia. He has not been crowned by the elder generation; malevolent fate has not even allowed him to be one of the four or five or six greatest living poets. A serious contemporary has remarked of the present volume that 'in nearly all our poetical coteries the poetry of Kipling has long been anathema, with filed sports. Imperialism and public schools.' This is wide of the mark. Mr. Kipling is not anathema; he is merely not discussed. Most of our discerning critics have no more an opinion on Mr. Kipling than they have on the poetry of Mr. John Oxenham. The mind is not sufficiently curious, sufficiently brave, to examine Mr. Kipling. Yet the admired creator of Bouvard and Pecuchet would not have overlooked the Kipling *dossier*."

Kipling has been considered in many aspects- the Bard of Tommy Atkins, the exponent of Anglo-Indian life, the Laureate of the Empire, the poet of Wheel and Axle, Lever and Screw, and a most compelling Voce from the Jungle.

6

Rudyard Kipling's Non-Fictional Prose Travelogues, Letters and Autobiography

Kipling has done a lot of prose writing. He has written books like *A Book of Words*, a book of speeches and address. He has written many books of travel letters and his superb autobiography.

A Book of Words

This book contains Kipling's speeches and addresses on various matters of life and art. It begins with his speech on literature. He spoke to the Artist's General Benevolent Institution in 1907 about the claims of art. He spoke on values of life at McGill University, Montreal in 1907. 'Imperial Relations' is his speech to the Canadian Club, Toronto in 1907. 'Growth and Responsibility' is his speech at the Canadian Club, Winnipeg in 1907. 'The Handicap of Letters' is his speech to the Royal Literary Fund in 1908. 'A Doctor's Work' is his speech at the Middlesex Hospital in 1908. 'The Spirit of the Navy' is his address at a Naval Club in 1908. 'The Ritual of Govt' is his speech at Brighton in 1910. 'The Verdict of Equals' is his speech to the Royal Geographical Society in 1912. 'The Uses of Reading' was his speech at Wellington College in 1912. 'Some Aspects of Travel' was his speech to the Royal Geographical Society in 1914. 'The War and the Schools' was his address at Winchester College in 1915. 'The Magic Square' was his speech to the Household Brigade O. C. C. in 1917. 'The First Sailor' was his speech to the officers of an East Coast Patrol in 1918. 'England and the English' was his speech to the Royal Society of St. George in 1920. 'The Scot and the War' was his speech at Edinburg University in 1920. 'The Virtue of France' was his speech to the Sorbonne University in 1921. 'The Thesis' was his speech at a banquet at the Sorbonne again in 1921. 'A Return to Civilization' was a speech at Strassbourg University in 1921. 'The Waking from Dreams' also. 'Surgeons and the Soul' was his speech at the Royal College of Surgeons in 1923. 'Independence' was a Rectorial address at St. Andrews in 1923. 'The Classics and the Sciences' was his speech to University College, Dublin in 1923. 'Work in the Future' was his address to the United Kingdom Chamber of Shipping in 1925. 'Stationary' was his speech to the stationer's company in 1925. 'Fiction' was his speech to the Royal Literary Society in 1926. 'The Spirit of the Latin' was his speech at Rio de Janeiro in 1927. 'Our Indian Troops in France' was his speech at La Bassee in 1917.

From Sea to Sea (1899)

This is a book about Kipling's correspondences and occasional articles written for the *Civil and Military Gazette* and the *Pioneer* in India from 1887 to 1889. The book has two volumes. Vol I. has *Letters of Marqhe* i to xix and *From Sea to Sea*, i to xxiv. The contents with details of vol 2 are as follows: 'The City of Dreadful Night, Among the Railway Folk, The Giridih Coal-Fields, The Smith Administration, Hunting a Miracle, A Letter from Golam Singh, The Writing of Yakub Khan, A King's Ashes, The Bride's Progress, 'A District of Play,' 'What It Comes To' and The Opinions of Gunner Barnadas.

The official publication of Kipling's Indian, Asian and American letters of that time as *From Sea to Sea,* from which some of the more violent disparagement of America had been left out, could only have partly removed the general impression of an angry, hostile young man.

Kipling, as an imperialist, tried to impose racial and European views on America as well. England and America, the two great Anglo-Saxon lands could find a common purpose in the better ordering of the world by their superior powers of obedience and self-sacrifice.

The failure of the United States of reality to answer to this dream was only part of a long process of disillusionment that

Kipling, with other British visionaries, was to experience in the last years of his life.

But it cannot also be neglected completely as it has been by most writers on Kipling. Some critics, underestimating the potential force and the actual intellectual capacities of what used to be called right-wing Imperialism, but is now more satisfactorily named right-wing radicalism, in Edwardian England, perhaps because it never won power and failed in its aims, have preferred to ignore this aspect of Kipling's thinking, dismissing his political ideas as silly and immature. All revolutionary views, whether of the left or right, are silly and immature unless and until they succeed. Kipling's, of course, where they are successful, filtered through the imagination. Critics think he was an artist, not a thinker.

Nor was the practical programme 'silly.' These critics forget, that if Joseph Chamberlain had not suffered a stroke at the height of his powers or if Bonar Law had been a less unsuitable leader, Kipling might have been the Laureate of a powerful British imperial movement however short-lived that power would necessarily have been. His extreme views were shared with differences of detail by the intellectuals of the right of his time—by the *Spectator* and the *National Review,* by the St Loe Stracheys, Amery, Milner, the Maxses.

Kipling (like his more intellectual associates) conceived of society in terms nearer to the great Continental social theorists, Weber, Pareto and Durkhem, laying emphasis on groups within society rather than the historical or ethical development of society as a whole. But there is a danger in this approach to Kipling through his ideas. He disliked democracy, because it fostered the herd mentality and lawful protest.

Both writers Mar Beerbohm and George Orwell has criticized Kipling harshly for this. It is this that Professor Alan Sandison, Kipling's harshest yet finally most completely appreciative critic, has emphasized in his essay, "The Artist and the Empire." From the moment that Kipling left India in 1889 one part of him looked at everything he saw and asked: is it to be the corner-stone in the Anglo-Saxon fortress (from 1911 or so he would increasingly have been willing to say Anglo-French fortress), that must be built to shore up the world against the forces of despotism, anarchy, frivolity, meaninglessness.

India, from which it all started, soon had to be forgotten, since his respect for its old native culture gave it no place in this new white man's world. England, when he reached it, was found to be built upon shifting sands. America, above all, was to remain a delusive hope for most of the rest of his life.

A Fleet in Being

This book is the notes of Kipling's two trips with the channel squadron, collected from the *Morning Post* of 5, 7, 8, 9, 10 and 11 November 1898, published the same year with an illustration by Norman Wilkinson on the front cover.

The New Army in Training

This book is a collection of Kipling's reprint of articles, first published in *The Daily Telegraph* of Dec. 7, 10, 14, 19, 21 and 24, 1914.

France at War

This is a book of articles by Kipling. *France at War* has the following six chapters.

1. 'On the Frontier of Civilization'
2. 'A Nation's Spirit'
3. 'Battle Spectacle and a Review'
4. 'The Land that Endures'
5. 'Trenches on a Mountain Side'
6. 'The Common Task'

The Irish Guards in The War

Kipling loved the Irish, and its regiment called The Irish Guards in which his own son John Kipling found and died in France during the World War I in 1914. Kipling wrote this book about the history of the Irish Guards in two volumes. The Volume One has chapters like 'Mons to La Bassee,' 'La Bassee to Laventie,' 'The Salient to the Somme,' 'The Somme to

Gouzeaucourt' and 'Arras to the Armistice.' Volume Two has chapters like 'Lous and the First Autumn,' 'The Salient and the Somme,' 'Rancourt to Bourlon Wood' and 'Arras to the End.'

The critic Edmund Blunden did not like the book. He observesd, "The fact is that Kipling appears not perfectly to understand the pandemonium and nerve-strain of war; it seldom surges up in his pages of that appalling misery which brought seasoned men down in the shell holes beyond Thiepval, as they went up to relieve the Schwaben Redoubt, crying, and whacked to the wide. He makes constant stern attempts at actuality; he constantly falls short, in expressions merely strained, in sheer want of comprehension."

Kipling's unwritten epitaphs to John are to be seen in the two grinding public tasks he undertook after his son's death—the long, arduous and searing preparation (written with agony and bloody sweat, Miss Ponton tells us) of *The Irish Guards in Wartime*, which was not finished until 1923, and the inspection of war graves, first in Flanders, and then as far afield as Gallipoli, Palestine and Mesopotamia, that he undertook as a Commissioner of War Graves in the years after the war. By using his impressions of the Flander cemeteries in the celebrated story 'The Gardener' (1926), he was able to come closer to his feelings for his dead son than in any other fiction.

LETTERS OF TRAVEL (1920)

From Tideway to Tideway (1892) is the first section in this book. In Sight of Monadnock, the first essay describes Kipling's arrival at New York by sea and his tour of the city; trip to New England by train in winter and how to walk on snow-shoes makes a snowman in the shape of Buddha in honor of the mountain. 'Across a Continent' is about Kipling's description of New York, a trip to St Paul Minnesota, and on to Canada. 'The Edge of the East' is about Yokohama; and about the crops, land-prices and costumes of Japan. 'Our Overseas Man' is about clubs and club-houses. 'Some Earthquakes' is about tea production and a bank failure. 'Half-a Dozen Pictures' retains mental images of beautiful and striking scenes from all over the world. 'Captain Courageous' touches on seal poaching and returns to the Canadian Pacific Railway with some account of 'Boom town.' 'On One Side Only' continues a tour in summer; mutual envy of city and their hosts; the perpetual servant problems. 'Leaves from a winter Note-Book,' the last essay has Autumn, wood-cutting and other preparations for winter in New England. There are details about bear-hunt and other animals; snow and its dangers; great interest in activities of neighbors.

'Letter to the Family' (1907) is the second section of the book which begins with 'The Road to Quebec' as a political treatise on Canada and the empire, with impressions of Quebec. 'A People at Home' is about the Canadian clubs that meet for lunch and a speech; the different attitudes and characteristics of different peoples. Preparations for winter, development of country by railroads, and a glimpse of a beautiful girl who could personify Canada. 'Cities and Spaces' has details about a private car on the Canadian Pacific Railway with Canadians returning home and new ones arriving. Further thoughts are on the development of the country and a wish to take Members of Parliament round the Empire to learn about it. 'Newspapers and Democracy' is about country newspapers and their big-city counterparts; reporters who treat their subjects reasonably. The law and the 'imported stuff,' with remarks on the English, especially the man who nearly died of thirst beside a river because he had no glass. The book has many other essays. 'Labor' is about foreign labor in Canada and difficulties with the homegrown article. 'The Fortunate Towns' is about Kipling's tour of Winnipeg and other cities of the Wheat Belt. 'Mountains and the Pacific' is about Kipling's visit to Calgary, the Dane who made good, railway through the Rockies, and on to British Columbia, Sikhs in Vancouver; Whale-catching and processing. 'A Conclusion' is about strength and beauty of Quebec and Victoria; the 'anti-Empiricists' and the quiet, hard-working people who make good emigrants.

'Egypt of the Magicians' (1913) is the third part of the book. 'Sea Travel' is the first essay here. 'A Return to the East' is about a trip to find the sun in Egypt; Serang awakes childhood memories; old-fashioned ship with poor service and accommodation. 'A Serpent of Old Nile' is about Suez, the division between East and West, where the child brought up in the East will find that he has come home, Zagazing and the engine coughing in the desert, Cairo and more memories of India. 'Up the River' is about Cairo, an unkempt place; its extraordinary government and polyglot European population; the Old City, the University; and the soldier who thought well of the place. 'Dead Kings' is about tourists and archeologists in Egypt. 'The Face of the Desert' is about the Nile and the desert; Adam and Eve in the Garden of Eden; smugglers and the men who catch them; Omdurman, Gordon, and the Mahdi. 'The Riddle of Empire' is about Halfa, on the frontier where armies and river-fleets once gathered. There are details about the Sudan Administration — armed chiefly with binoculars— and how the inhabitants were reconstructed after Omdurman.

Souvenirs of France (1933)

This is a little book telling of Kipling's travels in France from the time of the Exhibition of 1878 to his meeting with Clemenceau after the 1914 war.

The author's love of France and the French runs all through it.

Conversely, it may be said that his affection for France grew into a love affair; for the most part of his private life to which we shall come later. In *Souvenirs of France*, published in 1933, he spoke publicly, as he perhaps never would have done of England, about himself in relation to France, recalling his boyhood visit with his father to the Paris Exhibition, his subsequent discovery of France by motor car, his early discovery of French literature and its influence, even referring to the Boer War time of his unpopularity with the French and of French written attacks upon him.

At home, his political influence might have been considerable, when at last decent conservatives ceased to associate with the blackguardly Lloyd George and the Coalition came to an end in 1922. Baldwin recognized this when he once wrote, "I had a breakfast with Kipling at Brown's Hotel, and two hours' talk ... I was highly pleased to find that he had come to the same conclusion about the Government that I had, and by the same road, after almost as long and anxious a cogitation. We have common puritan blood and he said a thing I have often acted on. When you have two courses open to you and you thoroughly dislike one of them, that is the one you must choose, for it is sure to be the right one."

Something of Myself

This is Kipling's posthumous autobiography as Mr Carrington completed and published it after the author's death.

The book has the following eight chapters.

1. 'A Very Young Person'
2. 'The School before its Time'
3. 'The Years' Hard'
4. 'The Interregnum'
5. 'The Committee of Ways and Means'
6. 'South Africa'
7. 'The Very-Own House'
8. 'Working-Tools'

The book end with an index which is unusual in a autobiography.

W. Arthur Young and John H. McGivering observe that, "The germs of many of the books and stories are mentioned, so that the reader is left with the uneasy feeling that he has read it before.

7

Rudyard Kipling's Vision of the British Empire

The British ruled India and many other countries for more than two centuries. So the British Imperialism was very strong in the nineteenth and twentieth centuries. English intelligentsia encouraged this. Ruskin himself held the colonial expansion as a task worthier of England. Carlyle supported it.

In 1872, Disraeli announced that the three great objects of the Conservative party were the maintenance of English institutions, the preservation of the empire and social reforms.

The British in India had a jolting in 1857, but they recovered. They gained a grip over the country, and thought that they were leading the natives towards the light of civilization.

The transfer of the government of India from the Company to the Crown effected a closer association between the Governments of India and that of England.

The British started their civil service. They established the railway and post and police departments. In 1911 King George V visited the country.

Lord Curzon, on the grounds of better and more efficient administration partitioned Bengal in 1905. To most people in India and Bengalees in particular, it was understood as an application of the policy of divide and rule.

Curzon's successor Lord Minto and John Morley did reforms. Sujit Bose observes, "If this was then, the political condition of India during Kipling's time, it was certainly one which could inspire thoughts of the permanence of the British empire in the British mind. Kipling explicitly approved of the presence of British in India. In most of his short stories, and poems, Kipling propagates the myth of the justifiability of British rule in India. It is Kipling's tone of confidence which prompted Rider Haggard to hail him as the 'true watchman' of the British Empire."

The Victorian Age was the heyday of England's prosperity and glory.

The British ruled a quarter of the land and its citizens were one-fourth of the world's population. Kipling believed the divine right of the British rule in India.

Kipling clearly said it in 1897 '... We're about the one power with a glimmering of civilization in us. As you say, we've always had it somewhere in our composition.' The point to which we arrive is that everything about the English is noble. Kim, after whom the novel is named, is sumburnt and looks as black as an Indian, but within the apparently black skin flows English blood and that is the deciding factor which puts him on a superior platform.Norman Page refers to Edmund Wilson's claim regarding Kim's gradually becoming a sahib. Edward Wilson claimed that the book deals with the gradual drawing of Kim's consciousness that he is really a sahib. Wee Willie Winkle, the child-hero of the story which bears his name, is a child aged six and three-quarters. The superiority of the English blood, as seen in *Namgay Doola*, is potent enough to retain its class for generations, even after it is mixed with blood of the Asiatics. *Namgay Doola*, stands apart from his fellow Tibetans as a man of exceptional caliber.

Nineteenth century Bengal was well comparable to the Golden Age of Pericles. On the social, political and intellectual levels, the Beegalees were the leaders in the country. It was the age of Ramakrishna Paramahamsa Vivekananda, Bankim Chandra Chatterjee and other stalwarts. The British however, believed that even the competent Bengalees were in competent to rule themselves.

One Lord Satyendra Prasanna Sinha of Raipur was appointed a member of the Governor-General's executive council. But Kipling prefers to believe that the Bengalees were complete failures as administrators. Kipling ridiculed the Bengalees superiority.

Paul Theroux in his preface to *Saros Cowasjee's Stories from the Raj: From Kipling to Independence* states: "'No one is ridiculed more heartly than Girish Chander De, M.A., the educated Bengali in Kipling's 'The Head of the District.' The successor of Yardely-Orde, the deceased English Deputy Commissioner of a North West Frontier Province district, is a Bengali called Girish Chander De. The sharp contrast between the administration of an Englishman and that of an Indian makes Kipling's opinion clear that in order to save the subcontinent from falling into uncontrollable chaos, it is imperative that the English must continue their presence in this country.

In the story 'His chance in life' we find Kipling advocating the racial ideology that even a Eurasian is superior to an Indian. For ex, Michele De Cruz is the Eurasian who is pitted against the Indians in the story. Because he has a white drop of blood in him. Kipling seems to think that the white man has a divine right. His character Jan Chain is a sort of God. This was the Stuart Kings' divine right to rule inherited by the common Englishman, specially those who went out to administer the outposts of the British Empire.

A natural result of Kipling's prejudice was his presentation of the relation between the Indians and the Englishmen as that of servants and masters. Kipling's 'The Story of Muhammad Din' begins with the following statements:

'The polo-ball was an old one, scarred, chipped, and dinted. It stood on the mantelpiece among the pipe-stems which Imam Din, khidmatgar, was cleaning for me.'

Kipling thinks Indians were the servants of the British. Unfortunately the ignorant people like the Bhils accepted the white man as their master.

Kipling wanted his British readers to realize that the popularization of education would result in the creation of Girish Chunder Des and Huree Chunder Mookerjees rather than the necessary Imam Dins and that the second type was more than for the permanence of the British Indian empire.

Lord Dufferin who came to India in 1884 said this: 'The British nation and its rulers have been called upon to undertake the supreme government of this mightly empire.' Ideas such as these gave birth to what came to be known as the White Man's Burden. What exactly did Kipling mean by white Man's Burden? Carrington explains:

> 'In the eighteen-nineties, the phrase 'a white man' did not only mean a man with an unpigmented skin; it had a secondary symbolic meaning; a man with the moral standards of the civilized world.'

It is a shame that Kipling did not learn about the British exploitation of India. He simply sings!

> Take up the white man's burden-
> send forth the best ye breed-

Kipling's white characters are hard workers, trying to enlighten Indians about civilization.

C.E. Finlayson, who appears in 'The Bridge Builders,' is one such Englishman who is doing his duty to the limits of human endurance. The life of Scott, a character in 'William the Conqueror' is similar to that of Finlayson. A life of sacrifice, duty and responsibility, it is reminiscent of the military code which Tennyson has so lyrically presented in *The Charge of the Light Brigade*:

> 'Their's not to make reply,
> Their not to reason why,
> Their but to do and die...'

Kipling Thinks that the ultimate result of the British taking up the White man's burden is the establishment of their beneficent rule in this country. The trusteeship principle of Burke finds practical application In Kipling's concept of the White Man's Burden. The theory of paternal relationship went on well with the theory concerning the White Man's Burden.

The vast distance of 'fifteen hundred miles,' is covered by railway in only 48 hours and Kipling's characters Scott Martyn and his sister reach the southern province to dedicate themselves to the service of the famine-stricken people.

The other was the passing of Government of India Act in 1919. Apart from the constitutional changes of 1919, Indians were admitted to the War Cabinet and the Imperial Conference. It follows therefore, that for the English, the maintenance of British imperialism in India was a moral compulsion. It is interesting to observe that sometimes Indians seen to be attesting the British use of force. They admit that their brethren exhibit such behavior as to justify the use of force by the British.

One aspect of Kipling's philosophy of imperialism, as has been noticed earlier, was the limitation of popular education. Indeed Kipling considered the educated sections of India to be the enemies of British imperialism in India. It seems Kipling or the British did not realize the threat the western education offered to the ruled. Angus Wilson, in his introduction to the Centenary edition of Kim says: 'Kipling and most of the British did not regard the nationalist Indian middle class, mainly centred in Bengal, as serious force.' For Kipling, the British Indian Empire was a necessity. It was necessity to justify Britain's claim to ethnic and political greatness.

Louis Cornell in his book *Kipling in India* observes, "The dominant theme of recent Anglo-Indian fiction has been the lack of understanding between Indians and Europeans. Forster's *A Passage to India* is the most notable example, but it is a subject that has fascinated such lesser writers as John Masters, John Berry, and many others."

As C.T. Buckland, one of Kipling's contemporaries, wrote, 'The more an Englishman sees of India, the less competent he feels to write about the natives of the country. They are a good and loveable people..., but we never seem to come to a true and thorough knowledge of them. The substance eludes our grasp, and we find ourselves contemplating an imaginary shadow.'

Kipling's vision of India reflects his consciousness of this gap between the dark and the light. Although his 1887 stories explore the possibility of bridging it, Trejago's love for Bisesa ends in disaster, and Strickland's disguise comes to an end with his marriage to Miss Youghal. Tentative efforts such as these serve only to emphasize the impossibility of real communication between the races.

As we might expect, what Kipling sees on the other side is a partial and somewhat distorted version of the world of the native Indians. It is a version based on Kipling's own experience, to be sure, and as such it is true to the facts as he saw them; but his experience of India was sharply limited by his being a member of the conquering race. This general prohibition against contact on the domestic level- a prohibition that was Hindu in origin, rather than British –meant that no Englishman could see into the heart of Indian life, nor was Kipling an exception.

It was as a reporter that Kipling became acquainted with the opposite end of the social scale- the Indian aristocracy. The activities of a prince became matters of public concern, as do the activities of a criminal. Carring-ton records some of Kipling's experiences with Indian aristocrats as early as 1884, when an Afghan *sirdar* tried to bribe him in order to win the *Civil* and *Military* Gazette's favor.

Like many of his contemporaries, therefore, Kipling admired the virtues of an India that had perished in the Mutiny of 1857, an India of memory and tradition.

But in the early months of 1888 Kipling was sent on another journey for the *Pioneer*, this time to Calcutta, where he was forced to take notice of the clerisy. His first response to the Indian metropolis reminds us of his provinciality. He expected to find 'real live city,' an Indian counterpart to London, but all he could think of at first was the stench that permeated every corner of the town. 'Shovels, not sentiments' adequately sums up Kipling's rejection of the Indian middle class and its ideals.

It is perhaps significant that Kipling's critique of Congress is s outspoken that one of the persons he refers to assaulted the editor of the *Pioneer*. But the essay itself need not concern us at length, for Kipling merely rehearses arguments that were current in Anglo-Indian circles: that Congress did not represent the Indian masses; that the delegates had no clear purpose; that they were incapable of conducting an orderly meeting, let alone the affairs of a subcontinent.

Kipling achieves his most complex portrayal of native India in a story that has not been much discussed by critics-'On the City Wall,' first published as part of *In Black and White* in December 1888. It was a story that takes little account of the conventions of the narrative art: the ostensible climax, for instance, where the reporter discovers that he has unwittingly helped a revolutionary to escape from the police, is too minor an incident, placed too close to the end of the tale, to seem in proportion with the rest of the story. At his best, this character Mulvaney (in the story 'The Incarnation of Krishna Mulvaney') becomes larger than life. Tougher, stronger, more imaginative than any man could be, he takes on heroic size and enters a realm that is outside normal human experience.

The twenty-two-year-old newspaper reporter who wrote 'The Man Who would be King' was no longer an apprentice. For six years he had to write prose and verse on demand; each year his output had grown more copious, his style more individual and assured. India had provided a strange environment for Kipling, but on the whole Kipling could –and did count himself fortunate in having lived there.

Benita Parry in her book *Delusions and Discoveries* writes, "The history of Kipling criticism reproduces the history of Western attitudes to the modern imperial experience. His contemporaries at the turn of the century reacted very immediately to his writings, finding in them political beliefs and social ideals which some admired and others deplored in 1899, W.T. Stead, an outspoken imperialist, praised Kipling as the interpreter of the popular consciousness and the inspiration for the popular imagination, while Herbert Spencer attacked him for abetting the recrudescence of barbaric ambitions and sentiments. Kipling's imagination was daring, his themes diversified, his tales always more than pegs on which to hang ideas, and textual analysis of his prose can proceed without reference to his imperialist postures."

A Select Bibliography

Beresford, George C. *Schooldays with Kipling*. London: Gollancz, 1936.

Birkenhead, Lord. *Rudyard Kipling,* London: Weidenfelt, 1978.

Bodelsen, C.A. *Aspects of Kipling's Art*. Manchester: Manchester University Press, 1964.

Brady, N. *Son of Empire: The Story of Rudyard Kipling.* 1945.

Brion, M. *Rudyard Kipling.* 1929.

Brown, Hilton. *Rudyard Kipling*. New York: Harper, 1945.

Brown, Hilton (ed). *The Sahibs: The Life and Ways of the British in India as Recorded by Themselves. London*: Hodge, 1948.

Carrington, Charles. *Rudyard Kipling: His Life and Work.* London: Macmillan, 1955.

Chandler, Lloyd Horwitz. *A Summary of the Work of Rudyard Kipling, Including Items Ascribed to Him*. New York: Grolier Club, 1930.

Clarles, C. *Rudyard Kipling: His Life and Works.* 1911

Clemen, W. M. *A Ken of Kipling.* 1900.

Cohen, Morton. *Rudyard Kipling to Rider Haggard.* London: 1965.

Eliot, Thomas Stearns (ed). *A Choice of Kipling's Verse.* London: Faber and Faber, 1941.

Falls, C. B. *Rudyard Kipling: A Critical Study.* 1915.

Hart, Walter Morris. *Kipling the Story-Writer*. Berkeley: University of California Press, 1918.

Hopkins, R. Thurston. *Rudyard Kipling: The Story of a Genius*. London: Palmer, 1930

Jarrell, Randall (ed). *In the Vernacular: The English in India: Short Stories by Rudyard Kipling*. New York: Doubleday Anchor, 1963.

Kipling Birthday Book. Complied by Joseph Finn. London: Macmillan, 1896.

Kipling, John Lockwood. *Beast and Man in India.* London: Macmillan, 1891.

Knowles, F. L. *A Kipling Primer.* 1900.

Livingston, Flora V. *Bibliography of the Works of Rudyard Kipling.* New York: Edgar H. Wells, 1927.

________ *Rudyard Kipling: Craftsman*. Revised ed. London: Hale, 1938.

Martindell, Ernest W. A *Bibliography of the Works of Rudyard Kipling* (1881-1921). London: The Bookman's Journal, 1922.

Maugham, W. Somerset (ed). *Maugham's Choice of Kipling's Best*. Garden City: Doubleday, 1953.

Page, Norman. *A Kipling Companion*. London: 1984.

Munson, A. I. *Kipling's India*. 1915.

Parker, W. B. *The Rebellion of Mr Kipling*. 1890.

Pontoon, D. *Kipling at Home*. 1942.

Rutherford, Andrew (ed). *Kipling's Mind and Art*. London: Oliver & Boyd, 1964.

Shanks, Edward. *Rudyard Kipling: A Study in Literature and Political Ideas*. London: Macmillan, 1940.

Stewart, James McGregor. *Rudyard Kipling: A Bibliography Catalogue*. Ed. A.W.Yeats. Halifax: Dalhousie University Press, 1959.

Stewart, J. I. M. *Rudyard Kipling*. London: 1966.

Tompkins, Joyce M.S. *The Art of Rudyard Kipling*. London: Methuen, 1959.

Weygandt, Ann M. *Kipling's Reading and It's Influence on His Poetry*. Philadelphia: University of Pennsylvania Press, 1939.

Wilson, Angus. *The Strange Ride of Rudyard Kipling*. London: 1977.

Wright, Arnold. *Baboo English* as *'Tis Writ: Being Curiosities of Indian Journalism*. London: Unwin, 1891.

Annexure 1

Biographical Notes

1865. Born in Bombay.

1871. Sent to England.

1878. United Services College, Westward Ho!

1882. Rejoined parents in India. Employed on editorial staff Lahore *Civil and Military Gazette.*

1887. Assistant editor Allahabad *Pioneer.*

1889. Returned to England.

1890. *Plain Tales from the Hills.*

1891. Voyage to South Africa, Ceylon, New Zealand. *Life's Handicap. The Light that Failed.*

1892. Married Caroline Starr Balestier. *Wee Willie Winkie.* The *Naulahka.* Honeymoon world tour. Settled in Vermont U.S.A.

1893. *Many Inventions.*

1894. *The Jungle Book.*

1895. *Soldiers Three. The Second Jungle Book.*

1896. Returned to England. Settled at Torquay. *Captains Courageous.*

1898. Cruise with the Home Fleet. Settled at Rottingdean. *The Day's Work.*

1899. U.S.A. Serious illness. Death of his daughter Josephine. *Stalky and Co.*

1900. South Africa. *From Sea to Sea.*

1901. *Kim.*

1902. Settled at Bateman's, Burwash, Sussex.

1904. *Traffics and Discoveries.*

1906. *Puck of Pook's Hill.*

1909. *Actions and Reactions.*

1910. *Rewards and Fairies.*

1914-18. During First World War his only son John was killed in action.

1917. *A Diversity of Creatures.*

1920. *Letters of Travel.*

1926. *Debits and Credits.*

1928. *A Book of Words.*

1932. *Limits and Renewals.*

1936. Jan. 18th, Kipling died in Middlesex Hospital.

Note: The dates given of Kipling's prose works are of first publication in England.

Annexure-2

Indian Response to Kipling

The following are some of the PhDs done on Rudyard Kipling:

Gupta, Sunder Lal. *The poetry of Rudyard Kipling: A moral-sociological consideration.* DU, 1993.

Jamiluddin, K. *The Indian background of Kipling's fiction and poetry.* LU, 1952

Krishna, F.E. *Rudyard Kipling: The Anglo-Indian world of his novels.* Rajastan, 1982

Lakhani, Chandrakala Shivchandra. *A study of Indian life as revealed in the fictional writings of Rudyard Kipling.* Nagpur, 1989.

Saksena, M.M. *A study of Rudyard Kipling's fiction with special reference to his craftsmanship.* Agra, 1959

Verma, Ravi Prakash. *Rudyard Kipling: A study of imperial mythology in his fiction.* BHU, 1987

Index